Mrs. Queen's Chump

Idi Amin, the Mau Mau, Communists,

and Other ^*silly* Follies of the British Empire

A Military Memoir

J. J. Hespeler-Boultbee

CCB Publishing
British Columbia, Canada

Mrs. Queen's Chump: Idi Amin, the Mau Mau, Communists, and Other Silly Follies of the British Empire – A Military Memoir

Copyright ©2012 by J. J. Hespeler-Boultbee
ISBN-13   978-1-77143-029-6
First Edition

Library and Archives Canada Cataloguing in Publication
Hespeler-Boultbee, J. J. (John Jeremy), 1935-
Mrs. Queen's chump : Idi Amin, the Mau Mau, communists, and other silly follies of the British Empire – a military memoir / written by J. J. Hespeler-Boultbee.
ISBN 978-1-77143-029-6
Also available in electronic format.
Additional cataloguing data available from Library and Archives Canada

Cover photo and design by the author.

Photo credits: All photos contained herein are copyright J.J. Hespeler-Boultbee.

Extreme care has been taken by the author to ensure that all information presented in this book is accurate and up to date at the time of publishing. The publisher cannot be held responsible for any errors or omissions. Additionally, neither is any liability assumed by the publisher for damages resulting from the use of the information contained herein.

All rights reserved. No part of this publication may be reproduced, stored in a retrieval system or transmitted in any form or by any means, electronic, mechanical, photocopying, recording or otherwise without the express written permission of the author. Printed in the United States of America, the United Kingdom and Australia.

Publisher: CCB Publishing
              British Columbia, Canada
              www.ccbpublishing.com

for Cuauhtli Emiliano

Also by J. J. Hespeler-Boultbee

A Story in Stones:
*Portugal's influence on culture and
architecture in the Highlands of Ethiopia
1493-1634*
Foreword by Richard Pankhurst

©2011 – ISBN 9781926585987

Author's Note

The events and dialogues related in this volume constitute memoir rather than history, little more than morsels of a much broader story now almost forgotten – the slimmest and faintest of links between a tumultuous reality and the enigmatic mists of memory. What follows is culled from events occurring some sixty years prior to being noted down, more or less in sequence, in these pages – a fact that might be seen to ruffle the edges of hard evidence. Such are the fickle diversions of Time when married to the whimsical art of storytelling. The reader will judge.

Certain historical characters will be recognized. However, many names have been altered or fabricated in order to avoid embarrassment or inconvenience to any number of people for any number of reasons.

The author especially acknowledges and thanks Tristan Trotter for his most valued assistance in the preparation of the manuscript. Almost from the day I began this very personal assignment yours has been a strong encouragement.

With the wink of a watery-eye and a tip-o-the-hat, I happily offer greetings to my dear friends and journalistic cohorts of Portuguese revolutionary days, Art Moses and Mick Lowe. You have both known for many years of my involvement in these events, and have urged me to write about them. So here they are, and we'll open other notebooks, *brevemente* ...

My dear wife's long-suffering patience and understanding has been a blessing throughout the months this work has been in progress. Dearest Alemie, I salute your forbearance and your many, many kindnesses.

JJH-B, Victoria, B.C., Canada – October 2012

Contents

KENYA 1
1. A Schooling 3
2. The Mau Mau 36
3. Early Days at Nyeri 47
4. Rogue 69
5. Digging Holes 87
6. Tracking 91
7. Nurses 95
8. My Brother's Tale 100
9. A Very Large Corporal 116
10. Ambush 127
11. Spurs 132
12. White Knees 137
13. Amulet 139
14. Horseback Golf 143
15. The Rhino Cull 146
16. Watercolours, Animals and Sixth Sense 150
17. Christmas Up a Tree 166
18. The Mountain 169
19. Aden and On 185

MALAYA 199
20. Malay Jungle 201
21. Sebastian's Bicycle 209
22. Ulu 221
23. Snakes, Pineapples and Bees 244
24. Taking Off 250
25. The Garrison Welcome 252
26. Mess 257
27. Train to Kuala Lumpur 264
28. Alice 276
29. Drill 282
30. Out with the Tide 294
31. Home 320
32. Aftermath 325

KENYA

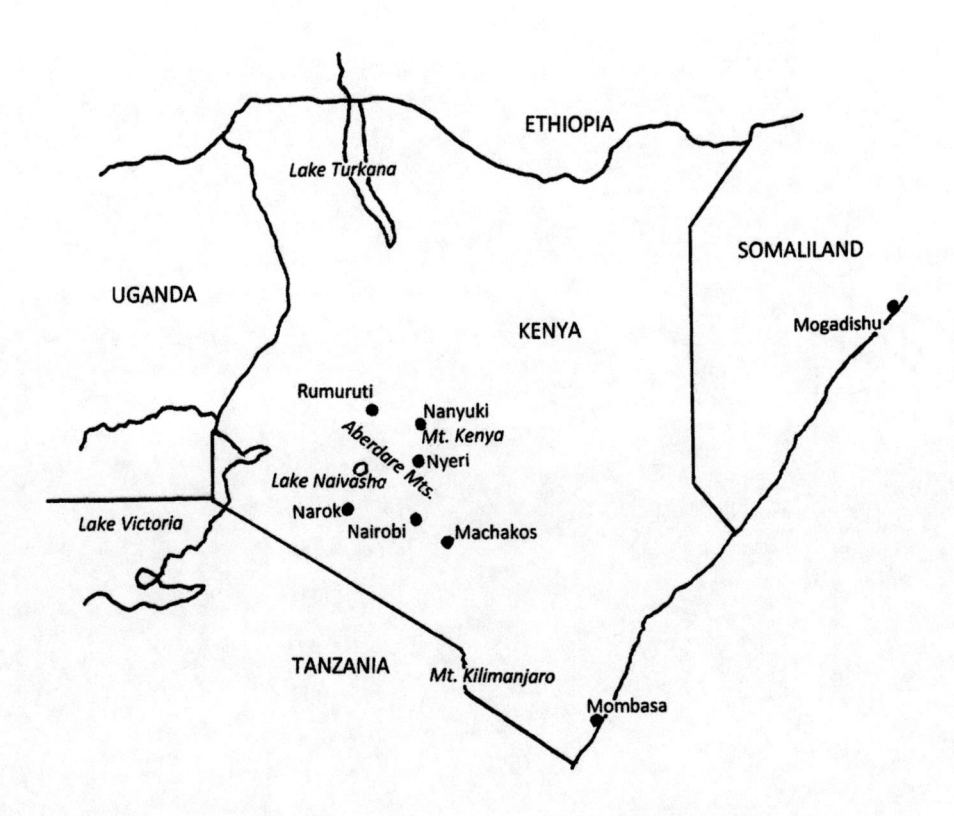

1. A Schooling

For the most part England's very private "public schools" were established with a singular goal in mind: to provide hundreds of cadres of moderately well-educated loyalists to go out and govern the British Empire. It was hoped they would prove to be men of substance who could think on their feet – administrators and policemen, soldiers, engineers. Two-thirds of world wall maps were pink tinted throughout the 1800's and up until about 1960, signaling that indeed the "sun never set on the British Empire." No one in Britain cared to take the French too seriously when they contended this was because "an Englishman cannot be trusted in the dark;" nevertheless, graduates of this Spartan educational system, chipper young squirts not unlike myself, were anxious to get on with the next adventure down the line, and that was somewhere "out there" in the vastness of Empire.

But by mid-twentieth century the only problem was that when we finally did make it out into the great wide world, more than anxious to do our bit, the Empire was in manifest disarray.

This is a personal account from that time – the mid-1950's. Queen Elizabeth II had ascended to the throne by then. Some sixty years on as I write she is still very much in place. Arthritis may distort and cripple my bones but it has not yet entirely succeeded in overburdening my memory – though it may have tinted it a bit. When they're not busy fading away, old soldiers do like to take their time buffing up their occasionally outrageous stories. Still rather full of hopes and dreams, always a bit of the cockeyed optimist and certainly a mite irresponsible, I would like to imagine that at heart I am only a slightly older version of the young man I was then. I have always told stories, and over the years friends and family have said "you must" write them down. It is true, unfortunately, there is not an extensive bibliography of the events with which I was occupied in those years. There are certain records and chronicles here and there, but for the most part I shall launch into this project with my God-given grey matter, and from the comfort of my Canadian haven mull those events that, over the years, have been so instrumental in leading me to where I am right now – at my desk in a small apartment overlooking the delightful garden that separates me from the side entrance to St. John the Divine Church in Victoria, British Columbia.

From the end of the Second World War until the early 1960's, Britain had instituted what was known as National Service for all men attaining the age of eighteen – a two-year military call-up into one or another branch of the services. Everyone had to register; there were few deferments. Compassionate grounds were occasionally considered. Now and then a candidate for service was unfit for medical reasons. Depending upon marks and the general progress of his studies, a university student might sometimes receive permission to postpone service until after graduation – this often to the benefit of some military branch requiring a specialist. Nationality counted little. Resident foreigners were high on the list for prompt call-up, no matter what nationality. The official thinking appears to have been that if Britain was good enough for residence, then the recipient of the Crown's hospitality was justly charged for it through his gracious offering of service in the military. If one did not agree with this premise then one forfeited residence, thank you very much, and would be obliged to leave Britain for wherever – and promptly.

Certain privileges were open to students of the "gentlemanly schools" – the British class and caste system at its most blatantly snobbish that generally produced "good chaps" often qualified for little more, upon completion of their formal studies, than an understanding of cricket, or knowing instinctively (through breeding, of course) what was acceptable wearing apparel for any given social function. If these favoured fellows fared well through their basic military training – and to their credit they often fared extremely well indeed – they tended to be the young men who made up the bulk of the officer ranks of the *pukkah* and line regiments. And such privilege was perhaps the most important point of the English public school system; for if these young lads were indeed right prats but for their innate grasp of what constituted a "jolly good chap," at least a certain mettle had been instilled in them through the sheer brutality of a schooling that served them quite well once they were in uniform. They usually made good soldiers and competent officers.

Malvern College, often considered among the top dozen of England's public schools, had been booted from their magnificent premises during the Second World War. The location of the school, its grounds and numerous buildings on vast acreage in one of the rural western counties lying close by the Welsh border, proved to be a godsend to Britain's military establishment. In 1942 the entire place was taken over for the early development of the TRE – the Telecommunications Research Establishment – experimenting and applying early forms of radar and radio jamming that would ultimately contribute to the defeat of Germany's Luftwaffe. The establishment was staffed in large part by Canadians.

Once the school body returned to its premises at the conclusion of the war the headmaster decreed, in an expansive moment of brotherly and Commonwealth gusto, the initiation of an "instant tradition" – the acceptance of a moderate number of Canadian students into the school. The parents of most new pupils had had to sign their progeny onto the school waiting list at birth, so the break given Canadians was most welcomed – by Canadians, and my mother in particular. It was because of this device that my brother and I were accepted into the school, and found ourselves in company with sixteen other students from Canada scattered among the ten houses of the college. Mother was especially happy on two counts: one, it seemed to satisfy her requirement for a school of sufficient status to measure up to the aspirations she held for her two darling boys; and two, being a boarding school, the arrangement permitted her to be rid of us for the bulk of the school year. We were aware she found us a handful, so we understood that. In fairness to our mother I should add that I do not for a moment believe her parking us in a boarding school was an element of personal selfishness; considering the social alternatives open to her at the time she made the best choice of school she could, and she did so with our benefit in mind. That said, the circumstances did permit her the occasional solo or accompanied expedition to the south of France, or Italy, from which she also derived great benefit – and pleasure and education. She would send her sons postcards, and regale us with many wondrous stories when we would see her again during our holidays.

Many societies consider boarding schools a cruel abandonment of children, but if it is, I truly believe in Britain it is a cultural thing as well – a tough-love method for a parent to cast offspring into what is thought to be a useful and lifelong stream of his or her peers. Right or wrong, while there are ample numbers of those who condemn the system, there are plenty who feel there are few better forms of education. Certainly I feel both my brother and I profited from such schooling. Our mother's excursions added a sparkle of adventure to our education, and whetted our appetites to embrace the world that awaited both of us.

I had no immediate plans past school graduation. For a couple of years the prospect of National Service had loomed on the horizon. Like the rest of my school fellows, I was a military cadet in the collage corps associated with the Worcestershire Regiment. I enjoyed the activity, and was good at it. All my friends had made up their minds that the next best adventure, and one they could not avoid anyway, would be the inevitable two years of National Service. My brother served from 1952 until 1954. With such an example there was no question but that I should swing along in step. I offered not so much as a hint of resistance to the idea, and it was the same for all my fellows at school. I knew I could avoid service by citing my father's cattle ranch in Canada, claiming it my intent to return there; but it was not my intent to return, and I said so. One simply did not say no to the anticipation of a duty so debonair, a prospect so cavalier, so dashing, as a stint in the British Army. We had been bred to it. And besides all this, the burning of draft cards was not a concept that took hold for another decade. No question of "no."

My call-up date was set for early October 1954, which permitted me a whole summer to wallow in Greek sunshine. I was eighteen years old. It was the last holiday I was ever to spend with my mother, and the two of us made the most of it. Mama was not in the least concerned I was being torn away from her and the hearth of our magnificent Buckinghamshire home to face the rigours of two years in the military. As with my brother before me, she considered it with no greater solicitude than if I had been returning to school for another term. That there was an off chance we might have to face danger did not phase her one bit.

"It'll be good for you!" she said. "It'll stiffen your back, maybe even give you some conversation skills. Great adventure! You'll see something of the world ...!"

How right she was. Dear Mama, nothing marshmallow about her.

*

The ten weeks of my basic training were to be with the Green Jackets at Winchester, a rifle regiment originally formed during the Indian wars in the forests of North America. I followed in my older brother's footsteps; he, too, had joined the Green Jackets for basic training, been commissioned into one of the Home Counties units, and from there seconded (loaned) to a Tanganyika battalion of the King's African Rifles. In 1952 his unit was on operations in Kenya as part of the British fight against the Mau Mau uprising.

Nobody among my crowd actually understood Mau Mau, neither could we get much of a firm handle on any of its political implications – or if, in fact, there were any. Certainly no one had anything like sympathy for the organization. Nowadays a more politically enlightened public, if it has even heard the term Mau Mau, would be inclined to consider it one of the forerunners of an heroic African liberation effort. But in Britain in the mid-fifties the sect was understood to be no more than a large gang of murderous thugs who had taken to chopping people into small pieces. They were considered "terrorists." The general consensus was that they constituted a bunch of wild and unruly natives run amok, that a noose or a bullet would be too good for them. They had attacked law-abiding white settlers, and were venting their savage blood lust by hacking people to death using machetes (they called them *pangas*) manufactured, ironically, in Birmingham. Someone might have calculated it was all in search of political liberty, but then the natural and common sense rejoinder to that argument, to which there was no reasonable response, would centre on the sheer idiocy of offering political liberty to such a rabble. Indignation was the initial reaction; ungrateful natives were obviously unable to tell when they were well off, living as they did under the magnanimous protection of Britannia's generous mantle. "Independence?" They weren't ready, wouldn't be for decades, and their ferocious actions manifestly proved the point. Kenya was one of Britain's most cherished African colonies. Thousands of Brits had gone out there as settlers, and had turned the whole countryside into a most productive garden …

Mau Mau, they called themselves. Was it a tribe? Savage lot, whoever they were. They would have to be dealt with – severely put in their place. Order and confidence would have to be restored. All we knew about the uprising was gleaned from the lurid details of a screaming pro-settler daily home press. Later a film, *Simba* (starring Dirk Bogarde, Donald Sinden and Virginia McKenna), came out that confirmed our worst impressions of ungrateful natives and added to the mix of our general ignorance. American writer Robert Ruark had stumped around the colony on safari. Among a collection of Africana was his sensational page-turner, *Something of Value*. Both film and book left people more confused than ever.

And so my brother went off to what we assumed was war, myself to follow shortly. Both of us could have avoided service altogether by simply returning to Canada, but we did not – at least at that time. My brother turned out to be a worthy soldier; for a time he was aide-de-camp to the governor of the colony and we thought maybe he was having himself a whale of a good time. I envied him, and even thought I might be sufficiently noticed to follow him in that post, too. Not to be. My lot turned out to be the daily slog, and although green and immature until the last day of my time in uniform, by quite early on I had begun to perform that most un-military of activities – the attempt to reason, to think things through and try to come to my own conclusions. For two years I queried (at least to myself) every order I was given. Dangerous. I began to realize that, though committed for a defined length of time, on the whole I did not care for soldiering. I loved the adventure of Africa when I finally got there, and of Malaya a little later on; the savannah and the jungle, the variety of people and landscapes, the animals, the richness of smells and sites. What a rush to the mind of a boy whose head was full of fantasies. But soldiering? No. Not a clever move on my part. Considering that I might have opted out by returning to Canada, I began to regret my earlier decision not to.

Many months later Corporal Idi Amin, laughing as he was prone to at his own jokes, said to me:

"You good man, sah! Very generous! Mrs. Queen get good mileage outta you!"

Indeed Mrs. Queen did get good mileage out of me. And when people subsequently asked me, as invariably they have on many occasions, why the blazes I hadn't spoken up in time to avoid military service I used to find it difficult to explain myself convincingly. Often I would exit the conversation feeling very much the chump. It has become a little easier for me to talk about it of late – which is, after all, at least one good reason for my choosing to write about it all now.

*

The Greek holiday did my spirits good. It had been filled with adventure and history and mystery, leaving me pumped and ready to take on whatever next was thrown my way. My return to our bucolic country home some weeks before the end of the summer proved to be a quiet period permitting me to ready myself for what I supposed was to come. I had no realistic idea what I was in for. What eighteen-year-old gives a damn, anyway? He'd have to be remarkably well-centred to figure that one out correctly. I had learned from my brother that basic training would be a tough experience, but I had been in the cadet corps at school, and was sure I knew most of the ins and outs. I was a capable cadet. Nothing should surprise me.

Thousands upon thousands of men have gone through basic training in the British Army and I remain convinced that, but for the details, we all have many of the same stories to tell. It was hard, and it was hell, but all of our observations are little more than variations on a theme.

The non-commissioned officers – NCO's, our instructors and fairy godmothers – used to tell us they would break us, and then rebuild us into soldiers. Perhaps that is what they did – break and remodel. I watched them really break a few in earnest – but not many. One I remember well.

His name was Cobb, a wretch whom the inflictors of basic training did indeed break – or at least, I think they did. In the end he managed to get himself sent home absolutely unfit for military service. The answer to the question I retain at the back of my mind could go either way: did the system beat him, or did this one crafty fellow ultimately defeat the system?

"Square bashing" was what initially brought it about for Cobb. Walking was no problem, but when marching he could not co-ordinate his left foot with his left arm, nor his right foot with his right arm. When he set off walking for his tea break in the NAAFI*, no problem; he'd step off with one foot, swinging the alternate arm. We watched him. The sergeant watched him.

"You can do it!" the sergeant would shout in jubilation.

"Yeah, sure serge – I can do it! Just watch me do it!" Cobb would answer with the voice of the moron we all supposed him to be.

But right after tea break, when we got back out on the square to march up and down, there would be Cobb stepping out with his left foot – co-coordinating a resolute and simultaneous forward lift and swing of his left arm, determination all over his face.

"NO!" the sergeant would bellow in utter fury, and Cobb would dissolve into a puddle, jabbering and blubbing, the voice of the sergeant a castigation far too harsh for him to bear.

"You bloody idiot! What are you? A moron? Left foot – right arm! Get out here so we can all watch your moron antics …"

"Moron …" repeated the downcast recruit.

Our drill sergeant did not possess great quantities of patient

---

* NAAFI – Navy, Army and Air Force Institutes – on-base club-cum-café facility for the lower ranks

psychological skills. An occupational hazard of his calling, perhaps, left him barely above a moronic pathology himself.

Cobb would be forced out of the squad to march up and down where we could all see him; his humiliation was so complete his shoulders sagged noticeably.

"Stand up, man! Stand up! Pull your shoulders back – *Kee*-hrist!"

The sergeant wasn't helping much. Cobb, terrified, exaggeratedly contorted his shoulders so that he looked like a pretzel that hadn't been totally un-kinked, then resolutely stepped out – left foot, left arm. And the sergeant would wheel in a circle, cast his eyes to the heavens as though calling to the gods for an understanding of what it was he had done to have been singled out as instructor to this miserable wart on the face of humanity ...

Then he did a decisive but I have always thought a rather stupid thing: for each mistake Cobb made, the whole platoon would be punished.

For hours on end, day after day, the whole lot of us would be marched up and down, turned left and right, brought to a halt, wheeled about, back and forth, back and forth. Cobb would be on his own, struggling to obey but often, due to some quirk in whatever he had for a crafty brain, he'd be off somewhere twenty paces to our rear trying to figure what had gone wrong, and why he wasn't able to keep up.

The sergeant would scream at him, and then we'd all be punished with cut NAAFI breaks and more hours on the infernal square.

If ever any of us had started off with sympathies for Cobb, they sure didn't last. We came to hate him. Many of us began to think he was acting up. How could anyone so dense ever possibly pass a medical exam to get into this man's army, anyway? We shunned him, we punished him, so sure were we that he was doing it all deliberately.

And it was not just on the parade square. Whatever we were doing – bayonet drill, guard mounting, peeling spuds in the kitchen on k.p. duty – there would be Cobb, getting it wrong, and getting the rest of us into trouble.

On the firing range the hawk-eyed sergeant, watching us in total expectation that something was about to go terribly wrong, stood glowering behind Cobb as the wretched fellow attempted to find a place to insert a single bullet into his rifle. He was lying down, the targets some three hundred yards out front, and he could have had no idea the sergeant was watching him. Yet I recall thinking at the time that if Cobb had any sensitivities at all he would have realized the rest of us were right there, watching. Glowering.

He couldn't figure out how to open the breach bolt. The sergeant gave him no help, but didn't take his eyes off him. It was a relief the fellow didn't know where to stick the bloody bullet; the stupid bugger might have wheeled about and shot any one of us.

Stumped, he pulled his rifle back under his arm and tried to insert the bullet into the spout. Wouldn't fit. Stumped again. This time he pushed the rifle forward, and discovered the butt trap – the little brass lid that lifted to reveal space for a lanyard and a small cleaning oil bottle. He lifted the trap, removed the lanyard and oil bottle, then – triumph! – popped the bullet inside, closed the trap lid.

Slowly he brought the rifle sight up to his eye, pointed it more or less at the one remaining target, way off in the mist – the rest of us had finished the exercise. Only Cobb was holding things up.

He squeezed the trigger. Nothing happened. He scratched his head.

"Got an itch, have you?" the sergeant growled.

Cobb made no reply. He removed the bullet from the butt trap and held it, confused, turning it over in his dirty fingers.

"Where's your itch now, Cobb?" Deep sarcasm.

Cobb grimaced a gawky smile and grabbed at his crotch.

"Aye!" acknowledged the sergeant, knowingly nodding his head at the perceived wisdom he was sure Cobb did not possess.

"You can't find the hole to put the bullet in, can you Cobb?"

Cobb by now had rolled onto his back looking up at the sergeant, grinning idiotically and quite unable to say anything intelligent. He continued to hold onto his crotch.

"Aye," the sergeant repeated. "Cobb can't find the hole!"

Then he bent down to within two inches of Cobb's snotty nose and screamed at him:

"You'd fuckin' find the hole if there was fuckin' hair around it, wouldn't you Cobb!"

Cobb found his voice.

"Yes, serge!"

The sergeant looked wild as he turned away. We all heard it. We all laughed. Perhaps Cobb thought he had said something funny. He had, but I'm not convinced he was too conscious of what it was. Maybe. He started laughing because the rest of us laughed – but his laugh was a cackle, the deep unsure cackle that might precede some horrendous B movie slaughter. It unnerved us, and we stopped laughing while the object of our unsympathetic mirth continued to cackle.

"*Kee*-hrist! Let's get away from here," the sergeant said, and we all started packing up to return to barracks.

In the trucks going back the sergeant said to the corporals:

"Cobb stinks. He couldn't have taken a shower in a month. When we get back, have some of the lads take him into the showers and give him a scrub-down."

And that's just what was done. Cobb was escorted into the showers by some of the biggest and meanest lads in the platoon, protesting but not quite sure what was in store for him. The corporals handed out long-handled stiff-bristled concrete brooms.

"Use these. Scrub him up really good ... Clean!"

Cobb didn't have a chance. Stripped naked, his scrubbers were also butt naked – four of them, and they relished the job they had been told to do. Cobb was knocked to the duckboards and generously soaped all over. If he cried out and tried to get up, he was knocked flat again – and the brooms were put to work. Squirming and writhing about in agony, the wretched fellow was scrubbed raw till he bled in his crotch and arm pits. His hair, neck and face were not spared, nor the soles of his filthy feet. By the time the boys had finished with him Cobb lay shivering and whimpering on the shower room duckboards.

No one went to his assistance. At lights out his bunk was empty, and still no one went to see why he wasn't coming out of the shower room.

In the morning we found his gear heaped on his bed precisely the way it had been left when the scrubbers had come to escort him to the showers. His boots were gone, but there was no sign of Cobb.

At breakfast the NCO's told us what had happened. At about three o'clock in the morning, the patrolling guard discovered Cobb on the barrack square. He was totally naked but for his boots. He was found marching up and down on the tarmac, wheeling about like a drunk, turning left, turning right, giving himself the commands – "Left turn!" "Right turn!" "Squad halt!" "About turn – quick march!"

The guards watched him for a while – left foot, left arm.

They went to his assistance, and he collapsed in the centre of the square. An ambulance was called and he was taken away. Later in the morning someone piled his gear into a kit bag and that was taken away too.

No one ever saw Cobb again.

Basic training was brutal, no question. The constant shouting was unbearable, and the more so when we were obliged to shout back our acknowledgement of the original shout. It was no different for the rest of us than it must have been for the wretched fellow who had been removed. In a way, I think some of us envied him. Some said he was just putting it on, an act to get himself thrown out.

Others didn't think that at all. Cobb just couldn't be any other way. He was a genuine nut, a real nut, they would say. He shouldn't have been permitted to get past the medics in the first place. Whatever was said or done to him (even prior to the shower room incident) had succeeded in breaking his spirit – as our NCO's had promised would happen to all of us.

Something must have worked in the NCO's favour. By the end of ten weeks of madness we were a fighting unit – and quite capable of marching in right smart step.

*

There is another recruitment story I have found myself recounting over the years:

Because of its proximity to London, the Green Jackets depot at Winchester did much of its recruitment within the capital. The unit was well endowed with east-end Londoners whose youth, in those days, were some of the toughest characters to walk the streets since Charles Dickens. They didn't have a name for themselves exactly, but everyone who wasn't one of them dubbed them "Teddy boys." In both looks and demeanour this group of people comprised a whole level of society that had adopted a dress code reminiscent of the Edwardian era, and an attitude that would have suited the Artful Dodger. The whole reflected a way of life – a tough, bellicose belligerence, an "up-yours!" expression of the grey street scene that then centred on the disinherited portions of dockside London (and then spread out). Scary.

Teddy boys usually went hatless (unless the hat was outrageous), but from top to bottom, and without too much exaggeration:

A lengthy and unusually thick and greasy duck-tail haircut, the carefully coiffed tresses combed to lay over each other at the back of the head in the general shape of a duck's arse; sideburns; a dark velvet jacket, three-quarter length in cut to hang down well below the bum (this was the Edwardian bit), with a high collar, often in contrasting colour, and narrow sleeves with cuff buttons to match those running down the front of the garment; a heavy belt hitched a pair of quite amazingly drain-piped trousers, sometimes so sheer it was not unimaginable that a shoehorn might ease access; the shoes themselves had two-inch high double or triple crepe soles for cat-like silence while prowling about the streets, but were built heavy enough to deliver a powerful kick. Accoutrements often included a length of bicycle chain, knuckle dusters, switch-blade knife – or any other imaginative tool convenient for street fighting or Paki-bashing. The stance was prowl, the glance scowl, the language foul.

On one occasion just prior to my leaving the barracks for officer training I was asked, along with a few other soldiers, to accompany the duty sergeant to the railway station in order to assist directing an intake of recruits up to the barracks.

It so happened the station lay close to the barrack gate, down a gully more easily accessed by a narrow footpath than by the road. Past experience had shown recruits tended to get lost if left on their own to find the barracks, so a greeting party was sent out to meet each intake and guide the poor blighters up the pathway.

We watched as they stepped off the train – a group of perhaps thirty Teddy boys.

"Oi-oi!" said the serge out of the corner of his mouth. "Here they come! Aren't they a bunch of lovelies, just! Look at 'em!"

They were indeed quite a sight.

Few if any of them knew one another, so they sheepishly shuffled about cracking their knuckles and preening their outrageous dress code in an embarrassing effort to establish each individual's impossible alpha position amidst such an unhinged assortment of peers. It didn't work well, so when the sergeant approached them with a cheery "Good afternoon, gentlemen!" they were of a mind to pay attention to him.

"Welcome to Her Majesty's Green Jackets Depot! Good to have you all aboard! Now if you would be so good as to pick up your suitcases and follow the corporal there, he will lead you up that pathway to the barrack gate. It's only a step ... not far at all, really ... Shall we be off?"

None of us had ever before heard the sergeant express himself in such reasonable tones.

A few mumbles, but mostly silence as this chromatic crew of sulky street dandies struggled up the short hill with their cardboard suitcases filled with God alone knew what assortment of oils and lacquers and Edwardian baubles and ruffles.

"This way, if you please," said the corporal, leading off, the auxiliary soldier escorts trying to look both stern and indifferent walking alongside.

The recruits followed like sheep till the party arrived before the closed barrack gate. The main entrance itself was wide enough to permit trucks to pass. It was closed, but there was a narrower foot gate to one side allowing passage for just one person at a time.

Bringing up the rear, the sergeant once again addressed the mob in a muted and most friendly voice.

"Listen carefully, please. There is a corporal standing on the other side of the gate, there, the chappie with two stripes on his arm ... He has in his hands a clipboard with a list of all your names. As you step through the side-gate, give your name to him so he can check you off – then move over into the roadway and form up in three lines ... Understood? Right then! Let's go!"

It took a few minutes for the mob to move forward and step through the gate, each man pausing to acknowledge his name. No one quite understood what it meant to "form up in three lines on the roadway," so they straggled about kicking the dust and looking angry enough to tell this man's army what they thought of it.

The sergeant was the last man through the small gate. He came through like a bull, and must have appeared about as dangerous.

"You miserable shower of shit-faced little punks! I told you to form three lines – so get into three lines! Corporal! Help these dandy sons of their mommies to form themselves into three lines, and then turn their fucking heads towards the barbershop. Move this shit heap!"

The Teddy boys were startled to be addressed in this manner, but by now they were anything but sure of themselves, so complied – and shuffled off, the corporal barking at them from up front like a dyspeptic terrier, the sergeant swearing and cursing them from behind. The other soldiers, myself among them, marched alongside, boxing them in so to speak.

They were taken directly to the barbershop, where a team of three regimental barbers, in seconds, flashed their electric shears to give a bristle buzz-cut to every one of them, scattering their precious coifs across the concrete floor. An orderly wielding a dustpan and broom quickly swept their status into a tin garbage can and put the lid on it. I have never seen such startled looks. One or two of the recruits burst into tears. As they stepped into the bewilderment of the sunny barrack parade square, each man was told precisely where to stand – "and don't fucking move!"

When all was done – and it must have taken no more than twenty minutes to shear the thirty men – the squad, still lumbering their cardboard suitcases, was marched directly to the quartermaster to be issued with a kit. Crepe-soled shoes were removed – boots had to fit. But that was all that fitted. For the rest, khaki dungarees, khaki underwear, khaki socks were hurled willy-nilly into their faces with a "Put these on right here, right now!" Each man was given a brand new beret, "to keep your stupid brains warm now you've lost your tresses!"

"Now!" bellowed the sergeant. "Open your fancy suitcases, and remove your wash kit – your toothbrushes, toothpaste, washcloths, and the picture you need for wanking. All else goes in the suitcase, including the clothes you have just removed. Close them up, and you'll find labels over there on the table to re-address everything back to your mommie at home! If you need to have brown paper and string, we'll give you that for extra parcels – but they also get addressed home to mommie. Get the picture? EVERYthing else you came with goes straight back to mommie!"

Once each man had completed this chore, he was issued with two tin plates and "eating irons" – knife, fork, spoon – and with khaki sheets, khaki pillowcase and two khaki blankets. Once more told to stand in a three-lined squad beside the drill square, each man by now pulverized out of any semblance of the creature he had been when he had alighted onto the station platform two hours previously, complied willingly. The squad was turned left and marched off at the regimental stride of one hundred and twenty paces a minute – a good-paced trot – and brought to a halt before the barrack block that would serve as dormitory for the balance of basic training.

"Get washed up! In fifteen minutes you form up outside here again to get fed in the canteen. If any man's not here, he'll receive no food till tomorrow breakfast – and he'll have a bit of explaining to do to me, as well! Look sharp!"

That was the start of it. From that point on there would be no let-up at all till they finished their basic training ten weeks later.

But ten weeks later they were soldiers. They had learned to stand up straight instead of slouching like mean street scrappers; they were smart in their uniforms, trimmed of excess hair, knowledgeable of their more conventional weaponry – and proud like hell of their cap badges. Every single one of them had lost flab, gained muscle and weight.

Amazing transformation!

*

Kind words from the drill sergeant:

"Am I hurting you, soldier? I bloody should be! I'm standing on your hair!"

*

"Your mother may love you, soldier. I DON'T!"

*

"You dozey little man, you – you miserable streak of fuckall! If you don't wake your bloody ideas, I'll chop your feet off, sharpen your shin bones, and drive you through the square! WAKE UP!"

*

WOSB – the acronym for War Office Selection Board – was a four-day exam administered to those within the ranks who, being well-educated and having completed their basic training, were considered to possess sufficient leadership qualities to be brought forward for officer training. The opportunity to take this exam was generally offered to anyone who had attained the equivalent, or more, of high school graduation. But it was by no means a foregone conclusion everyone with an education would necessarily make it to officer rank. One or two soldiers with whom I served in the ranks during basic training had university degrees, sat the WOSB exam – and failed lamentably. They were free to sit the exam a second and even a third time, but quite often they would wind up serving out the whole of their military contract in the ranks. I suppose there was also a certain element of preference involved; some fellows I knew genuinely did not wish to be lumbered with the responsibilities of command.

This was not my case. I wanted to become an officer. I was confident, felt I was capable of command and had the qualities required. I saw myself in that category, and couldn't conceive serving out my two years in the ranks. Soldiering on would be all very well, but not at base level. It wouldn't at all have suited the element of snobbery involved in the way I looked at myself in the mirror. I had been raised a gentleman, or thought I had, and saw myself as someone above the herd, worthy – possibly in the most perverse of ways – to be a leader rather than a follower of men. My school books told me this, or I thought they did; my fantasies about myself told me this. I did not wish to do what others told me to do. I wanted the chance to make up my own mind, to command as generals command, and saw myself possessed of the capacity not only to do just that, but to convince others I would know better than they did.

No doubt a psychiatrist would be able to have a field day with such elements of grandiose self-conviction, the sheer Walter Mitty-ishness of it all; and yet the attitude fitted rather well with the whole concept of superiority being pumped out in the English public school system of the day. Thinking back on this over a lifetime of unequivocal lessons of enlightenment, I admit embarrassment at the sheer naïveté of such notions, except that I am now in a position to see how schools like the one I attended for five formative years were the crucibles of pomposity, and how it was this exceptional pomposity that formed the kernel of Rule Britannia. Pompous notions of superiority provided the backdrop for both its raison d'être and its utter cruelty – the base elements of the appalling British class system that controlled empire. Pomposity, indeed, and the protocols it engendered comprised the engine of empire.

I remember once having the temerity to express to an extremely wise sergeant how I doubted my own capacity to accept the orders of others.

His acerbic answer:

"Laddie, you'd best have another think. You'll never be able to give orders until you can take 'em."

In hindsight, and as a matter of record (it took years to din this into my skull), I can now admit to knowing little better than others – then or at any other time. It took a while for that to dawn on me. When it did, the collapse of psyche was almost catastrophic.

But for now, confident candidate at WOSB, I had the world by the arse and was about to show everyone at large what a sterling candidate for officer training I was.

And then I went and failed the exam.

There must have been a mistake. Um-m-m ... crushing ...

But I rallied, and passed the exam next time round. In fact of sixty in that new in-take, only two of us passed. It was the same exam, and I performed precisely the same way – except for one thing. The essay.

As confident men of the world we were tested in all spheres – our physical fitness, our varied capacities to lead other men in difficult situations, in tactics, in the conversation that comes of a wide general knowledge. Gathered in small sessions, we had to discuss the news of the day with senior officers – and somehow make sense of it. Our examiners wanted to know what newspapers we read; we were assumed to be intelligent creatures who read the newspapers avidly and had a good grasp of current affairs, so at the end there was that infernal essay. We were given a choice of one of several subjects on which to write:

"The significance of the Suez Canal"

"The importance of the mid-Eastern oil fields to the British economy"

"The Arab/Israeli question"

"Murmansk"

"Malta and the Med"

"The future of the partition (India/Pakistan)"

... and so on.

My companions licked their pencils ... and heads down.

The trouble was none of the above appealed to me. I could have fudged it for a page or two, but in terms of pithy comment resulting from solid knowledge – well, I was definitely on shaky ground. As a schoolboy I had a rather better grasp of the daily news than most; I used to spend hours reading the newspapers in the school library, particularly enjoying the editorial and commentary pages, and I had kept up the habit throughout the months of service at Winchester. But what this activity actually did for me was to make me less certain about the world around me, not more certain. Idealism? – none of it; I was confused (a word that recurs frequently in these pages).

As luck would have it, the last essay choice available was a throw-away – just in case one hadn't a clue about world affairs, yet wore the right old school tie and was a jolly good chap anyway:

"Someone who has influenced my life"

Ah-ha! Saved!

Leaning to it, I wrote the word "NANNY" in bold letters at the top of my page – and then proceeded to write the most loving and eloquently laudatory paean I could muster to the dear lady from Esquimalt, British Columbia, who had coddled and mothered me more than my mother between the ages of one and seven.

The papers were gathered in after an hour, and as soon as I had handed mine over I had a sickening feeling in the pit of my belly. It would be considered too flippant, I thought ...

There were a few startled glances as our papers were shuffled between one officer and another in a first peremptory scan ... A raised eyebrow or two. I thought I heard one old fogey mutter the word "nanny" with a question mark.

Later, when the essays were handed back to us, graded A, B, C or D, mine was marked with a large encircled A.

It worked as if I had been anointed, and within a few weeks I was unpacking my kitbag at Eaton Hall officer training school near Chester.

Six-foot four inches of impeccably-clad and polished soldiery, his voice booming off the walls of the welcoming salon of the palace of the Duke of Westminster: Sergeant-Major Michael O'Keefe of the Irish Guards, my intake's chief instructor. "Micky," but only behind his back.

"Gentlemen – my name is Sergeant-Major Michael O'Keefe. Welcome to Eaton Hall officer training school," says he to all of us and none of us in particular.

The peak of his cap came straight down across his nose, forcing him to hold his head bolt upright so that his eyes were forced down and he had to glower under the cap to be able to look straight ahead – and so over the tops of the heads of most people. Thirty of us sat, silent as Trappists at compline, listening to his every brr-r-ed syllable.

"In deference to the gentlemen you are considered to be, and the fact that you will become officers at the conclusion of your training here, I shall address you, individually, as 'Sir.' In deference to the fact that I am your instructor, each of you will likewise address me as 'Sir.'

"But there is a difference: you'll mean it; I won't!"

And so began four months of rigorous and intensive training at Eaton Hall – a rambling old palace standing in its own parkland acreage, surplus of one of the richest men in Great Britain and which he had turned over to the military presumably to add a morsel of ostentation to the officer class waiting in the wings – and possibly also as a tax write-off. A magnificent extravaganza of Victorian era false Gothic, Eaton Hall was actually falling apart – and today is no more. The place was torn down in the years following the end of National Service in 1961. But while I was there, the sumptuous hall (main building of the estate) formed the core of our quasi-officer existence, while the grounds and surrounding buildings, in the manner of most British military barracks, comprised offices, lecture theatres, canteens – and training fields. At any one time there must have been at least several hundred officer cadets going through the place; it was the principal National Service infantry officer training establishment in the country.

The training, by intent, was hell. The basics at Winchester had been rigorous and physically demanding; but the officer training at Eaton Hall was considerably tougher on both body and brain – exacting in ways that continually left cadets uncertain, pushing themselves into zones in which they were forced to question whether or not they fitted the cloth – or even wanted to. We were deliberately kept in a stomach-churning state of high suspense for four months. A failure at the end of such high-charged effort would have been unthinkable – and yet some did fail. Many of these young men were following in their families' military traditions, stepping earnestly into their fathers' and grandfathers' footprints. No small number was descended from those who had given their all in two world wars, and memories were yet delicate and fresh. The cerebral dance was the product of an intense desire not to let the family down. Those whose parents had never served were generally so anxious to make their stance and prove their mettle that they, too, were hyped to the n'th. The pressure was on to measure up to the best, and although none of us really knew what the best was, we all thought we did. The prospect of failure was too horrible to contemplate.

The pressure, of course, was in order to see if we would crack – and so, consequently, we felt forced to push ourselves in all we did. Exhilarating or mundane, serious military matter or idiotic playtime, we ran at every aspect of our lives as though whatever was before us was a brick wall we had to knock over.

One of the terrors we were told about early on – "it's coming, so be ready for it!" – was the pivotal forced march with which we would have to contend in the last week or so of our training. Failure to make the grade on that, we were warned, and you'd be out. Under the watchful administration of Sergeant-Major O'Keefe and the continual buzz of his hornet-like team of non-coms, we undertook to build ourselves towards a pinnacle of fitness. First it was a run in gym kit over a two-mile stretch. After that came a fast two-mile march in boots and battle dress tunics. (This, we were told, was the "soft stuff.") About the four-week point we were running the same course – but in full battle kit (boots and gaiters, battle dress trousers and tunic, steel helmet, full grenade pouches, sixty-pound pack and a rifle weighing in at just over nine pounds). A week or so after that the two miles went up to three. Yet another week and we were running the distance without a break; then a mile was added. In the end we were running a total of nine miles (fourteen-and-a-half kilometres) in full battle order – non-stop.

There was a stout cadet in the squad who had tremendous difficulty keeping up over any significant distance at all. He was a personable fellow and we all liked him immensely. He was also popular with the instructors, so all of us were pulling for him to get past this significant hurdle. The poor man was terrified of what was in store weeks before the actual event, but he steeled himself and refused to beg off or accept anything less than was being undertaken by the rest of us. In the end he managed extremely well; the rest of us had had time to devise a method of putting him in the centre of the squad and "carrying" him when he started to lag. He said it nearly killed him, but he stayed the course on the day of the final test and surprised himself.

Field exercises in north Wales were a big thing. We had lots of practice riding about on tanks, holding on for dear life as they smashed their way over field and gully in a desperate bid to teach us what "the real thing" would be like if ever we had to cope with it. One poor soldier fell off, as I recall, and had to be invalided out of the army with a permanently buggered back. We had to learn about rocket launchers and mortars and, when these didn't provide us with sufficient make-believe clout, there were "thunder flashes" – explosive sticks that went bang when ignited, thus simulating grenades or any of the other unnerving battlefield noises. They were loud enough to burst an eardrum, but not sufficient to remove a hand unless you were still holding it when it went off.

Our rare off hours were usually spent in the bars and dance halls of Chester. For the most part we were painfully conscious of the "gentleman" our schooling assumed to be buried somewhere inside each of us, and so were careful to be on our best behaviour. It did not eliminate entirely the occasional bout of inebriated high jinks – like the time when one of our number, scion of a family of undertakers, drove a bunch of us to town in the hearse his father had given him for transport. It had been re-painted bright yellow, and contained no fewer than fourteen gentlemen and their ladies when its owner attempted to take a shortcut through the wall of a village church graveyard, navigating between the headstones. The ladies (some of whom were to show up later in dainty crinolines at the formal Eaton Hall summer ball) were told to seat themselves quietly on the church's pews, while the rest of us waited for the local constabulary, scratched our heads and tried to think up some plausible excuse. It was fortunate for us that the village vicar showed up before the police. He was upset, naturally, but as our vehicle had not actually knocked over any of the gravestones the good reverend said he would refrain from creating a fuss – with the proviso that we return the following day and replace that portion of the dry stone wall dislodged by the vehicle as it bore us onto the premises.

Pranks were often forgiven by a sometimes bemused school authority, as on the occasion when a number of cadets discovered an eight-oared rowing shell in the duke's boathouse, and decided we needed to know if it would float. It did, so eight of us jumped in, along with one extra for cox, and inexpertly manoeuvred it out to the middle of the River Dee's swift stream. Despite the coxswain's shouting and best efforts (he had told us he once coxed for Cambridge) we couldn't manage to turn about, and so drifted past Chester's riverside parks and walkways – crowds gathering and calling advice – until, in agonizing slow motion, we managed to put it over the local weir. The shell was reduced to matchwood in an instant, and the ungallant crew rather sheepishly had to splutter ashore, each individual trying in his own way to muffle his shame. Our chagrinned cox, the only man among us who should have known what he was doing and so been able to avert the catastrophe, stormed off in humiliated rage.

*

Most of our adventures were by accident rather than by intent, but we were usually quick to spot the humour and so turn what might have been disaster into pantomime. A serious incident occurred that summer which permitted me a rare opportunity to see the inside of a gaol cell, and which had – at least for me – more than the customary elements of the surreal and the absurd.

Much of our training relied on what the Americans like to call the buddy-buddy system. Englishmen in those days would not have chosen to use the term "buddy;" it was too American, and to have incorporated it into the lexicon of an organization as intrinsically xenophobic as the stiff-upper-lipped-officer-class-in-training of the British Army would have been a no-no. But the idea was precisely the same: students were paired, and they worked together through much of the programming, bouncing ideas and actions off one another the better to gain a grasp of whatever point was being considered. Generally it was a good system and worked well to the advantage of both students and instructors.

Early in our training I buddy-buddied with Guido Bondaccereli – who looked and sounded like a toffee-accented Englishman, but whose paternal antecedents clearly held Italy close to their bosom. His nickname, naturally, was Eye-Tie and he revelled in it good-naturedly.

There was little that was not good-natured about Guido. In training we went through miseries together – scrambling over fences and hedgerows, clawing and crawling on our bellies across ploughed fields, jogging in full battle order on inhumane forced marches, or in the classroom writing exams.

In all instances Guido's personality, his optimism and cheerful up-beat humour raised the morale of everyone around him. I considered myself incredibly fortunate to have been paired off with him, for the two of us became fast friends and were able to help one another over (or under) many a hurdle.

One evening the two of us were selected as part of the detail for guard duty – pickaxe handle clubs our only weapons as we took up our position at one of the side gates into the barracks. Not a lot of traffic used this gate at night; it was principal access for deliveries of equipment and foodstuffs. But about three o'clock in the morning a covered three-ton military truck rolled up and the driver poked his head out the window.

"You goin' to open up the gate for us, mates?"

Guido and I did exactly what we were supposed to do; we noted his number, the time he entered, and had him fill out a standard form. Then we threw wide the gate.

"Thanks maties!" he called out as he rumbled through. "I'll be back in a jiff..."

Half-an-hour later he was back again. This time we noted the time of his exit, and out he went, business complete.

"Ta, me mates!"

Guido and I returned to the guardhouse to finish up a game of chess.

Another hour passed, and a jeep from within the camp screeched to a halt outside the guardhouse. It was the highly agitated camp adjutant asking if we had allowed any vehicles to enter. We showed him our clipboard. He studied it carefully.

"Shit!" he muttered, and stormed off as quickly as he had arrived. Guido and I again returned to the chess board.

Not fifteen minutes later another car drove up, also from inside the perimeter of the barracks, this one bearing the camp commander. He told us that someone had driven to the armoury, beaten up the corporal in charge, and made off with quantities of rifles, Bren guns and ammunition. It was a heist of major proportions.

Guido and I were questioned, of course. We had seen little and could not even provide adequate description of the truck's driver. We were not held responsible. Our actions in letting the trucker in, and then letting him out again, were correct. The laxity, for laxity there surely was, appeared to be the process required of us, and from that day on a much closer inspection of all traffic passing the barrack gates became standard procedure.

There was further alarm when, within a day or two, the same kind of stunt had been played out at several other barracks in England, and the word quickly went about that the Irish Republican Army was on the move again, equipping itself. There were stories on the radio and in all the newspapers, and a certain bemused consternation throughout Britain – jokes concerning the preparedness of the British Army in the face of what were assumed to be little more than ragtag Irish fanatics (leprechauns, no doubt) dressed up as British soldiers in order to bamboozle their way into barracks all over the country. Surely to God the whole Irish Question was not being raised yet again? But it soon went about that Irish patriots were, indeed, the people involved. That was quickly established. But no one at that key point in time had the least idea how serious these actions really were, or how they would lead inevitably to the "Troubles" – and the bloodshed – that were to plague all of Britain and Ireland for the next forty years.

Guido and I continued our chess match.

Some weeks after this incident our platoon was led out on a map-reading exercise. It was summer 1955 and while most of Britain basked in balmy sunshine, the uncooperative mountains of North Wales sogged themselves into a customarily mournful season of fog and drizzle with only now and then a brief break when the sun would deign to show itself. Chester was a short truck drive down the road from North Wales, and the mountainous terrain provided the perfect setting for the purpose of our exercise. As usual, we were divided into pairs. We were stripped of all personal belongings – money, personal identification, even my pocket knife had to be labelled and dropped into a bag held out to us by one of the corporals. Each pair was then issued a large scale ordnance survey map of the area and a compass, and we were given a coordinate at which we would be picked up later that evening ...

The road was little wider than the truck itself. As we lumbered on, the grumbles emanating from the engine and gear box indicated our transport's aversion to the terrain we were negotiating. We would stop each mile or so for a pair of cadets to drop out of the back of the vehicle like condemned mariners walking the plank; on the road below the Welsh mist would close over them in much the same way the cruel sea would swallow its victims.

"This is Hansel and Gretel country," said Guido as it came to be our turn, and the tail lights of the truck from which we had ejected ourselves had disappeared into fog.

"Where the hell are we?"

"Buggered if I know!"

We studied the map, turning it this way and that. We were none the wiser when we oriented it north-south according to our compass; all roads marked on the sheet switch-backed hither and yon, and there was no way of telling which one we were on. Contour lines might have indicated something, at least the steeper and more prominent hills, but the mist ensured we could see none of them – or even if they were there.

"Tell you what," I offered brightly. "Let's find a hill and climb to the top of it. We might come out above this fog, be able to make out the lay of the land – and so plot where we are on the map ..."

Good idea, agreed Guido, and we tried to figure out where there might be a hill to climb.

"I reckon we go this way," he said, scaling a low stone wall and vanishing instantly.

"Hold on a jiff! We ought to try to stay within sight of each other ..."

"Fat chance of that!" came Guido's voice out of the fog. "I'm headed for Brigadoon."

For an hour we laboured up and up, the obscurity of the cloud never thinning. There was not a hint of a road or a trail, nor of a house. Not a living thing stirred. We called out, and our voices echoed back as if bouncing off high cliffs – but we could not see them.

Then in front of us, gradually from the mist as though we were approaching the face of a cliff, there loomed a gigantic stone wall. As we approached we could see it ran away on either side of us and so into ... fog.

"There might be a house on the other side. Let's climb the damned thing ..." and I cupped my hands on top of my knee to give Guido a leg up. Standing on top of the wall, he looked down on the other side.

"It's a pig pen."

"Is there a door out of it?"

"Yes. It's over there, on the other side. Here – I'll give you a hand up."

I scrambled up next to him. The wall led away left and right, and we could see it enclosed a number of other farm buildings.

"Let's just jump down here with the pigs, and we can go out through that door ..."

Both of us jumped down into the muck of the pen and so set off the pigs. Squealing and nervous, they ran about bumping into one another and churning an already filthy muck into a veritable quagmire of mud, urine, pig food and pig shit. A huge sow took umbrage and ran at Guido. He had to be quick on his feet to get out of the way, diverting it by hurling a chunk of cabbage at its head. Unconsumed portions of pig dinner littered the floor. Our uniforms, damp from the fog, now began to assume the shades of the pen itself.

Sloshing across to the wooden door leading out of the place we realized it could not be opened from the inside. Only then did we notice something we had not seen when we jumped in: the inside floor level was lower than outside. The height of the stone wall surrounding the pen was considerably greater on the inside than it had been when we climbed up from the outside. Scaling it now in order to get out again was a manifest impossibility.

"There must be a farm house nearby," reasoned Guido. "Let's just shout."

So we both shouted ourselves hoarse – and eventually there came a woman's voice from the other side of the wooden door.

"Who's that in there with my pigs?" she enquired crossly.

Relief at last!

"Ah, madam! Thank Goodness you're there. We jumped into your pen from the other side, and can't manage to open this door. Would you be so kind ... and we shall explain ..."

A bolt was slid back, and the door opened a crack – just enough for the woman to see the two of us. She was a terrifying sight. She wore huge gumboots, and above them a heap of fabrics which might have been dyed in the muck of her pen. A knotted scarf tied up her bramble patch hair. There was a scowl on her face, and fire beamed from her angry eyes. In her hands, and jabbing at us with steadfast intent, she wielded a sharp-pointed two-pronged pitchfork.

"I know who you be!" she screeched. "You stay where you are, if you know what's good for you!"

And she slammed the door shut in our faces.

"George! Get on with you, and go call the coppers! I reckon we got us a couple of them damned Irish buggers trapped in here ... dressed as British soldiers, they are, 'an'all ..."

George called back his assent, and Mrs. Pitchfork addressed the two of us again:

"You stay right where you are, m'lovlies. We'll let the law look after the likes of you!"

George was gone a long time, but after a couple of hours he returned with a constable wheeling a bicycle and Guido and I were released from the pen, Mrs. Pitchfork standing at the ready behind us as we faced the law.

"Now what's all this 'ere?" the policeman enquired, flicking open his notebook with a dirty thumb.

"Who are you?"

I answered first, spelling out my complicated name while he laboriously wrote it down with the stub of a pencil.

"We're both officer cadets from Eaton Hall. We are on a map reading exercise, and have become lost in this mist ..." I started to explain.

"Where's your identification?" the constable asked, reasonably enough.

"Our ID, our money, and everything – it was all taken off us before we started out ..." Guido attempted to explain.

"And who are you?" asked the constable, his pencil stub poised.

"My name is Guido Bondaccereli ..." he began with the correct sing-song pronunciation of his venerable family name.

This was too much for the constable. He snapped his notebook shut.

"Well, whatever you call yourselves, you'll both come along with me ..."

Producing a pair of handcuffs, he secured the two of us together under the cross-bar of his bicycle and marched us off, down a road that ran on the other side of the hill we had climbed earlier. There were two more policemen and a black paddy wagon waiting for us at the bottom. Unceremoniously, Guido and I, plus the constable and his bicycle, were bundled into the back of the vehicle.

In the police station at Harlech we stood before the high desk of a jovial sergeant, and once again attempted to explain ourselves. A group of curious constables in blue serge stood about with broad grins on their ruddy Welsh faces.

"We'll have to verify your names, you understand?" the police sergeant cheerfully sang his explanation. "Yes – I'm sure you can understand that. We'll telephone, and probably have confirmation by breakfast. In the meantime, make yourselves comfortable in the cells at back. Now, how do Irishmen like to take their tea, do you suppose …?"

He was laughing. Everyone was laughing.

It came to me then, and my saying so was the cause for a moment of even greater hilarity among the contingent of the arresting officers: it's a fair bet, I told them, that I am the only Canadian serving in the British Army in North Wales who was ever arrested for being a member of the Irish Republican Army – while in company with an Italian.

Guido thought that was amusing, too.

*

Sergeant-Major Michael O'Keefe was a long suffering fellow. Occasionally one could see it in his eyes when something occurred to offend his military sensibilities – sometimes in the way he would cast them, rather hopelessly, towards the heavens; at other times a pained expression that rumpled his brow and might have caused a searing stab to his temples. He seldom raised his voice in anger; on the other hand, he seldom addressed us as anything short of a gaggle of morons. And yet his quiet and reasoned tones had no trouble at all penetrating our thick skulls at distances of up to a quarter-mile. His eyelids would flutter closed, and one could almost hear him mutter under his breath, "Jeez, Josef an' Mary … May the Good Lord Gawd 'elp us!" A measured quietness, but it carried well.

One of our final exercises was to be the four-day battle camp at Trawsfynydd, another wee Welsh mountain hideaway where, we were reliably informed, it always rained.

Creature comforts were non-existent, or few at best, and so before embarking I decided I needed an umbrella. I did not have one of those fold-up types that might have fitted into my pack. The only one I had was a long crook-handled thing that wouldn't fit in a duffle bag, let alone a backpack. But I was determined, so I took some darkened string and tied my jolly brolly along the left side of my rifle. It would have been a perfect solution had we just jumped on the trucks and driven off; unfortunately the sergeant-major formed us up for an inspection prior to boarding.

Standing to attention, I was able to pull my rifle close into my side so that my baggy trousers covered most of the brolly. He failed to see it from the front, but as the sergeant-major passed behind me I heard him stop.

"What the blazes ...! What's this I see?"

"Are you looking at my umbrella, sergeant-major?"

I was on the brink of laughter, and so too were a few of the lads who knew what I was trying. It was impossible to see the sergeant-major's face, but that was not necessary to know its colour. His words came purple.

"I can't believe it! I've never seen anything like this before in my bleedin' military life!"

If it had been up to the sergeant-major alone I believe in that moment he would have had me hurled from the gates of Eaton Hall into the dust and oblivion of some English roadway. But as good fortune would have it, he was making his rounds with our senior instructor, Captain Selwyn Pocock, a good humoured officer with a sparkling sense of the absurd who had taken quite a liking to our entire squad, and was proud of his instructional achievements with us.

"Let it go, sergeant-major ... The man obviously feels he will be needing an umbrella at Trawsfynydd, and is even showing some considerable initiative in getting it there. It's not as if we were on parade ...

"Besides," he added, "I might need to borrow it."

Sergeant-Major Michael O'Keefe snorted, and I never heard another word on the matter.

*

Trawsfynydd was not just a battle camp where live ammunition was used in exercises in order to let us know what it felt and sounded like; it seems the place was deliberately designed to scare the bravest heart. For instance in one "live-fire" exercise, machine guns were set to whiz an arc of fire just a few feet above our heads as we crawled across the ground – and I'll swear it's not until Sure Death is so close that you really know what it is to keep your head down in the mud, and to sneak your way through it flatter than a lizard. Of course someone told us (it must have been one of the NCO's trying to rattle the willies out of us) the grisly story of one lad who panicked and stood up to try to run for cover, with predictable results. In point of fact the arc was designed to swing about twenty feet overhead, but we weren't to know that – and the deafening certainly of its proximity didn't convince us otherwise.

The camp lasted throughout one week – seven of the most miserable days I have ever spent anywhere; they took a year-and-a-day to unwind. It rained continuously; the mud was up to our knees. Whether water was dumped on us from above or ricocheted up onto us from the ground, we were constantly soaked to our bones. I think our battle dress uniforms even absorbed humidity from the air; they were sodden and uncomfortable the entire time. The battle dress garment in those days was nothing like the slick fabric apparel of today's fighting soldier. Cut from a heavy wool weave, it clung to one's body when wet like a claustrophobic blanket of dog hair saran wrap. Worn over a sweaty and unwashed body for a week, it had an indescribably vile and pungent stink to it. Moreover, the gods of rain did not favour my umbrella.

Once back in our quarters at the hall we had a mere two days to polish ourselves to perfection for our graduation parade. All our kit, including the bedraggled pieces of it we salvaged from battle camp mud, had to be cleaned, ironed and polished till the whole kaboodle gleamed for a rigorous final inspection. It was a daunting task, and two days were barely enough to prepare for it. My umbrella, having proved its ineffectiveness during our week of drenching Welsh mountain misery, had been abused beyond reclamation. I wanted, now, to present myself and all my kit as the pinnacle of disciplined military perfection – so I pitched the damned thing out.

As it turned out Eaton Hall was to test us right up to the very last evening before we assembled for our "passing out" – the graduation parade.

On our final evening, the commandant held a formal mess dinner – an affair that was as flamboyant and intimidating as ever we would find in our various regimental depots. The dining salon was so decked out in splendour it would impress a whole gaggle of dukes and earls: shining silver chalices and fruit bowls, polished cutlery, decorative porcelain, crystal glasses, candelabra, and a host of mess stewards dressed in their regimental livery. Those participating in the dinner were no less impressive: all graduates were obliged to turn themselves out in their best bib and tucker which in our case was clean, tailored and pressed battle dress. The officers, members of the school administration and senior training staff, were all in what we called their Number Ones – red or white mess jerkins with medals, piped trousers and gleaming patent leather boots. It was intended to be a congratulatory farewell dinner, but also a none-too-subtle means of introducing each of us, who would become officers on the morrow, to something of the pageantry of the British Army. The colourful formality differed in detail from regiment to regiment, but in its overall aspect was pretty much what we could expect in any of the regiments to which we were about to be posted. In essentials this evening was set up as our last lesson. From this point on we were to be officers and gentlemen and this dinner, above all, was to be a gentlemanly affair.

It is probable that none of us actually required instruction as to how we should present ourselves, or how we should behave, but nonetheless we had been cautioned – not by our chief instructor, Sergeant-Major Michael O'Keefe, but by his boss, Captain Selwyn Pocock. For this final initiative, evidently, an officer and gentleman had been delegated to instruct officers and gentlemen. For some reason it might have been unacceptable – unseemly – for a sergeant-major to instruct gentlemen on how to deport themselves as gentlemen: how we were expected to behave at table, to sit up straight and talk politely with one another, minding our use of language and refraining from profane expletives; how to use our knives and forks properly; which glass was intended for which particular beverage – the difference between a water goblet and a wine glass. The port, we were informed, should always be passed around the table to the left. (Possibly a gentleman's gentleman, but never quite a *pukkah* gentleman himself, a good sergeant-major would have known his place, lacked a certain finesse, perhaps. He would not have been expected to know about such things.)

Captain Pocock was a familiar figure to us, of course. Only an occasional instructor, he was nevertheless the officer responsible for our overall training and the man to whom the sergeant-major would report. O'Keefe's use of language on us was rough, to say the least, for he treated us as the scum he had always said we were, and if ever there was humour in his voice it was invariably well-tempered with a biting sarcasm. I believe he regarded most officers as toffee-nosed snobs, and so had even less regard for us miserable juniors.

But this was not Captain Pocock's way at all. From the beginning his manner with us had been gentle and reasoned, familiar – but not quite; always as though he expected from us nothing but the highest standards in everything to which we applied ourselves, whether it was field tactics, physical exertion, classroom learning – or mess conversation. He in no

Mrs. Queen's Chump

manner shied away from displaying his capacity for a generous level of tolerance and humour – as he had so readily shown with my umbrella escapade. As a group we liked and trusted him, so our lesson from him concerning our good table manners was rather informal, given and received more as a matter of understanding between the gentlemen we all thought we were.

One of the points of his instruction concerned our formal toast to the queen. He told us how, at a certain point, the commandant would rise to his feet from his position at the head table and, ringing his small table bell, lift his glass and pronounce:

"Gentlemen, The Queen!"

The word "gentlemen" was the cue. On hearing it we also were to rise to our feet and lift our glasses. When the commandant pronounced the words "The Queen" we were expected to follow with strong voice: "The Queen!"

It was ritual. The way it was done.

The dinner passed well. The commandant made a short speech – he must have made it a hundred times – about how all of us had been carefully selected to become officers in our various regiments, how great an honour it would be to serve our monarch, our country, our "colours," and how the greatest empire the world had ever known now required our services and devotion. He woofed on a little pompously, some of us thought, but we chimed in with "Hear! Hear!" at appropriate intervals, encouraging him to blather on a bit more. He knew none of us personally, and we had only ever seen him at some distance, so he could hardly get chummy with us.

His speech was followed by a briefer and more relaxed word from Captain Pocock, who spoke to us of our training, some of our individual accomplishments, and how basically he was well satisfied with our efforts. There was a hint of humour in his voice, and like the rest of my companions I felt his words were not just warm, but sincere. He finished with a little joke (he, too, must have told it a hundred times) about how our performance had out-shone other squads in training at the school. Proud smiles of good fellowship all round ...

The commandant tinkled the little bell beside his plate and rose to his feet, glass in hand.

"Gentlemen ...!"

As instructed, we all stood up and raised our glasses.

"... The Queen!"

"The Queen!" we all repeated in unison.

There was an instant's pause, a charged silence. Then:

"Where ...?" came the loud and rather too highly-pitched voice of one would-be graduate at the end of our table. Perhaps the port had passed his way once or twice too often.

Bending down and lifting the curtain of the table cloth, the offending cadet proceeded to seek for Her Majesty under the table.

Consternation – for a moment suppressed.

"Sir!" boomed the voice of a suddenly outraged commandant, glowering down the length of the table.

Captain Pocock pushed his chair back and stood up. His face had gone as white as his mess jerkin and his eyes bugged. Striding to the end of the table and standing behind the offending cadet, he said:

"Come with me, sir. This instant!"

The offending cadet was still smiling rather stupidly, rather drunkenly, as the captain escorted him out through the dining room door.

Dinner resumed immediately, and nothing more was said of the matter.

But we learned later the mouthy nit was expelled from Eaton Hall on the spot, reduced to the ranks for the balance of his service. One ill-conceived and poorly-timed joke, one ill-conceived action, one ill-conceived word – and the man's military career was, as the saying goes, toast.

☐

2. The Mau Mau

Defining Kenya's Mau Mau insurrection (1952-61) requires juggling a number of political concepts, and discussion around these could go on from now till doomsday. It is likely no one will ever get it right because all sides got it so terribly wrong from the beginning. It was a war, to be sure, a scrubby one of violent hatred, paranoia and superstition, and barely a whisper of decency or magnanimity. In the end campaign medals were awarded. Mine are in a box, and will likely remain there, a curiosity. At times I have been tempted to pitch them out; for all that they are pretty baubles, they represent to me some powerful kind of jinx. But they are stamped with my name, and I cannot throw them as far from me (even gritting my teeth) as I would; they boomerang back, and I see them over and over ... They're there. Yet I cannot wear them on Armistice or Veterans' Days. I don't feel comfortable standing in line with other veterans. To me my medals represent a sadness, an embarrassment, even a shame – not a personal shame, I hasten to add. The shame, to my mind, lies with the events themselves – a particularly black period in Britain's contemporary history that speaks yet unwritten volumes about western white man's malignant legacy.

I was curious, no question – as curious as any perky young man, strong like a sapling and ready to step into the world, when first made party to the great events of the day; but quickly an unwilling accomplice, a most critical witness.

Sweet reason is not unreasonable to an eighteen- or nineteen-year-old, but who's going to listen? It has taken me many years to come to a point where I can feel comfortable writing of these things.

*

On the one hand the Mau Mau could be seen as the first of the twentieth century African freedom movements – an inspired collection of fighters determined to overthrow Britain's colonial mastery of Kenya. This, at any rate, tends to be the contemporary view held by most Kenyans themselves. Without specific intent the Mau Mau insurrection led the way to all other independence movements in the latter half of the century. Quite incidentally it peeled away what Britain so desperately wanted to keep secret, thereby exposing her to unprecedented global censure and criticism. There were many bricks in the empire wall, and dislodging them was difficult. Kenya was one of the more intractable of Britain's bricks, but once the loosening process had begun the wall could be neither repaired nor replaced. Disintegration and collapse was inevitable and the downfall of empire followed as a matter of course.

On the other hand, and at a polar extremity of political thinking, Mau Mau has been described – and also quite correctly – as the ultimate in frightening savagery, a cutthroat band of ignorant and apolitical terrorists hell-bent on slaughter, driven to their actions by superstition and their own terror of contravening a series of vile secret oaths members had been sworn to uphold. The objective of these oaths: to kill or otherwise drive white men from the land – and to enforce the loyalty of recruits to the Mau Mau agenda. But in their frenzied zeal the insurrectionists finally killed far more of their own than their enemy. In one sense, then, the Mau Mau insurrection may even be viewed as a civil war.

In an attempt to paint a picture of the phenomenon, the New York Times of the day described Mau Mau as being a manifestation of the frustrations of a backward people whose collective mentality and limited economic capacities prevented their ability to keep pace with the civilization it had encountered.

So what was Mau Mau?

As a political movement the Mau Mau incorporated extremities of polar viewpoints. It was seen by the British and the white Kenyan settlers as a dangerous anarchistic rabble of cutthroat thugs, something worse than mere terrorism, if that can be imagined; among the majority of ethnic groups within Kenya itself it was also viewed with considerable alarm as a terrorist movement; yet among the tribes most deeply affected, the movement had many followers who considered it to have legitimate political purpose and direction. Kenya's African political leaders – Jomo Kenyatta foremost among them – had had a well-developed political agenda for decades. Demonized by the British as a communist sympathizer because he had spent time in Moscow, Kenyatta was arrested on trumped up evidence as Mau

Mau's chief instigator soon after the emergency was declared. His trial was the proverbial mockery of justice, and he was sentenced to seven years of hard labour in a remote region of northern Kenya. Ignored entirely was the fact that, since the 1920's, he had continually championed – in speeches and writings – peaceful change, and prophetically warned of the risk of violence long before its onset.

The Kikuyu people, the largest ethnic group in the country, had suffered greatly at the hands of their British overlords. It was principally their lands in the high fertile agricultural areas in the vicinity of the capital, Nairobi, that had been taken over by the settlers. The Kikuyu had been shunted off, and they were to become, in large measure, the serfs and houseboys of the whites.

Yet the Kikuyu themselves were divided. There was a politically astute, largely urban class; and there was a largely uneducated rural and peasant class. Among both, feelings were high and confusion was rife. Many Kikuyu simply did not know which course to follow. These groupings were divided into those who believed in a peaceful political solution – for whom Kenyatta presented himself as leader – and those who believed there was no alternative but to take up arms. The Mau Mau, as it came to be called, was the activist group that had given up on negotiation between white and black; its senior members had broken with the Kenya African Union (KAU) led by Kenyatta, and they were the ones who decided instead to achieve their aims through coercion and violence.

The actual insurrectionists were led by a number of diehards – Dedan Kimathi, Musa Mwariama and Stanley Muthenge were three of the "big ones," all of whom were ultimately killed by the British; and Waruhiu Itote, more generally known as "General China," who lived into old age and, by the end of his life, was much revered by his countrymen. It was this group who, along with others, operated the gangs in the Kenya forests – the Mau Mau. They were marauders, outcasts driven by British and settler forces into the high and remote zones surrounding the urban areas in order to survive. As the years of the euphemistically called "emergency" wore on, these gangs came under continual harassment from the far greater military sophistication of their opponents, and were quickly forced into disconnected fragments. The British intent was to dislodge and dislocate the insurgents, to isolate them from one another and keep them on the run. The rebels became trapped by the inefficiencies of their individual groupings, by their lack of food, armaments and logistical supports of all kinds – and, finally, by their own terror mechanisms as well as the terrors perpetrated by the British opposed to them.

Upon entering this area of Africa in the previous century, making Kenya a protectorate in 1895, the British had introduced money and taxation – systems which the Africans disliked intensely. The British assumed ownership of all native lands, redistributing them among themselves and relentlessly squeezing out the Kikuyu. Kikuyu men were prohibited from working lands claimed by others, and so were forced to work for British overlords. By 1930, ten years after Kenya was proclaimed a colony, there were thirty-thousand white settlers; by 1945 just three-thousand settlers owned forty-three thousand square kilometres of the finest (formerly Kikuyu) lands – but they cultivated only six percent of it. The whites grew fine crops of exportable coffee, and became exceedingly wealthy; the Africans were banned from growing coffee.

The British had faced stiff African opposition from the start: the Kikuyu had risen against them periodically between 1880 and 1900; there had been the Nandi revolt that ran for ten years, 1895-1905; the coastal Giriama were involved in a major year-long uprising in 1913. There had been the women's revolt in Murang'a district in 1947 and, in 1950, the so-called "Kalloa Affray."

It was the Kikuyu who were hardest hit by British colonialism. Britain's colonial government had seized seven-million acres (twenty-eight thousand square kilometres) in what became known as the "White Highlands" – Kikuyu lands in the hinterland surrounding Nairobi. The Kikuyu are an enterprising people; within the urban areas they had set up stores and businesses which contrasted severely with the rural peasant status of their fellow tribesmen. By the late 1940's the Kikuyu themselves were a deeply divided people, some considerably wealthier than others.

In 1919 the British had set up a Legislative Council, initially for whites. The Indian population, originally brought in by the British as workers on the Uganda railway, had grown quickly by using the railway to expand their businesses into the colony's interior. Right at the outset this community made known its demands for representation, which was granted to them only in 1927.

The Africans, chiefly Kikuyu, formed the East Africa Association in 1921 in order to press their demands for the return of appropriated lands. Their voice was ignored, the group outlawed by the British in 1925. Immediately the Kikuyu Central Association was formed, and in 1928 Jomo

Kenyatta was appointed the organization's general secretary and editor of its newspaper, The Unifier (*Muigwithania*).

Throughout the 1930's Kenyatta's group agitated for legislative representation, return of their lands, greater access to education and respect for traditional African customs. Despite constant warnings of unrest and even bloodshed, the British did nothing – continuing to refuse African representation in the legislative council until 1944. At this time there were fourteen representatives for thirty thousand whites; six representatives for one hundred thousand Asians; one representative for twenty-four thousand Arabs; and one representative (chosen by the Lieutenant Governor) for five million Africans. This last figure was increased to five in 1946, and to eight in 1951 – the year before the outbreak of the Mau Mau insurgency.

The Mau Mau movement involved mainly the one tribe, the Kikuyu – "Kukes" as they were called disparagingly by settlers and army alike. At the time of the uprising they were by far the predominant ethnic group in Kenya, especially in the urban areas but also in the rural regions surrounding the capital and other centres. Smaller tribes, the Embu and the Meru, also speakers of the Kikuyu language, were likewise affected. But the shrill argument that Mau Mau was part of a mid-century communist conspiracy was an excuse popularized by the propaganda arm of the British Government and, though enthusiastically endorsed by Kenya's white settlers, had always been a difficult claim to believe. Nowadays this line of thinking has been well and truly debunked.

The meaning of Mau Mau is uncertain. I have heard it claimed the name was taken from the group's early activities in the region of the Mau escarpment. Another possible origin for the name is the acronym for the Swahili words *Mzungu Ande Ulaya, Mwafrika Apate Uhuru* – a loose translation for which might be "send the white man away; grant the Africans their freedom." Others claim it to be an anagram for *uma uma*, Swahili for "out out." Questioned after his capture in 1954, Mau Mau General China said he thought the term Mau Mau might have been derived from a European mispronunciation of the Kikuyu word for oath – *"muma."* Yet another derivation, and one to which I've given some credence, is that the term is of Portuguese provenance. The word *mau* in Portuguese means "bad;" doubled, the word becomes an adult's admonition to a child for being naughty or throwing a tantrum: *"mau mau!"* – "behave yourself!" I base this conjecture simply on the fact that the expression has existed for centuries, albeit it in a language other than either Swahili or English, but taking into account the historic fact of the strong Portuguese presence and cultural influence in all of East Africa dating back to the late 1400's. In any case, the British used the term pejoratively, and it stuck. Leaders of the Mau Mau themselves preferred to refer to their organization as the Kenya Land and Freedom Army (KFLA). Such a title was shunned by the British. To have used it might have granted their enemies (at least internationally) a measure of legitimacy that neither the British nor the British settlers in Kenya would have countenanced. Soldiers and settlers who fought the Mau Mau were quick to come up with a disparaging abbreviation for their adversaries; they called them "Micks," or "Mickies."

Although the Mau Mau was on the rise through the summer of 1952 and there had been some early indications of trouble, Governor General Sir Evelyn Baring, arriving in September of that year, had been given no warning whatsoever from the Colonial Office. Nor had his predecessor tipped him off. Within a month Mau Mau activity had become so intense that Baring wasted no time in declaring a State of Emergency. Operation Jock Scott was launched that October; roundups of Kikuyu suspects were launched throughout Nairobi and the city's hinterland. More than twenty thousand people were removed to a screening camp at Langata; thirty thousand more were deported to reserves. In these wretched areas the Mau Mau had virtually complete internal control, and murder was a means of exercising it, coercing individuals and increasing membership.

The British employed public executions (by hanging) and torture in their effort to establish control on the reserves and within the filthy camps they maintained. Arthur Young, the colony's Commissioner of Police, pleaded with Gov. Baring to take note of British torture – "horror in the camps" – and resigned his position in protest in 1954 after less than eight months on the job.

Historians writing about the Mau Mau uprising cannot help but note the ruthlessness of the response of the British government and settlers within the colony. Elements unleashed by the British governing powers behaved every bit as savagely as they liked to point out the French had behaved in Algeria during that colony's fight for its independence (1954-62). If pure statistics tell a story, the British were in fact far crueler than the French. The British hanged twice as many of their victims as had the French in Algeria – and a great many of them in public. A mobile gallows was carted from town to town. Hanged corpses were displayed at crossroads and junctions. It was the sort of terrorizing behaviour that had been repudiated in Britain over a century earlier. Opinions expressed in recent studies suggest Britain's responses in many instances were just as savage as the Mau Mau actions they were intended to counter, a desperate knee-jerk reactive counter-terrorism to which perpetrators felt they were entitled because they themselves had been terrified. It was a hideous cycle.

The emergency remained in effect until the appointment of a new Governor General, Sir Patrick Renison, in October 1959. Within a month he had declared hostilities over – but still the killings and oath ceremonies continued, some in the forests, some in the villages, and even within the detention camps. There was no marked let-up until 1961.

Terror can compel obedience or breed opposition. There were as many, or more, Africans – Kikuyu – fighting against Mau Mau as there were members of the organization. The movement had lost wide popular African support after the Lari massacre, an incident that occurred during the night of March 24/25, 1953. In an effort to wreak vengeance on Kikuyu loyal to the British, the Mau Mau had descended on Lari in force and slaughtered some one hundred and twenty inhabitants – mostly women and children. It marked a definitive turning point.

A major element of the Mau Mau that frightened and nauseated both the military and the settlers was the system of oath administration. Oath-taking ceremonies were designed and performed by the Mau Mau precisely to distance an inductee from society at large, force him or her to become an outcast of church, or whatever societies and allegiances had been of prior importance to the individual. The concept was that the oath-taker would thus become more malleable to the idea of accepting the dictates of the Mau Mau. Many Bantu peoples have secret societies, just as secret societies also exist in a European context. The difference (cultural, to be sure) is that a European would view his particular society as totally voluntary, so permitting him to be in full agreement with and bound by its traditions or honours. But among the Kikuyu an oath was a magical undertaking. It had the power to terrorize and kill. With diabolical ingenuity the hard core of the Mau Mau administered a series of oaths precisely to terrorize their own people into supporting their cause. Once an African (possibly one imbued with superstitions) had taken the oath – forced to it at knifepoint – he became a member of the club, so to speak, and would only violate the oath upon pain of death. Much later in the game, and just as diabolically, the British propaganda machine invented a "cleansing oath" – the *thengi* – a counter-oath that freed the oath-taker from previous oaths and obligations, and thus his or her membership in the Mau

Mau.

Though the government forces had virtually cordoned off a gigantic area – one hundred miles by seventy miles – by the end of 1954 fully one third of the Kikuyu population was in gaol. Mau Mau leaders Dedan Kimathi and Stanley Mathenge had fled to the forests at the outset, from which they launched raids on farms and attacked remote police posts. Operation Blitz was launched in 1953 with sweeps of the mountainous Aberdare forest (average height eleven thousand feet); Operation Anvil followed the next year. A resettlement programme – so-called "villagisation" – began in June 1954. Kikuyu farmers were removed from their land and forced to live in specially-prepared containments. For the time being this process solved the problem of a massive expansion of what had become known as "the pipeline" – a system of appalling detention centres described in the British press as "Kenya's Belsen" – a "gulag." Torture was rife.

I myself recall an incident one afternoon on the outskirts of Nyeri when the jeep in which I was a passenger was forced to the side of the road by armed white men going in the opposite direction. Tied to the hood of their vehicle was the bloated dead body of a man they had killed earlier that day. I do not know if they were soldiers, police or a gang of the vigilantes we called "Kenya cowboys," but they had been parading their trophy before the town's populace – not quite a public hanging, but presumably intended as some form of public warning.

On another occasion I was passing near my own company headquarters office, a large marquee tent, and was drawn to enter it by loud shouts and hair-raising screams. There were two officers of the company present, along with a number of *askaris* and others I believed to be police. Strapped onto the top of one of the desks was a captured Mau Mau suspect who was being questioned as to the whereabouts of a group of rebels, presumably people he knew, or the rest of his own gang. To encourage response, or possibly just because the man was helpless and it was possible to torment him, one of the *askaris* was tickling his bare legs with a bunch of stinging nettles. The man's dirty feet had bloated up like rugby balls, so much so I couldn't make out his toes. They had developed bleeding and suppurating fissures. He had defecated, the closed air stank and the space inside the office was crowded so I remained for no more than a few moments. I was outranked by all the officers present, so even now am able to take refuge in the knowledge that there was little I could have done. To my shame I said nothing, then or later.

Hundreds of thousands of urban Kikuyu were banished to tribal reserves throughout the years of the emergency. Such "detention centres" had quickly become overcrowded and basically uninhabitable. Dubbed "the pipeline," they were appalling knock-offs of the concentration camps that had been favoured by Nazi Germany a generation earlier. They ensured that thousands of innocent people would die of malnutrition and starvation, and thousands more would die of floggings, torture and disease. These camps (there were fifteen major camps, many more smaller ones), along with the resettlement programme set up throughout the vast area of Kikuyuland known as "villagisation," were crucibles of violence and disease. Tuberculosis, typhoid, measles and malaria were rife. In these places alone men, women and children died by the thousands.

The British euphemism for the events of that time and place remains, even today, "the emergency." The term sums up quite a mess quite tidily, sweeping any nasty bits under a thick layer of self-serving obfuscation. The same sort of thing was to happen years later when Northern Ireland was wracked by forty years of war – "the troubles." Hearing such terms should sound an alarm that there is something much more sinister afoot; they form a signal, a soft-pedalled lingo for mayhem on a grand scale. Details will out in time, long after this volume will have gone to press: in January 2011, some three hundred boxes of secret documents relating to the Mau Mau were found to have been clandestinely transported to Britain at the time of independence in 1963. With the idea they may throw fresh light on excesses committed by both sides, a high court has demanded they be thoroughly examined. So amidst a combination of official dodging, paralysis, lies and, in the end, the expiration of time – the full story of the Mau Mau is gradually seeping into the domain of public awareness concurrently with those obscure bits of it that will be forever hidden and unaccounted for. One has to be extraordinarily alert to prevent victors from writing a full explanation of history.

Few people remember the Mau Mau now. I have spoken to members of my own generation whose recollections, after fifty years and much brow-furrowing, draws a blank. They have never heard the term, they say, no memory whatsoever of what the two repeated words signify. If I try to talk about the subject to anyone under forty years of age the result is frequently a furrowed brow, a "duh moment" that can sometimes surprise, even embarrass, those who might be expected to know. The term Mau Mau, the historical event of it, has simply dropped off the spectrum of general knowledge. Africans tend to remember, of course. For them, looking back, it is considered to have been a period of heroic action against centuries of oppression. What were "terrorists" to the British are today presented to contemporary Kenyan school children as independence seekers, "freedom fighters" for the oppressed of the former colony. In Kenya today where, for political expediency there had settled over the whole Mau Mau era a cloud of amnesia, there is now talk of erecting memorials to celebrate the dogged nine year fight for nationhood. In Britain a continuing and shameful amnesia appears to offer greater comfort.

What were the total casualties?

Statistics vary. The two figures that most people counting agree upon are that one thousand and ninety victims were hanged by the British security forces – many in public – and four thousand six hundred and eighty-six insurrectionists were killed by the Home Guard – forty-two percent of total security force kills. All other numbers are up for grabs.

The former colonial government claimed eleven thousand five hundred and three were killed on all sides, but this does not tally with independent assessments. David Anderson, in his book *Histories of the Hanged: Britain's Dirty War in Kenya and the End of Empire*, claims twenty thousand died; Caroline Elkins, in her book, *Britain's Gulag: The Brutal End of Empire in Kenya*, claims upwards of seventy thousand died.

In all, some one hundred thousand suspects were listed as imprisoned by the British in camps; anywhere between one hundred and fifty thousand and three hundred thousand are thought to have perished in the combined miseries of the detention camps and as a result of "villagisation." No one knows. There has never been a full or accurate tally.

For their part, the Mau Mau are claimed to have killed one thousand eight hundred African civilians and thirty-two white civilians. Two hundred British soldiers and police are listed as having died in Kenya during the period of the emergency, but I have been unable to discover satisfactory explanation as to precise causes. I must assume that accidents and disease are responsible at least in part.

Ultimately the British defeated the Mau Mau militarily. But as a result of rebel actions and sacrifices, and possibly more because of the savage response to them on the part of the British, the movement's more sophisticated and politically-minded cadres certainly achieved a principal aim: the Africans of Kenya were granted their independence in 1963.

☐

3. Early Days at Nyeri

Michael Barker and I were fellow cadets, developing a friendship during our time together at Eaton Hall. He had intended to enter university to study theology, eventually to follow his father as a minister in the church, but decided instead to get his National Service out of the way before embarking upon what he foresaw as the even more onerous demands on his future. He calculated that life as a seminary student would preclude those certain types of adventure open to most of his contemporaries and, in any case, he felt he should "do his bit."

In the initial days of training, when each individual in our unit was unfamiliar with his new surroundings and just beginning to form tentative links with the man next to him, it was not unusual to broach, albeit circumspectly, the most sensitive areas of personal enquiry. Sometimes this might be achieved in those rare moments of relaxation when we would sit together during a NAAFI tea break; other times we might be grouped in our barrack quarters, sitting on our beds, polishing our cap badges and belt brass. One man would talk about his studies, another about his family or girlfriend; not infrequently we would talk about what we were doing right now, how our present activity might bear on the greater life we all instinctively knew was in front of us. Conversation was rarely bawdy. Bawdiness was very much of the basic training barrack room; at Eaton Hall we were now gentlemen. Life was looming large and extremely serious.

Someone asked Michael:

"If you go on active service, how will you feel when you face an enemy and perhaps have to kill him – or even submit to being killed yourself?"

Unintelligent question for a perspicacious mind, but that was hardly our level at that particular time of our lives. We were young men on the threshold of responsibility, in so many ways green as little apples clinging to the tree. It was a curious time of our lives.

Michael answered that were he a low-ranking soldier, a private without rank, a believer in God or not, he would be obliged to fight and put his life on the line – like a soldier. But here and now, on the eve of graduating as an officer, he felt his circumstances had changed – that he must assume if ever he was faced with a life-or-death situation he would now be in a position of command and this would imply responsibility for the lives and well-being of those under him. He could not reasonably ask others to do what he was not prepared to do himself. He hoped he would acquit himself in a manner consistent with what is generally expected of a British officer – and if that meant killing an opponent well, that's what he would try to do. As to the possibility of being killed himself, all of us would be taking chances with that one every day, wouldn't we ...?

The rest of us thought his response signalled a sterling attitude. Well done, sir. These were our immortal years. Honour was a quality we all recognized; a quality that had been dinned into all of us as part and parcel of our English schooling and upbringing. It had many faces, and all of us preferred to think that we could recognize them if and as they were presented to us. Kill or be killed did not have any significant resonance.

In due course most of us graduated from OTS. The day after our graduation dinner Michael Barker went off to his assigned home regiment and I to mine. We shared addresses, as one does, but when we separated on that last morning amid the excitement of whatever lay before us, we both knew it would likely be a long time before we would be able to meet up again, hoist a pint and share stories of all the adventures upon which we were now embarked. Who among us had the slightest idea what all that would entail? Despite the best of intentions there was a part of me, I suppose, that never expected to see him again. Many of us, even as late as our final day at the school, had no precise knowledge of where we would be headed. In the end I was commissioned into one of the Home Counties regiments and promptly seconded to the same Tanganyika battalion of the King's African Rifles in which my brother had served, and which was then fighting the Mau Mau in Kenya. Michael Barker had also put in for the KAR, but it was not his first choice. He had signed up for other units as well, so was unsure which posting would come through.

*

I was destined to spend almost a full year on active service in Kenya. My battalion was stationed all of that time at the Beck Farm in Nyeri, a huge spread of land – the greater portion of it under the cultivation of coffee with the owner's home and compound at its centre; a smaller portion of the farm, closer to the town, was leased to the military. This last was still large enough to serve as tented barrack quarters for perhaps one thousand men, plus all their vehicles and equipment, and it included a spacious farm house which was used as the officers' mess. Being stationed there meant that, for the most part, our platoons were on operational patrols within the local district – various sections of the dense Nyeri forest, and segments of the forest that ran up into the Aberdare Mountains. These were all considered significant centres of Mau Mau activity. Many square miles were mapped out as no-go zones – areas where no one at all was permitted to roam, night or day. These were great swaths of the local countryside encompassing many villages under strict curfew. To be caught there during daylight hours would involve detailed questioning at the least, and possible arrest; at night one would run the risk of being shot on the spot, no questions. It was an impossible encumbrance for the local inhabitants who had to cross these areas for their needs of home – food and firewood and water. Daily there were "incidents." Some were frightening, some occasionally amusing, as in the time when an old villager, demented and not in the least intimidated by our presence, performed a silly dance before me in the dust of the roadway. But usually our encounters with locals were sad, the elements of fear, suspicion and hatred close to the surface. Rarely were they ever jovial or happy meetings. Now and then they were violent.

For those of us charged with controlling movement, all these incidents were packed minute-to-minute with elements of excitement and urgency, if not quite alarm. We had the weaponry, and the top-down encouragement was for us to use it. Life was scary for the locals; not so much for us. We were well armed, had the numbers, the backup and the authority. The locals were fearful of us.

For most of us patrolling these zones, particularly as newcomers, it was a full and onerous experience. We had been well trained, but the night-time intrigue was still new to us. It caused us pause because I think all of us, though young and untried, were reasonable people at heart. Many of us found it difficult to produce a rationale for resisting the bully tactics so clearly written into our orders, but we were not long away from civilized Britain and I believe there were those of us who had doubts about what we were being asked to do out there. It was a balancing act and by and large we performed it quite well. There was no question of us going off the deep end. Occasionally might we hear that some nut case on our side of the divide had blown his stack and started shooting the place up. Usually it would turn out to be one of the locals, someone – a settler, quite often – whose family had been too long exposed to the terrors of nightly solitude on a remote farm; or likely just someone who had been drinking ... On the whole the National Service fellows were remarkably stable and fair minded – just lads doing their best to work through their orders.

But this entailed both the sharp and the blunt ends of colonial racism, invariably unpleasant for someone who, new to the colony, simply did not know how to feel comfortable being overtly racist. One has to learn, from early childhood, how to be a bully. When bullying was required, or when we might have thought it was, it did not come easily. Every day there was something new, many new unexpected psychological conflicts.

I turned from nineteen to twenty years old during this period of my life, and the adventures that so naturally accompany an outdoor existence in Africa were the very essence of my existence as I thought it should be. But young officers like me, "one-pippers," had left our boarding schools only the year before. Each of us was a different shade of inexperienced green, and we still harboured ideals we had brought away from an exceptionally privileged life in England. Justice, fair play, cricket and the difference between a gentleman and a cad ... these were things we had learned to measure. We had been trained to fight, and well-trained; but I do not believe the killer instinct had yet been truly instilled in any of us.

Plonked down into the middle of this nasty emergency it quickly occurred to me this was in no way the heroic war fought by many of our fathers against Nazi Germany. This was a sideshow, part of an unsavoury effort to keep unruly natives in check and to tidy up the fringes of empire. Junior subalterns are seldom if ever asked for their opinions about anything, nevertheless a few of us did have some difficulties assessing whether or not holding empire together was actually worthwhile – and in trying to answer that one, those of us who were not so blind or cowed that we couldn't read what was plainly writ on the wall, were perplexed. Our "elders and betters," senior British officers we encountered in the mess, assured us there was nothing finer than empire, that it was the epitome of perfection – and it was hard to argue. None of us had yet lived long enough. But soon after arriving in Kenya I for one, and I was not alone, was having doubts about that. Had there been a real fight to fight, well enough; any one of us would have been up for it. But what we were being asked to do, now, was in no way an honourable fight.

Opinions are generally considered worthwhile only after a period of concentrated thought – and soldiers are not supposed to think. Junior subalterns are particularly vulnerable, for it is they who have the closest link to the men who are actually doing the dirty work. A thoughtful subaltern can be a liability.

The Mau Mau was no real enemy. Armed with knives and crudely-built firearms made from curtain rods and door bolts activated by elastic bands, they were terrified of being caught by us and desperately tried to avoid confrontation – or being shot in the back. We were picking the fight, not them, and for many of us it did not feel right. If ever I tried to figure out what the dishevelled little fellow at the business end of my sub-machine gun might have been trying to say to me (never mind that I could tell by his wide eyes precisely what he was thinking), I realized it was up to me whether he lived or died. But his survival in that vertiginous moment (a fragile lump of time at the point of my weapon) was not "living" for him; and had I chosen to pull the trigger there was no way I could have avoided accepting responsibility – or that my action would have been anything else but cold blooded murder. Yet I probably would not have been questioned too thoroughly.

I hazard a guess that most of us who were newly arrived in the battalion felt this way. It brought about a helpless anger, the morose sadness you might feel when you know you are trapped into an impossibly unacceptable situation. This was not a war. It was a piece of theatre. Above all it was a humiliation – for us as well as them.

Our humours were turned black or bawdy. Many of us ran up big bar bills in the mess. Drunk was good. Manly, even. Back in officer training school I had been able to convince myself that I was prepared to kill in battle for something like a *cause*; even to be killed. Yet according to my naïve assessment now (though I would not have cared to admit the naïvety), to shoot a man in a no-go zone because he happened to be there – even to point my weapon at him – made a terrorist of me, not him. How could one just open fire in such a circumstance? Where was the generosity in allowing an "enemy" to survive when it was so plain that all he wanted in that instant of confrontation was to be allowed to survive? Survival was the one thing all of us wanted, though confessing it to our mess mates, especially our seniors, would have been something like a degradation.

Our carefully-nurtured values, those we were so sure contained the kernel of truth, the unshakeable certainty of our well-honed sense of decency and civility, were being turned upside-down and given a right spanking. It was particularly so because another group of junior officers, most of them senior to us by at least one pip, and who had been out in these Highlands much longer than the rest of us, were anxious to chalk up kills. Were we, the newest of newcomers, destined to think like them when we had been out here a little bit longer?

The reasoning of these seasoned, slightly senior junior officers (and this much came out in numerous conversations during our mess drinking bouts) was that if we had been trained to kill, then our only means of fulfilling ourselves was to do just that. It may not have been expressed exactly that way, but that was the message; it would be difficult to mistake even oblique sentiment when its expression is actually so loud and clear.

These senior juniors, several of whom had been blooded themselves, wanted to assist us newcomers to join their fraternity. It was as if they were offering us a game to be played in dead earnest. The presentation was light and airy, but there was a hidden desperation, a darkness that hinted at the need for justification. In the convoluted logic of such thinking, soiling the innocent might have made each of them feel better. Some of them might have suffered nightmares as they slept in their cots, but in essence killing was a simple thing, something they were supposed to do – the reasoned consequence of a longer training than the junior juniors had yet had. Armies are supposed to break things and kill people; as these things go, this battalion was normal. It appeared to possess a fairly average complement of psychopaths – although the newest of us had yet to be measured.

Among hundreds of my stored mementos, a single photograph haunts, and I look at it even now. It is a transport back to the instant it was taken. It evokes a single moment as photographs are supposed to – but this moment is different. For me it freezes smells, textures, words, the faces of those walking by, or who just happen to be standing there. Emotions are harder to detect, but they are there too. Looking at that photograph across the space created by nearly sixty years I can feel again the immense weariness, the lameness, the boredom – the outsized inadequacy that stops youth dead, prevents him from taking hold of all his moments when he might use them with grace and creativity. A woman wails, terrified. Behind her, all around her, rise the moans of humiliation, resignation – the low clamour of people penned behind barbed wire mere metres from that soldier leaning against the side of the military Land Rover. The sun warms his body. The dust cakes in his nostrils. The cigarette in his hand is part of the same boredom that has tipped his slouch hat to the back off his forehead. The face in the photograph reads blank. For at least a couple of hours he has been watching a process that started at first light, and by now it is infinitely monotonous. The whole scene (and the viewer becomes a part of it) is now only a charade. The thought of bullying these villagers "on stage" for much more of this day is crushing, numbing. I have never taken to boredom easily or kindly, and yet here, in the right now immediacy of this photograph, one can see in an instant how monstrously, how tediously repetitive are the nuances of "military contract."

The Land Rover in the Kikuyu village made a sad and lonely backdrop to the photograph. This was no adventure.

Village raid ... the infinite monotony that stops youth dead

We were constantly receiving "red hot" information – often a load of crud, but anything of the kind had to be followed up – and so one day, in the earliest hours of the morning, we were called out to stage a raid on a Kikuyu village. It was a commonplace operation.

The entire battalion surrounded the village's *"pangie"* pit, a dry moat two metres deep, perhaps four metres across, itself completely encircling the outside of the village's fence and filled choc-a-bloc with sharpened wooden stakes – *pangies*. This pit and fence surrounded hundreds of squalid mud-and-wattle houses that huddled tight into the settlement.

Pangie pits were to be found at all villages in the emergency zones – thousands of vicious stakes immovably imbedded into the baked mud of the moat floor, needle-sharp and just inches from the one beside it. Anybody unlucky enough to tumble into the pit would be impaled instantly. Nobody entering it could possibly escape serious injury or death – which was the intent. Such pits served to keep villagers in and the Mau Mau out when they came seeking food or shelter. The only way into or out of such defended villages was via the roadway that led through a single main gate and past a Home Guard post; the *pangies* secured against entry or exit by any other route. If, in the early hours while we were encircling the place, we had discovered anyone even attempting to pass the pit, with a long ladder mayhap, the culprit would have been shot, or even tossed onto the *pangies*.

On this particular morning the procedure was routine as always: the villagers were roused from their beds, ordered out of their huts at gunpoint, and then forced to squat in the early morning sun in barbed wire enclosures set up within the village – men in one, women and children in another. Every village had its open spaces for a market or a playing field – and these served a useful dual purpose providing stockade areas. When necessary, army or police would arrive with rolls of barbed wire to accomplish the task, uncoiling it in double-quick time.

A military vehicle drove up right after we had entered the village centre. In the back of it were two Mau Mau turncoats from this same village, hooded against recognition by their clansmen. (Had they been recognized they would have been killed by the Mau Mau at the first opportunity.) The British would regularly press these sorts of individuals into service in order to assist with identification. The process started early and went on through the chill of the dawn hours into the sweltering sunlight of the mid-morning and afternoon, all villagers being led forward one-by-one between African police constables. They were paraded like recalcitrant school children before the two silent *ku kux klan* look-alikes. If one of these hoodies in the back of the car happened to recognize anyone as a Mau Mau sympathizer, he would beat loudly with one hand on the tailboard of the vehicle – anxious, now, to curry favour for himself by turning someone in. This would be the cue for police to drag off the poor wretch who had been identified. The *askaris* of the Kenya Police were not gentle, but might have done worse had they not been held in loose check by their white officers, who had to work in tandem with the military on these occasions. The army generally did not take kindly to its prisoners being poorly treated by the police, so sometimes it mattered which force would have made the original arrest.

Two former Mau Mau members have gone over to the British side and have agreed to act as informers within their own village. They are protected by the police. Were they to be identified by their own villagers they would instantly become targets for Mau Mau reprisal assassination. Having raided their village, and in an effort to conceal the identity of the informers, the British have dressed them in hoods so they may safely identify Mau Mau members within their own community. Isolated in pens by the military, every man, woman and child within the village is brought before the identifying team either for clearance or denunciation. The identifiers are not permitted to speak as their voices may reveal who they are; they convey their findings by a pre-arranged series of signals rapped out on a table or, as in this case, on the tailgate of the vehicle in which they are seated. The intensity of rapping will indicate the degree of a man's or woman's involvement with Mau Mau – very excited drumming calling attention to someone deeply connected with the sect. Those thus identified are immediately hauled away for interrogation – with the strong likelihood of beatings or torture to elicit further information.

Mrs. Queen's Chump

The Kikuyu villagers were divided. Seeing one of their neighbours dragged away, it was hard for them to remain neutral in the political climate of the time; those who were not themselves members of the Mau Mau tended to have little sympathy for gang members who were seen to be willing to kill their own as a means of coercing loyal membership. No matter their feelings, they understood the importance of remaining silent.

An intense grilling by low rank police officers, whites with translators, would immediately follow an identification. Not infrequently, generally when military officers were not present as witnesses, an interrogation would be accompanied by a thrashing.

Members of the military would stand apart. We neither liked nor trusted the Kenya Police. It was an unhelpful rivalry. The police considered the actions of the Mau Mau to be "crimes," and thus to fall within their jurisdiction. The military, on the other hand, felt they were fighting a war of sorts (many of us, as I said, had our doubts) and that the police, in almost all instances in which the two entities had to work things out between them, were interfering and incompetent. On occasions such as this particular village raid, the role of the soldiers was either to assist with the cordon about the village, or to patrol in pairs among the lines of huts. The police would ask the army to rummage through the squalid little homes, turning all their contents into the streets – but then they insisted they alone had the authority to seek for any concealed and illicit weapons. The whole theatrical experience was a well calculated exercise in brutality, no matter which force was actually in control – brutal tactics, brutal home invasions, brutal treatment of even the innocent.

It was a brutality, also, to my own tender sensitivities – one of which was that I would not for the world have cared to admit my sense of horror at the way we, the fair-minded British, were behaving. A cure for that might be for me to witness at first hand a Mau Mau atrocity – but the fact was, although I knew full well they had committed many atrocities, I saw none myself. There were far fewer of them by the end of 1956. The atrocities I did witness were those being committed by the British. From my lowly perspective as an infantry officer it was difficult to obtain a well-defined and overall picture. It did seem, though, that by now the Mau Mau had no wish at all to pick a quarrel with either the army or the police; that they knew they were heavily out-gunned, and what they wanted above all was to be able to come in from the dreadful conditions of living in the forests without food, decent lodging or any form of medical assistance. They existed in sorry state; it was not unusual for them to be shot in the back – indication they were desperately trying to get away from us. But then, if they did come in, they knew they would likely face trial and the chances were they would be sent to a labour camp, or possibly hanged.

*

My days were filled to the brim with new people, new events. During months of so much activity I barely gave a passing thought to the life I had left behind in Britain, or the people I knew there. A girl I had met in Windsor just before embarking sent me a photograph, and I stuck it up on the bamboo table I had rigged beside my bed. I could not recall her name so gave her photograph the nickname "Snips," and wished her a goodnight as I laid my weary head on my pillow. Michael Barker occurred to me once or twice, not so much as the friend I had barely had time to get to know, but as a mere "wonder-where-he-is-now" thought. Yesterday was already a long time ago. Mess brandy was cheap, and during the early days of my stay in Nyeri I was consuming large quantities of it. The faces of many people tended to fade in and out of the general fog of my consciousness.

All our various active operations tended to merge into a continual stream of duties, but in fact they fell into three categories: village raids of the type just described, team-style major operations, and bush patrols – about which I shall have more to say shortly.

I hated the raids; they were so hideously invasive and demeaning, as though we were placing our boots on the necks of the innocent in order to root out the Mau Mau.

The team-style work we attempted on those occasions when we would sally out as an entire battalion, likely in company with other battalions, were (at least in my limited experience) catastrophic cock-ups. As a noteworthy postscript to this second category, elements of the following anecdote may serve as template:

Returning to base one afternoon after a four-day operation at Lake Naivasha, the entire complement of regimental officers decided to meet up in the bar at Nyeri's Outspan Hotel. We were still dressed in our filthy bush attire and muddy boots – sweaty, toting our weapons provocatively and boasting. A few days earlier there had been "red hot" information that ninety Mau Mau would be attending a planning conference in the broad swampy area that surrounded the edge of the lake's waters. We didn't know exactly where, so rushed in – four battalions (close to four thousand men) screaming into position in trucks. Four days later we withdrew – not a trifle sheepishly. As a military exercise it had commenced with a great roar of intent, but in the end turned out to be something of a lip-biting embarrassment. No one would have read it that way that afternoon at the Outspan, however.

We drank a lot and shouted and swaggered overbearingly. The hotel staff was alarmed and tried politely to coax us down from a dangerous mob high; but we had the guns so they put up with us as graciously as they felt they had to. Midday wore on into the dark of early evening, and our tempo reached ever higher. Each officer attempted to recount how he had acquitted himself in an operation that, in point of fact, had been little less than a dismal military washout. In four days no one had even seen a Mau Mau. Score: hundreds of thousands of rounds of ammunition fired off fruitlessly, several Royal Air Force bombing sorties – and one dead cow.

The trouble was that when the four battalions had gone out on the op they had failed to synchronize either their mission or their method. When the rifle battalion directly across the lake from our unit opened up with small arms fire, the bullets zipped over the tranquil waters like angry hornets, the shoreline reeds providing us nary a mite of protection. We were forced to submerge ourselves, to sink our noses into the muck and slime at the lake's edge. Much later, after a detailed assessment of the fiasco, it was found that the tracks of about ninety men led out of the swamp across our backs.

We all blamed Brigade. Handy. Brigade Headquarters was set up behind barbed wire right across the street from the Outspan.

"Brigade! Who gives a damn about Brigade!"

The colonel's wife stood at the bar, a well-oiled and steely-black Patchett sub-machine gun slung casually over her shoulder, one booted foot up on the bar rail. As we lived in the dire-filled times of an emergency, everyone took to carrying a weapon. Settlers throughout the colony were suddenly wearing bush khaki clothing, Stetson hats and driving about, city or bush, in jungle-green four-wheel drive vehicles. Weaponry varied. Some of the old timers carried Second World War vintage Lee-Enfield service rifles, one or two the Italian or German counterparts, Carcanos and Mausers. Younger wags took to wearing pistols slung in holsters at their hips, and were derogatorily referred to as "Kenya cowboys." Ladies' fashion stores in Nairobi sold matching hats, handbags and holsters.

Mrs. Thornton claimed to possess some expertise with her choice of weapon.

"Ach, you don't know how to fire that thing …!" one of the junior officers scoffed at her – whereupon Mrs. Thornton stepped up to the bar, her colonel beaming approvingly from the bemused distance of a good half-quart of vodka, and proceeded to rake off the entire second row of bottles that had till now so colourfully lined the glass shelving behind the bartender. (He ducked.)

She missed one bottle, swung back and zapped it. It was good shooting.

There had also been a framed mirror that ran the full width of the bar behind the shelving …

The place erupted.

"Three cheers for Mrs. Thornton!" the juniors shouted, hefting the good lady onto their shoulders and trooping her about the barroom over the glass shards.

Someone started belting out, "For she's a jolly good fellow …," but tailed off when he realized others weren't taking it up, and that in any case the strains were lost in the general raucous hubbub.

In exaltation Mrs. Thornton fired off two triumphal rounds into the ceiling …

Moments later a forbidding and grizzled old stoat, browned by her years in the sun, her once delicate visage furrowed like the lands she had farmed for a generation, emerged like a tall ghost beside the bar. She was dressed in a white nightshirt and sported a tasselled bed cap. In her hand she clasped a 45-calibre service revolver.

"Who's been shooting bullets through my floor?" she demanded, scowling ferociously.

Mrs. Thornton was still atop the juniors' shoulders, the hot muzzle of her Patchett smoking and reeking of cordite.

"Mrs. Rutherford! How good of you to come and join us!"

In no time Mrs. Rutherford's loaded revolver lay carelessly on top of the

Mrs. Queen's Chump

bar, while she herself laid hand on a stiffer-than-normal tumbler of vodka and began to laugh and party it up as loudly as the rest of us.

So our days and nights merged into a continuum of totally irresponsible event, and it became ever increasingly difficult to separate one set of circumstances from any particular other.

"Brigade!" I muttered under my breath that same evening. Stepping out of the front door of the hotel and advancing across the street, unzipping my trousers as I went. I had the intention of splashing my indignation on a particularly offensive whitewashed wall that loomed among the headquarters outbuildings.

"I'll show you what I think of Brigade!"

In the dark I failed to see the coils of barbed wire that surrounded Brigade, and I quickly became entangled in it, falling on my face.

"Jeremy! Jeremy!" my fellow junior officers wailed, grabbing me by my boots and hauling me out of my predicament – across the barbs. My filthy uniform was demolished forthwith, and the tears and scratches on my face, body and extremities soon gave the appearance I had supped with a leopard.

"Oh dear!" I burped at breakfast in the officers' mess the following morning, having seen my visage reflected in the highly polished silver lid of the scrambled egg tureen. My sole consolation was that several of the other junior officers were to be in even worse condition. Nobody made comment.

*

There is an amusing postscript to this Lake Naivasha farce.

Many years later when I was working as a newspaper reporter in Regina, Saskatchewan, the local college hosted the first of what was eventually to become a long line of Commonwealth students. Peter Njuguna, a Kikuyu student, came to the city from Kenya to take a two-year preliminary course that, if he passed, would permit him to move on to an agricultural degree at the university in Saskatoon. I was writing about education for the paper and it was in this way I first came to know about him.

We became good friends and he would frequently come to the house for meals, or just to sit and talk about home with someone who had been there.

It was during one of these quite relaxed conversations that I learned he had been forced into the ranks of the Mau Mau when he was a boy of fourteen. Inevitably I told him about the debacle at Lake Naivasha, and he started to laugh.

He remembered the occasion well, Peter told me. His footprints were among those that passed over our backs when we were so distracted by the small arms fire coming through the reeds from across the lake, and our noses were pressed into the muck.

*

The Beck Farm was a big spread. It maintained its production of coffee despite there being a battalion of one thousand men bivouacked on several of the plantation's fields. One of the older and more spacious of the farm dwellings had been commandeered as the officers' mess. The more senior officers had their quarters set up within this house; the rest of the officers bunked down in tents that had been pitched in lines in a large garden area on the south side of the building.

But for the architectural design of the house, a spacious colonial style ranch dwelling typical of Kenya's Highlands, it would have been difficult to imagine the area we occupied as a farm. The battalion had been here for a number of months, and the overall aspect of the place was military encampment. Everything but the mess was under drab khaki canvas. The battalion headquarters and communications offices were housed in about six marquees pitched in a cluster less than one hundred metres to the east of the mess entrance. The HQ company billet was some one hundred metres beyond that. There was a level area considerably larger than a football field which was used as a parade ground and drill square to the north of HQ company, and to the north again in an east-west line were the ordered tent formations of the four operational companies – A, B, C and D. Beside D company, in the far north eastern corner of the farm property, and near its main entrance, was the camp's guard quarters. Just inside the gate was the motor vehicle yard – an independently-barricaded and gated compound where were parked all of the battalion's necessary transport vehicles – at least a couple of acres of trucks and Jeeps and Land Rovers, and the work sheds to keep them all in working order. At the extreme western end of the encampment, sunken fifteen metres below the level of the main camp area, was a wide flat space that could quite easily have hosted three football fields. When the whole area had been farmed this particular spread was employed in the cultivation of grain crops. Now it was empty except for a large area on which there had been erected a pair of goal posts. In their off-hours many of the *askaris* would assemble here, happily kicking a ball around in an impromptu game – and they would have continued doing so from dawn to dusk had they been permitted. As it was, the whole space was regularly turned into an after supper gathering ground, a social area where the soldiers would squat about bonfires to talk and laugh, tell their stories or beat their drums.

These *ngomas,* as they were called, were a nightly occurrence. Sitting comfortably in arm chairs within their mess atop the hill, sloshing back their ever so well-mixed pinks gins and brandies, most of the regimental officers tended to be scornful of this activity. Not only did the *askari* programmes go on well into the night, far beyond the bedtime hours of the average mess imbiber (and thus, so it was claimed, an impediment to sleep), but it was considered in all seriousness to be a pounding rhythmical reminder of the primal savagery that made it so necessary for us all to be there. Whatever message the African drums might have been beating out, the message received in the mess, nightly and with abundant clarity, was that Mother England must remain to carry her colonial burden throughout these parts for many years to come if ever there was to be the slightest hope of leading these poor blighters into the fold of modern civilization. The drumming was generally perceived as the infernal racket of unrestrained children, but something that had to be endured in preference to what might occur if the reins were pulled in too tight.

I did not have the courage to admit it too loudly, but I liked the drumming. In time it summoned me from my station at the bar, and I found I much preferred this form of entertainment to the constant round of boozy folk tales being spun out nightly in the officers' mess. At first I would step outside the mess into the darkness of the night and take up a position on the edge of the hill that overlooked the *ngoma* field. I was fascinated by the different rhythms and how, after a period of time, they would merge into a single voice. It was thrilling. However, I was not brave enough to go down there. It was nothing I feared from the *askaris*, though I had heard some of them worked themselves into frenzies – especially when they had a beer or two in their gut.

My real fear was the opinion of my fellow officers. I had heard them talk and knew how they felt. More especially, I knew how they preferred to draw a line between themselves and their black troops. The conventional military reasoning was that distance between officers and men created better discipline, made it easier to maintain essential lines of control. I recognized that argument, to be sure, but it did not satisfy me. I knew I would never receive a satisfactory or honest explanation of this officer-soldier divide from any single one of my colleagues in the mess. So I funked, said nothing. I would make it look as if I was complying with what was expected of me – but then sneak away to my solitary post on the hill. In consequence I suffered a rather knotted-up internal conflict, a twinge of guilt at the thought I was breaking faith with "my side." Even had I been permitted, I would not have known how to explain my thoughts to anyone. I would watch and listen to the drummers, secretly and in silence from my hiding in the darkness.

The first person I tried to talk to about this conflict was Nyamahanga Boke, the WOPC* assigned to my platoon. I was coming to know him quite well, and to feel a great respect for a forthright man who was a far more experienced soldier than I would ever likely be myself.

"The other officers in the mess don't appreciate the *ngomas*," I commented.

"We understand that," he replied, smiling.

"But you do it anyway …?"

"Of course. It's important to us, and it is enjoyable, too. You should come and join us. We are having a big one on the weekend, maybe roasting a buck. Come down there with me and I shall explain things to you … You will learn much about us."

So, come the indicated weekend, I took courage in hand and went down onto the field to meet with Nyamahanga. He had surrounded himself with a number of the fellows from our platoon, young men whose faces I knew because I saw them every day and worked with them, but who now stood before me in quite different light.

Nyamahanga moved among them easily, chatted and laughed with them

---

* WOPC – **W**arrant **O**fficer **P**latoon **C**ommander – a non-commissioned senior rank existing within each platoon just below the command position of the platoon officer and senior to the platoon sergeant. Up to the time I left Kenya, the British did not award commissions to East African *askaris*. When they started doing so, it was from the list of WOPC's that the first East African officer class was created.

Mrs. Queen's Chump

like an older brother. I enjoyed watching him. On the parade square, when we were all playing soldiers, he was their senior; down here on this wide open space, in downtime, he was just one of them. Yet their respect for him was plain to see. Towards me their affability, their friendliness, the easy familiarity of the pleasure they expressed at seeing me moving among them, abandoning in measure the officer-soldier formality that I knew my fellow officers would have insisted upon – all of this might have been different had my WOPC not been there. But for his presence I might have been instantly, catatonically, unnerved.

Good thing it was dark, I thought, for I was by no means sure of the role I was playing. The night hid any number of the apprehensions I knew, without coaching, were entirely of my own manufacture – not through any fear of the differences between our varying colours or cultures, but because I somehow knew my being there would have been cause for the severe criticism of my own colleagues and fellow officers. I was apprehensive of what they would think of me, of their approbation and my own ability to stand up to it. I think I recognized how the situation was testing me, that quite deliberately I was being infra dig. In a way I was pleased with myself and enjoying it, but I feared the scolding treatment I knew I would receive when I went back up the hill to the mess full of drunken officers, and I was not at all sure I would be strong enough to face them – or to face them down. Nyamahanga's presence was imperative in the first moments after my arrival on the field, and I am sure he knew it.

It was not only members of my own platoon who gathered about me, but others I recognized from different companies – faces I might have noticed on the parade square and never thought about. Now, suddenly, they were coming up to me with a measure of unabashed intimacy to greet me as though they knew who I was, and confident that I would know them – a confidence ratified by my nodding my head or smiling when I saw a familiar face. Nyamahanga never moved far away from my side. My sergeant joined us, a wide smile of greeting on his merry face. The two of them talked in dialect as I began to relax.

"Sergeant Zuberi says he is pleased that you have come to join us. It is a good thing that you are showing an interest in our customs. This way you will discover a better understanding of Africa, and it will be easier for you to learn Swahili ..."

Laughing now, the two of them surrounded by others from our platoon, led me to a stone at the side of the field, strategically placed as a seat of honour close to the fire pit. The carcass of a gazelle was turning on a spit, and someone pushed a tin mug full of barley beer into my hand.

"This tonight, this is *ngoma*. *Ngoma* is a feast, a party, a celebration. Not every night is *ngoma* ..."

"So what is the celebration all about this evening?" I asked Nyamahanga.

Broad smiles all around.

"Our leader has come to be with us!"

This was heady. Leader. It was not easy to see myself that way. The title did not readily fit me, and I was not entirely comfortable with it. Considering the word hierarchically, as if it were a vertical triumph of attainment, I realized the title depended precisely on how one saw oneself – and in that regard I definitely saw myself floating somewhere around lower middle. Not much of anything, really. Not one of the easy laughing mob; and certainly not high enough in the military pecking order to permit myself much more than a wince at what I felt were my own shortcomings. By bumbling along in my rather self-absorbed and sleepy fashion, I had barely scraped my way past the threshold of the officers' mess. I was well-trained, but I was not brimming with self-confidence, so in the mess I felt like a greenhorn among a host of sturdy gallants – my fellow subalterns leading their men into war. It was not unlike sitting down to banquet and, being unsure which utensil to pick up first, casting furtive glances sideways in order to see what the host would do first so I could follow suit.

Yet behind me, so to speak, were all these men – these merry men – of my unit, most of them probably about my own age, some possibly several years older. Nyamahanga, who would have been at least ten years older than any of them, was their leader – their natural leader – and here comes this jacked-up bullock with a glittering pip of rank newly granted by the British Crown and all of a sudden I have become the leader's leader. The weight rested uneasily upon my shoulders.

In my first months at Nyeri I had had difficulties with language, and relied on Nyamahanga as a translator. He was patient with me, and laughed a lot as he corrected my mistakes. This evening, tense at first, I was able to become more relaxed. Conversation with those gathered about me was stilted, but I noticed how even the simplicity of a single word somehow brought out the greatest pleasure and encouragement. I was seeing smiles this evening that I had never noticed on the parade ground or around the company office, and after a few more barley beers I dare say I was smiling pretty broadly myself. Several of the *askaris* had given renditions of songs local to their hometowns. One raised his voice rather softly and sang about a girl selling shellfish at a beach.

"He comes from Zanzibar," Nyamahanga explained, interpreting for me in a whisper.

When the soldier had finished singing, the men sitting with us burst into laughter and applause, teasing him about the girl in the song.

There were others who sang – in Luo or Chagga, and one in a Swahili dialect I thought I could understand, sort of. After each song there would be a few moments of raucous chatter, teasing and laughter, and then the next man would be encouraged to sing.

"Now you must sing us a song of your country," I was told, and suddenly all attention was turned to me – the *effendi*'s turn to make a fool of himself.

"I'll tell you what," I told them. "I'll sing a song for you, but you must learn the words. I'll teach you ..."

So they all sat eagerly in front of me, and I sang out:

"I got spurs that jingle-jangle-jingle ..."

... A popular country and western song which I remembered being made famous in my early childhood by Gene Autry. It tells the tale of a happy cowboy singing the joys of bachelorhood as he rides merrily along on his way.

I stifled my natural shyness, and made sure I gave the lads a bit of a show.

It was a hit! A couple of the soldiers rolled on their backs on the ground, yipping with glee. I couldn't have received a more appreciative endorsement if I had won a popular song contest.

Two of them jumped up and started gyrating to a hilarious buttock-wobbling dance.

"Jingle-jangle-jingle!" they sang, and whacked their butts together so hard they both fell over, roaring with laughter and encouraged by all the rest, some of whom also jumped up and started to dance – in an effort, I suspect, to become even more ridiculous. It was a show-stopper.

The words could not have meant a whole lot to them. Nyamahanga tried to explain, but it's likely they didn't mean much to him either.

In any case the "jingle-jangle-jingle" bit made an impact. For weeks afterwards as I would pass through the lines on my way to the company office, some soldier would be squatting on his haunches at the entrance to his tent, polishing the brass on his dress belt or cap badge, and chanting: "… jingle-jangle-jingle …" Occasionally I'd come upon one or two of them wobbling between the guy ropes to the buttock dance.

That evening I deliberately stayed late, until the fire had burned down and the first of the celebrants headed off to their tents. This way I was able to avoid returning to the officers' mess, and so to sneak unseen back to my own tent. I felt as though a spell had been cast over me, and I didn't want to disrupt it.

But the following morning at the breakfast table the adjutant zeroed in on me. The battalion commander wished me to report to his office.

Military men seldom mince words, and that morning I think Col. Thornton had decided to use his bullying tactics to scare the hell out of me.

"Not good to have you fraternizing with the *askaris*, sir …! What do you think you are doing …?"

He was a big man, with a brutishly unsympathetic glare in his eyes. Had he tackled me this way a day or so earlier, I have no doubt at all I would have been frightened out of my skin.

But Nyamahanga's calm and reasoned presence the night before had touched me; with absolute clarity I understood that my participation at the *ngoma*, my choosing to mingle with my WOPC and the men of my platoon, had been an act of integrity, an impromptu but honest and honourable initiation enthusiastically entered into by myself, true, but also by the men of my platoon.

Nyamahanga Boke

Mrs. Queen's Chump

There was nothing here to feel the least unsettled about, let alone shame. On the contrary, here and now in the cold presence of my commanding officer, I knew I had been greatly dignified – honoured – by the *askaris* who had so openly expressed their trust in me as their leader. True, they had little choice; they were assigned to my platoon (rather, I had been assigned to them). But there was no guilt to be spread around, and I for one had no intention of accepting any. Any question of laxity in discipline – there was none – would have been fabricated solely in the imagination of some jaundiced on-looker.

I was clever enough not to confront Col. Thornton with an argument; I was not intimidated by him, but I knew he was the embodiment of the British Army – the most sophisticated fighting force in the world, and that it was founded upon centuries of obedience and tradition – and pomp and class bullshit. It would have been idiotic of me to have considered for an instant that I could have reasoned with this man. How would it have sounded to him, I remember thinking at the time, if I had claimed, "Not me, sir. I'm different!"

A second lieutenant does not argue with the British Army.

Right then, in my colonel's office, I understood what was meant by "fraternizing," that it was something negative, but I knew his definition in no way applied to my own actions. I perfectly understood what he was attempting to say, but I did not – I would not – accept the mean-spirited and narrow definition of this bellicose senior officer that I had done something incorrect, as though I had somehow sullied the regimental tradition by choosing to be with the men of the regiment instead of its officers.

I was certain, moreover, no one in the officers' mess the night before had either witnessed or divined what transpired between myself and my men on the lower field. So I held my peace and did not respond when the colonel ran out of wind and found himself with nothing more to add concerning my "appalling laxity" of behaviour. Indeed, there was nothing I could say. But I knew, when I looked at his angry face, that he had made an assessment of my silence. I stood to attention before his desk, eyes fixed straight ahead about six inches above his brow. "Dumb insolence" – I knew he was thinking. I could almost hear him mutter it. Without saying a word I knew I had crossed this man as surely as if I had jumped on the toes of his squeaky spit-and-polish parade boots.

□

4. Rogue

Gundagai McGinty was an Australian, a full lieutenant shortly due for promotion to captain at the time I met him, and considering to sign on for more than his already contracted three-year commission. He never explained to me why he had joined the British Army; it could have been that his circumstance was rather similar to my own – nothing else coming down the pipeline in his life just then or, even more alike my own case, he was trapped by residency requirements so thought it was best to put his head down and just get on with it. We never discussed it. We hailed from vastly different segments of the Empire, alien enough from Britain that our fellow officers felt free to comment on the fact and often did. Gun was referred to as "The Oz," which might have been inoffensive enough, except that he didn't like it; my own sobriquet was "The Fuckin' Canuckin" which, uttered with smirks and intended in jest, was nonetheless irksome after I'd heard it the first time. But instead of complaining or taking the trouble to answer back, which might have given our tormenters a deal of pleasure, Gun and I had both decided, quite separately, to give measure to the differences our fellow officers chose to note so unkindly. We did this most effectively by demonstrating our brash colonial roots with as much exaggerated good humour as we could muster, a notable and quite deliberate lack of English officer-class posture and polish. Both of us tended to consider the mess overloaded with a slightly amusing but stuffy pedantry. From their viewpoint I think our colleagues considered our "attitude" rough-edged, bewilderingly "colonial" and doubtless minus a little tea-time polish.

Gun had been with the battalion for at least a couple of years before I arrived on the scene at Nyeri; he commanded considerable respect among the troops, and particularly among the subalterns, because of his knowledge of the bush and the forests, and his abilities to handle the work he was assigned. He spoke Swahili well. The troops he commanded trusted him absolutely, certain in the knowledge he would always stand up for them.

Each new subaltern coming into the battalion was given a three-week brush-up under the eye of a more experienced officer before being assigned to his own platoon, and it was my good fortune to spend that period of time with Gun. I learned a great deal from him and the experienced members of his squad, all of it knowledge that was to serve me well in the months ahead. In addition I was rewarded by a close association with the man himself.

Gun was several years my senior. Though on the verge of being promoted to captain he was being held back deliberately for reasons he did not discuss at first, but which I later came to see and understand. He was not a mixer. He kept his own counsel and never sought the advice of others. He was not a team player, and this counted against him.

He was stocky, powerfully built and extremely strong, all his movements exuding confidence. I once saw him carrying an ammunition box under one arm, and a man with a broken leg under the other. When he was able to pass off the ammunition box to another soldier, he broke into a run in order to ensure the wounded man could receive more quickly the attention he needed. Others might have helped, but it was an indication of his "get it done" attitude that he performed such a task the way he did.

His head was topped by a thick crop of blonde hair that fell over his forehead like a thatched roof. When he was angry or agitated, he would toss this mop with jerky motions up and over his right shoulder in a futile effort to shake it back; invariably it would flop forward again into precisely the position it had been before. It was like a nervous tick. He only wore a hat when regulations required it. On patrol in the bush he preferred to go bare-headed, with the result that his blondness was bleached almost white. The sun-parched skin of his face was drawn taut over the angular bone structure of his jaw, exaggerating eyes that danced under scruffy brows and were of quite different colours, one a vivid blue the other a milky green – a feature causing not a few people to query whether he could actually see from it. No trouble with his vision. It could be confusing to face him, difficult to choose which eye to look at.

To his face his fellow officers called him Gun. When he was beyond ear-shot they referred to him as "The Oz," always with a tinge of envy mixed with their respect because he had more kills to his credit than any other officer in the battalion.

Gun was a maverick, always on the verge of trouble, and if he got away with behaviour for which another officer might be castigated, it was because he was more on his toes than those who would criticize him. He was good at his job. It was the senior officers in the mess – the colonel and several of the majors and captains – who muttered about him the most, never actually levelling accusations, but rankled because his way worked, and it was so clear they should just leave well enough alone.

Gun operated his platoon as something of a separate entity within the battalion, his "headquarters group" consisting of a dog, a batman who was more of a shadow sidekick, and a young boy who looked up to Gun as would a son to a father. The four of them were always together. The dog was named Cuba, the batman Samadhi. The little boy was Kidogo – small in Swahili, a name Gun himself had chosen.

Samadhi was a rifleman in Gun's platoon, a man small in stature but big in energy. Gun had selected him as his batman long before I ever came on the scene and they had developed a strong bond of a quality easily misconstrued by other officers – particularly the seniors. Those who criticized the most could only see how this junior officer and his manservant openly laughed and kibitzed with one another. It was a relationship that, as a matter of course to the British officer thought pattern, was considered quite unacceptable. Officers should not be that close to the Africans; some had gone so far as to counsel Gun "for his own good" about how "this sort of thing" was frowned upon, that such fraternization could only rebound in some disastrous way on his military career. Gun ignored them, and no one had the balls to castigate him in such a way as to make a tongue-lashing stick – or necessarily even make sense. So when he was out of earshot his critics would grumble about him behind his back.

Piling a little insult on top of injury, Samadhi and Kidogo were surrogate masters to Cuba, a mutt dog whose exceptional intelligence only fostered further resentment. Instinctively the dog understood when he was to trot after Samadhi or Kidogo, or when to owe some higher fealty to Gun. Even more humiliating, when both Gun and Samadhi were busy with their military rounds to the exclusion of dogs, Cuba was perfectly content to have his ears scratched by Kidogo – prancing past senior officers, his nose in the air without so much as a hint of acknowledgement, let alone a salute. Indeed, the seniors were of a mind the foursome was a team of deliberate insubordination.

Filled with their own prejudices and absolutely unable to identify with such a close-knit working group, Gun's critics would have preferred to see him stand aloof like themselves, a respectable social distance between himself, his servant, his *askaris* and his dog. For the seniors with their unimaginative herd mentality it would have been impossible to consider there was something like friendship between these individuals – for if such a thing existed it most certainly should not be permitted. Most of the seniors who had an opinion to express were so stuck in their concepts of correctness between whites and Africans they would have found it impossible to conceive of a bond any closer than Kipling's to Gunga Din. And that was a poetic concoction ...

On the fringe of Gun's colourful headquarters group was a fifth entity: Hashimu, his platoon sergeant. Hashimu was a friend and fellow tribesman of Samadhi's. He stood slightly to the edge of the headquarters circle, an interpretive position between Gun and the rest of the soldiers in the unit. Because of this he, too, was held in some suspicion by those who so liked to look askance at Gun. Yet I think it was because of Hashimu that the most critical senior officers were decided to leave Gun pretty much alone. Sergeant Hashimu was greatly respected by the men under him, relating so well to the platoon as a whole – and its officer – that serious interference by others could only have caused rupture. These seniors were not blind to the close-knit manner in which Gun worked with his sergeant, and the sergeant with the men of the platoon. If there was a mystery present in all this, at least the seniors were able to give Hashimu his due. He was well-integrated with the individual members of the platoon, the *askaris* accepting him so well precisely because of the extremely close relationship he had with his officer. As an outsider it was amusing to witness the irritations caused by this complex play of personalities.

In the chips-down matter of getting the job done Gun's small unit stood out as exemplary within the battalion. Quite simply he was a better operations officer than all of the others; the biggest irritation was that he did his job so well. He had more operational success to his credit than anyone else; yet he was a quiet-spoken man – not the sort to seek credit, let alone brag.

This, then, was the group that was to take me in tow for three weeks just after I joined the battalion, and with whom I was to have my first lessons in how to operate effectively in Kenya's forests; yet I was never made to feel like a student among them, an outsider. I was pulled into the centre of the group, and not least of those who made me feel both welcome and at ease, and possibly even an asset, was Gun himself. I was privileged to be permitted to come close to him.

At the outbreak of the revolution Britain's response in the urban areas had been so thorough and so severe that key elements of the African organization had immediately been driven into hiding. Many fled into the urban jungles, but many more into the forested rural areas, especially north and northwest of Nairobi, the remote regions spread over the exceptionally rough terrain of the Aberdare Mountains and Mount Kenya. Within a year or so of the declaration of the emergency these two major regions had become centres of Mau Mau's most active campaigning, and thus the areas the British authorities considered vital to their control over the hinterland beyond the capital.

I enjoyed the Aberdares. I liked the jungle, and I liked our bivouac life under the canopy of the trees. Gun's first forest lesson for me was an explanation about food. Back at battalion headquarters prior to setting out he had had me unload the backpack I had intended to lug into the bush filled with tinned breakfasts, lunches and dinners.

"Break your bloody back, mate. Just take a jar of pickles if you like 'em – leave the rest to the *askaris*."

Indeed, the *askaris* knew all about bush cuisine. Each man carried a few small sacks of rice packed in among his shirts and socks and between them they had more than enough to feed the lot of us three meals a day. In addition they carried rashers of biltong – thin strips of salted and sun-dried meats that kept indefinitely and which, carefully prepared with the rice and seasoned with herbs picked in the forest, ensured that for the entire period of our small operation I was never aware of eating the same meal twice. It's just as well I listened to Gun on this one; once settled into my forest *basha* I discovered I had forgotten my can opener.

We patrolled every day, walking miles through forest, scrublands and bamboo; we would traipse down into darkened gullies, fording streams sometimes swollen to torrents, clambering up hillsides and out onto spectacular cliff edges. We encountered more animals than I'd ever seen in a zoo – gazelle, rhinoceros, buffalo, wart hog, giraffe, lion – and birds of such variety and colour I never knew existed. I watched the *askaris* tracking (animals or people made no difference, the method was the same) and I even fancied I'd become moderately proficient at it myself – or at least my instructors smiled and told me so. However, on the one occasion when I encountered a snake I blithely stepped right over it, not seeing it let alone recognizing it as a mamba. The soldier walking behind me sliced it into little pieces with his *panga*.

Gun knew his men well. He not only knew all their names, but to what tribe they belonged and the name of each man's home village. Beyond these details, he knew about their families and their headmen, he knew what each man had done for a living prior to joining the King's African Rifles, and when each man was due for leave or demobilization. His Swahili was fluent so that he had an advantage over many of the platoon commanders who had to rely on a WOPC or English-speaking African sergeant to communicate with their troops; and he deliberately spoke English with his sergeant, Hashimu, giving the man valuable language practice.

The *askaris'* liking and trust for Gun rubbed off on me – "the friend of my friend is my friend" – and without a great deal of effort I was able to use such privilege to my best advantage. Morale in the unit was high, and it pulled me along in all aspects of our daily operations; every man performed every task. I had never made my own *basha* before – the tiny banana leaf shelters in which we slept and took refuge from the nightly downpours. We dug a pretty fancy shit-pit, straddling it with a log high enough to rest our lower backs as we leaned in to use the facility. (A knotted rope led out to the pit so you could find your way in the dark – counting the knots so you didn't go a pace too far.)

I tried my hand at cooking, only to discover the Africans knew what they were doing much better than I did; but I did learn about patrolling and following a track, how many men it would take to perform any given task, and how they should be equipped. I became a highly proficient radio operator, and each night signalled our reports back to battalion HQ.

Many times during that three-week period we found indications of recent rebel movement, and though we would follow tracks for hours we failed to find any Mau Mau. Like us, the longer they spent hiding in the forest the more they enhanced their proficiency at using the undergrowth to conceal their movements – and they became extremely good at it. They were nowhere nearly as well-armed as we were, so their first imperative was to avoid contact with us. They knew the British penchant for shooting first and never asking the pertinent questions; they knew they moved and operated in these areas on pain of death. Coming up empty-handed was frustrating for us, but good training nonetheless. All of us were eager to be in on a "kill." We were engaged in a hunt. To our youthfully simplistic reasoning, it was the kill that was the raison d'être for the months of training each of us had undergone. In this I do not believe I differed greatly from any of my fellow subalterns back in the mess.

In the forest evenings, when sentries had been posted and the birds in the surrounding canopy had ceased their chatter, and when the *askaries* had snuggled silently into their *bashas,* Gun and I would brew up a tea, review the day's activities and, like any two young fellows cast together on quite the most extraordinary adventure of their lives, talk of home, of girls, of dreams and a thousand plans about what we'd do "when we got out." Gun wanted to remain on in Africa and start a safari business. He had found himself a woman in Nairobi, wife to another British Army officer, who was prepared to leave her husband and work in the bush with her lover …

"Does her husband know …?" I asked.

"Corse not!" he barked as if I was daft for asking.

For a junior officer to take a senior officer's wife as a lover, I knew, was a serious no-no – breach of military discipline, at least; insubordination probably and cause (I knew from my schoolboy reading) for most intense no-quarter duelling. If discovered there would be no sympathy whatsoever for Gun; and what of the lady herself?

Stories of carnal adventuring were commonplace. There was a saying in Kenya at the time, in the form of a question: "Are you married, or do you live in Kenya?"

From my most unqualified point of view Gun had many more manly qualities than I would have dared claim for myself. And as for amorous dalliances of any sort I was most painfully aware that I was fresh out of the egg. Lions at ten paces, no problem – any athletic buck might figure out how to get away from that one, or face his slaughter with courageous derring-do the way he had been taught in his years of consulting Boys' Own Monthly. Charging rhino, same. But a beguiling woman, one who could stir my testosterone, would leave me in a blind funk – angst which, after all, is no more than the growing pain one endures between gangly adolescence and the bravado of early manhood.

Yet while I may have been inexperienced and inept, I knew the chance Gun was taking was risky and foolish – but that maybe it was precisely why he was taking it. He didn't care. By taking after another officer's wife he was demonstrating a degree of recklessness encompassing far more than the sentiments he might have harboured for the woman herself. His feelings for the military he now served were overtly contemptuous. There was a history that pre-dated my coming on the scene. He wanted out, and made no bones about it in his forest conversations with me. It occurred to me this affair was just an extension of his general negative feelings about soldiering.

"I've had enough, mate. These Pommies are bastards. They actually think they're so right! The military types are no different at all from the bloody settlers they so despise. Racist bastards, they are – sick. The people that'll tell you who counts out here, the bastards running the show, are choking on the filth in their minds, I'll tell you. It doesn't take long for them to infect all you new guys. You may come out here with high ideals, but they don't last long with these empire builders badgering you!"

Then:

"I'll take Kidogo with me, o'corse. I'd like to take Samadhi and Hashimu as well, but I can't ask them to blow their careers the way I'm prepared to blow mine."

It all pushed me into silence.

*

Gun and I came to know this area of the Aberdares extremely well. At the conclusion of my three-week training session with him, I was given my own platoon and immediately sent with it back to the same area. There was Mau Mau activity there. They were clever and careful in covering their tracks, but still we found evidence of them. Time and again we would find footprints carefully brushed over with branches of foliage, or the remains of a recent fire, in most cases lightly sprinkled with earth or dust to disguise age. It was hard to conceal grasses flattened by someone sleeping on them overnight, or the sprig of a bush turned contrary to others growing right beside it. The extreme caution of our adversaries indicated they knew we knew they were in the vicinity; they would have known, also, if their intent was to surrender they would have to do so to an officer. If the *askaris* came upon them they would surely be shot – probably before any effort was made to question them. It was a sinister game; no "collect and return to go" cards, not even "jail." Out here in the bush the penalty for a misstep was lethal. But their incredible bush craft was brought forcefully home to me the day a small group of three rebels managed to sneak out of the forest with their hands up to surrender themselves to the police. They were in a terrible state – filthy, starving, terrified, constantly on the run. Under interrogation one of them told the police my name, pronouncing it "Bow-bi." I was summoned to meet the fellow. He recognized me and I asked him how he knew my name. He told me how, only a few days before, he had been concealed in thick bush so close to me that he could have reached out and untied my boot laces. At this time he had heard one of my *askaris* address me by name.

For a time Gun's platoon and mine switched places every three weeks, taking over the same zone and continuing to press for results in our hunt, and it was on Gun's watch that a call came through to the battalion headquarters late one morning. He had made visual contact with what he supposed was a large Mau Mau camp – he guessed fifty people in all. To take them on he needed reinforcements, and so my platoon was ordered out to meet up with him. It all came to nothing. My platoon stayed with Gun for nearly two weeks, and we fanned out daily patrols over a wide section of the countryside. All we found was an old encampment that had been abandoned some weeks earlier. So I returned to battalion headquarters – and the next day Gun's voice again came on the blower in the communications shack.

"This time for sure …!" he said with conviction.

He gave me a map reference, so once again I collected my troops and headed out to the rendezvous. Gun figured they had moved back into much the same area they had occupied before.

Unfortunately the battalion was not the only recipient of the radio message. I had just arrived on site and was standing with Gun surveying the supposed camp some several hundred metres away on the far side of a wide gully, when both of us heard the heavy drone of aircraft engines. In the next few seconds two gigantic Royal Air Force Lancaster bombers roared in over our heads, and dumped several bomb loads in the general area of the spot we were looking at. A few minutes later they made a second pass, but this time their drop fell well wide of the intended target area.

"Who the hell invited them?" Gun cursed.

"I guess they picked up the same map reference you gave me," I commented.

"Well, damn their eyes!" Gun shouted above the din of explosions. "We'd best get over there right quick and see what damage they've done."

We had to ford a river, and as we approached its bank we saw the body of a man being swept along by the current. At first we thought the RAF had done our job for us, but it soon turned out that the single kill of the day – if, indeed, it had been a kill from that day – was the corpse in the stream. The encampment that Gun had spotted was empty of life, but there was plenty to indicate a recent and hurried exit. Some cooked food was still hot in a pot on the embers of a fire, there was an assortment of filthy blankets and camp gear, even a few weapons – homemade rifles and a couple of *pangas* – had been left behind. Indications were that there might have been as many as twenty men.

"Stupid bastards!" Gun spat, referring to the air attack. "We could have bagged the whole bloody lot!"

Obviously at the first sound of aircraft the occupants of the camp had fled into the cover of nearby trees and bushes. By now they could be many kilometres distant.

There was no point in remaining. We radioed back to the battalion that we would return to base that afternoon, and within a couple of hours both our platoons were heading back towards Nyeri.

"What a cock-up!" was Gun's disgusted summary of events to the battalion commander. "If we'd needed air support I'd have called for it."

He stormed off to his quarters and didn't bother showing up for supper that evening.

In the following days we learned that Brigade Headquarters had indeed been alerted to Gun's map reference given over the radio, and had calculated that by flying in a couple of Lancasters they could offer substantial logistical support to whatever was happening on the ground. Gun requested an interview with the Brigade commander, and much later I was given to understand he made no bones about how helpful he felt the aerial bombardment had been. It was not the first time Gun had offended his seniors at Brigade. The terseness of his reports, delivered in the salty twang of his homeland jargon was well known.

"If any one of 'em had a spare brain, they'd be fuckin' dangerous," he snarled at me after coming from the interview. He had no use at all for those wearing red tabs on their collars.

"Career officers are generally so bloody stupid even their fellow officers notice it."

Several weeks passed before the battalion commander felt it necessary to revisit the same area to make sure the Mau Mau had not returned, and so of course it was Gun who received the order.

He didn't say anything. Gun had a way of keeping to himself when his mind was at variance with others around him. My guess is he felt a return to the same zone right then was premature – the Mau Mau would leave well enough alone, possibly not to return for a long time, if ever. The body of the man we had seen swept away in the river was not recovered; had it shown up the police would likely have been able to establish his identity fairly quickly. Identification would mean all relatives would be fair game for round-up and questioning. That would lead police to the names of associates who would be assumed to belong to the same gang, how many it consisted of and where they could be found. Knowing all this, survivors of the bombing would have scattered to the four winds.

All serving officers acknowledged what was generally referred to as the Africans' "sixth sense" – the uncanny ability, for example, to zero in on an event before it occurred, to possess knowledge of something so well that it appeared born of a wisdom our European minds have long since lost or misplaced. Gun's respect for this quality we all noticed in the Africans was something he considered sacrosanct, as if the level of communication and knowledge they possessed touched the spiritual – and so could not be questioned or doubted. It was probably on account of this he felt the bombing and scattering of the gang we'd been chasing, our inability to run any of them to ground on at least two occasions, had put a hex on the entire operation; nothing good could come of trying a follow-up so soon after a double failure. All this had something to do with the way in which we, as hunters, were singling out our prey.

He said little, but I was with him in the early morning when he loaded his men onto the trucks to head back to Aberdare. Something irked him. He passed the leash of his dog to Kidogo.

"You stay and take care of Cuba," he told the boy. "He is as important to me as you are."

He ruffled his fingers affectionately through Kidogo's curly black hair.

Then he looked at me, his eyes and shoulders expressing a long-suffering toleration, as if he knew the exercise was a waste of time and effort.

Mrs. Queen's Chump

"See you later, mate," he chimed, more than just a hint of sarcasm colouring his voice, and he swung himself up into the cab of his truck.

Back at battalion we did not hear from him for several days. It had previously been his habit to call in every evening with a report on his activities. This time, nothing.

Then one evening his voice came over the squawk box in the communications tent, flat, expressionless, urgent. He specifically asked to speak to me, but the wireless operator, the adjutant and the colonel were all standing right behind me as I sat down at the set.

"Jeremy – we've got a problem. Tell the C.O. I need two trucks here right away to pull us out ..."

"He's right here," I responded. "You can tell him yourself ..."

"I don't want to talk to him. I'm talking to you. Pass the message and make it stick – two trucks, right now. You know the zone. If I see no trucks within two hours we'll come out by foot ..."

Then he signed off, "Over and out."

"What the hell's all that about?" the colonel exploded. "He was given a specific order to patrol that zone for at least ten more days. Get him back on the line. I want to know what 'problem' he has!"

So we called, but Gun did not answer, and in the end the colonel acquiesced on sending the trucks. He needed to know – we all needed to know – what had happened. I was familiar with the road and drop zone, so was ordered to go with the lead truck.

There had been a problem, alright. Samadhi was dead. His body lay under a khaki poncho at the side of the road as we pulled up.

"Jesus! What happened?"

Two days before Gun had gone out on a routine patrol. They had moved into an area of high bamboo. There had been a storm the night before so many of the fresh shoots had been blown over and it was impossible to move quickly without making a racket easily heard a kilometre away. The hollow stalks of the bamboo clattered like drums. One had only to knock one against another and the noise would carry like a thunderclap.

They had stopped for a smoke break and were just lighting up when an angry bull elephant trumpeted behind one of the clumps, and started bearing down on them. The enormous animal ripped through the bamboo as though it was no more than grass, snapping the thick stalks with his trunk and feet. His ears stood straight out, flapping like ensigns as he charged forward and screamed with rage.

All the men, Gun among them, grabbed their weapons and fled downhill, vaulting and ducking the bamboo. As he ran he was suddenly confronted by a giant shoot that was too high to jump and too low to duck under. He hesitated, then put his foot on it and tried to use one leg to give him leverage.

But the shoot snapped. Gun fell to the ground and dropped his rifle.

Scrambling to his feet, he was aware of Samadhi standing just in front of him. The little fellow had stopped, thinking his officer needed assistance.

Gun looked at him. Something was wrong. Samadhi bent down and picked up the rifle. Its sling snagged, and it took him a moment to free it.

"Hapa bunduki yako, effendi," he said to Gun, passing the weapon over to him.

In the next instant the large grey mass of the elephant flashed by no more than an arm's length away from Gun and Samadhi was plucked from the ground.

Gun could only look on. He saw Samadhi held high above the elephant's head, coiled in its trunk. Then, with a snapping movement, his little batman was thrown to the ground and trampled as the animal passed over him and continued angrily downhill.

There was nothing to be done for Samadhi. But the elephant was still loose, and the *askaris* took after it.

An hour or so later they closed on it in a thicket, approaching from the rear. Gun held up his hand and the men stopped, watching their officer as he stalked around to the animal's head. As I heard the story later from Sergeant Hashimu, Gun was practically in tears, so angry and upset that he stepped right out in front of the animal.

The old elephant just looked at Gun now, quiet, anger spent.

Gun used a high powered FN rifle for the kill. Bringing the weapon to his shoulder and barely pausing to take aim, he took his shot from point blank range.

The elephant instantly dropped to its front knees and rolled onto its side.

He had felled it with a single shot to the eye.

The *askaris* ran forward to examine the carcass, and it was then they saw what had turned the animal rogue. A two-pound chunk of jagged metal had lodged in its jaw and had probably been festering there since the aerial bombardment four weeks before.

*

Samadhi was given a funeral with full military honours, though many of the senior officers thought the exercise was barely worthwhile. One or two of them let it be known they felt more for the elephant than for the batman, though there had been tacit acknowledgement the little fellow had acted with bravery in returning Gun's rifle to him at the last moment.

"Damned shame ... fine bull like that ... hardly sporting to run it down..."

Samadhi passed at slow drum beat between twin rows of *askaris*. One of the men audibly cleared his throat and spat onto the top of the casket as it passed.

A captain, witnessing what the soldier had done, stepped forward and spun the man around, slapping him hard across the face. He ordered the *askari* to be arrested and taken directly to the guardroom.

But at the conclusion of the funeral Nyamahanga Boke approached the English officer and saluted smartly.

"The *askari* should not be arrested," he explained. "In our culture it is a mark of deep respect to offer a man one's spittle ..."

"Don't tell me there's anything respectful about spitting on a soldier's casket!" the officer spluttered angrily. "Filthy savage superstition ...!"

Nyamahanga was summarily dismissed, the captain growling his deep disgust.

*

In March 1953, thinking the inhabitants of the Kikuyu village of Lari were showing loyalty to the British, the Mau Mau attacked and massacred over one hundred men, women and children. From the British standpoint it was the single incident of the emergency that best defined the barbarity of the movement. Settlers were unnerved and horrified. In Britain the newspapers were full of shocking detail and condemnation.

Gundagai McGinty had arrived in Kenya only a short time before this terrifying event, and he and his platoon were among the many troops ordered into the field as follow-up to try to find the perpetrators.

Gun's explanation of the incident to me was brief and, in a way, disconnected – as though the events he described as an on-the-spot witness had occurred to someone else.

One evening during our time together in the Aberdare Mountains we sat alone in my *basha* and he told me a story concerning the Lari follow-up, and how he happened to acquire Kidogo. I can hear his words even now, and they come across matter-of-factly. But at the time I found his story so compelling that, after he had left me and gone off to his own *bashas*, I sat for some time with my notebook and tried to capture his account more or less verbatim:

> "No one fixes bayonets in the jungle. Carrying a rifle or sub-machine gun is trouble enough in thick undergrowth. There are a thousand vines and branches to catch on the protrusions on any weapon; an extra thirty-five centimeters of bayonet would be a nuisance, hinder movement. And there is another reason besides: jungle fighting is a stealth and close quarters business. If one happens to see an enemy at all before the fight is joined it is seldom at a greater distance than a few metres – four or five – and then only for a second or two. Whoever gets off the first shot or salvo is usually the victor. For this reason the best arm is an automatic or a sub-machine gun, or even a sawn-off pump-action shotgun. Something fast and with wide spatter. Something you can operate from the hip. There is never time to take aim.
>
> "So bayonets are out. If you need the silence of a blade, a good knife is better. The bayonet is noisy in fact. It is designed for hand-to-hand fighting at a point when there is no time to reload rounds into the chamber. A bayonet is for demoralization, terror. With a strong arm and

the momentum of a man's charge, led by the weight of a nine-kilogram rifle, a bayonet can eviscerate any opponent in seconds. The thrust that does the job is usually accompanied by a banshee yell loud and blood-curdling enough to waken the dead and frighten the living to death. So if you're going to make that kind of a ruckus, might as well loose off a burst of firepower. It is faster, and has the added advantage of serving to keep down the head of an enemy standing behind the enemy you are attacking.

"Anyway, that's the logic. Bullets over bayonets in jungle – and I really don't know why I had armed myself that particular day with a bolt-action Lee Enfield – the short single-shot Mark IV jungle model. I don't like it much. I was not thinking, not anticipating I'd run into any action that day up in the Githu Aberdare ... The blade of my bayonet rattled in its metal scabbard on my belt, so I unsheathed it and fixed it onto my spout. I don't know if I felt any better armed. The thing was a nuisance. And it never occurred to me that I might use it.

"We picked up a fresh trail. One of the African trackers snapped his fingers to draw attention to it, and pointed silently at a turning over of grass blades and a scuff of mud. It was only minutes old, so I put the lead tracker on it right away and we all followed him at a run. We were in tall grasses parallel with the forest edge, so we spread out in an extended line.

"Within less than a couple of minutes, and only a few hundred metres further on, we saw them – a rag-tag group, maybe a dozen of them, moving ahead of us. They did not see us as we came up behind them, but then one of the *askaris* fired off a round so there was no further point in concealment or silence. The whole patrol ran forward firing into the brush directly ahead.

"Shouts. Figures darting all over the place. I saw one man drop, but in the same instant caught a glimpse on my low left of someone breaking through the undergrowth. I was closest, so ran downhill, burst through a clump of foliage and nearly collided with a small fellow momentarily trapped between a rock outcrop and two enormous tree trunks. Another second or two and he would have made a clean break into the dense cover, but I was right on top of him and it was too late.

He turned to face me, raising his arms, and I hit him with the bayonet. His face was as close to me as that lamp beside your head.

"I shouted at him. I do not know whether it was out of fear or loathing, or because in bayonet drill we had been taught to lunge and shout bloody murder at the same moment. The effect was intended to be devastating. His mouth dropped open releasing a cry of pain and terror that commenced way down in his bowel. Then he pissed himself. It soaked the foliage at his feet and splashed onto the front of my own trousers. My legs felt the wetness through the cotton fatigues, and the stench of his bad breath suddenly exhaled disgusted me. I drove at him with all my force in order to have done with this thing and to rid myself of his odious presence so close in front of me.

"His eyes popped open, wide like headlamps. First I read in them fear, then a beseeching, then pain. Finally surprise. It all came in rapid succession, then the lights went out. His arms had been down at his sides. He carried a *panga* in his right hand. As I came on and hit him, he gestured upwards, either to raise his hands and capitulate, or else to take a swing at me with his knife. At the moment there was no telling which, and by the time I got to question myself on this detail he was dead.

"I had aimed unconsciously at his navel but the blade went in high, in the centre but just under his rib cage. I forced down then on the butt of my rifle so that the blade turned upward behind his ribs lacerating his aorta. In the same moment, conscious of his *panga* and trying to avoid him swinging it at my neck, I lifted with all my strength and threw him up off the ground, backwards across the bough of a tree a little above the height of my own eyes. His right arm swung and his blade passed wide over my head. I turned and threw his weight up to my left, the entire bayonet now inside his body, the tip of it probably somewhere near the base of his throat. He started to slide onto the muzzle of my rifle, and to disengage him I pushed him violently backwards, draping him over the bough. His legs kicked once, twice, and his *panga* clattered to the ground. He was still as I drew the blade out of him. My left hand and forearm were covered in his gore.

"Telling it now, the whole action is drawn out, but I know it took place in seconds. Each move was a logical sequel to the move that preceded it. There was no thinking. Just instinctive action and reaction. The thinking came in the moments immediately following the action, and in the years that have come between then and now. I can tell you, the moment comes back, over and over ...

"He was just a boy, no more than fifteen or sixteen years of age. Maybe less. I never discovered his name, nor anything else about him. We buried him there deep in the Aberdare forest along with his companion shot in the first moments of the encounter. One of the *askaris* chopped off the hands of both of them before we threw earth over them. Wiring the thumbs of each pair together, he put them into a sack. Ostensibly this was so that the police could fingerprint them later, try to identify them. But that was a load of crap. Fingerprinting would do no more than prove the obvious: four hands, two dead.

"The hands of the boy were small, dirty under the fingernails but rather dainty. Sometimes I dream about the encounter. I see the boy's face. I would know him if he came through the flap of my tent. But it is the image of his hands hacked off from the rest of him that wakes me up.

"At the first sign of firing the gang had taken off, but the *askaris* had hold of one of them – a little boy. He was frightened and trembling, but far too small to know what was going on. It was Kidogo, the boy you see with me now – my little sidekick. He stuck to me like glue from that moment on. His family had been wiped out at Lari, so there was nowhere for him to go but to run with those who came to kill his family. He was on his own – so I'll take care of him now. I'll do what I can for him. He knows I'll eventually have to leave, but in the meantime I don't think he'd care to go with anyone else ...

"You know, later – before they learned that I hate their guts – one of the senior officers had the balls to tell me we'd done well, but I have never felt sure about that. Such things leave a mark, you know. Even when they do well soldiers seldom do good."

□

5. Digging Holes

Apart from the officers' mess, located in one of the farm's houses, the entire battalion consisted of lines of tents of every shape and dimension. It meant that sitting in one of the company offices trying to get on with paperwork, there was little immunity from whatever noises and distractions happened to float through the canvas walls from outside.

One afternoon as I was trying to work in our company tent – it was a large marquee – I heard a rhythmical voice chanting somewhere out of sight at the back.

At first it was just a rising and falling sound, and I tried to ignore it.

But then it started working on me, a muffled sound that could have come from some distance away, and yet was close and insistent.

"Go-dig-a-hole!" came the voice.

Then again, "Go-dig-a-hole!" – and again, "Go-dig-a-hole!"

It was repeated over and over, but in rhythm. Curious and rather irritated, I stepped out of the office and walked around to the back.

There I saw not twenty paces behind the marquee an enormous pile of dirt, and a hole with a young *askari* at the bottom of it. He had a shovel, and had dug himself so deep that his head was below the level of the surrounding land. Throwing huge heaps of loose earth over his shoulder he had created a small mountain around the rim of a very large hole, the surface of which was falling back almost as fast as he threw it up. His sweaty body and shovel worked to the rhythm of his voice.

"Go-dig-a-hole! Go-dig-a-hole!"

I looked down at him with considerable alarm because I could see the loose earth he was throwing out of the hole was sliding back so rapidly he was in danger of being buried alive.

"What are you doing down there?" I demanded.

He stopped digging and looked up at me. He was dressed in shorts, his dark skin glistening with exertion. But in the instant his shovel was stilled,

Mrs. Queen's Chump

the rim of the hole started to tumble back in and quickly covered his lower legs halfway up his shins.

"Dig-a-hole, *effendi*!"

"Well get out of there, right now," I told him. "Out!"

He tried to scramble out, but he couldn't get a grip on the sandy soil and was pulling quantities of it back on top of himself.

"Hold up your shovel," I said, grabbing it and trying to use it to pull him up.

With the help of another couple of soldiers who happened by, and with a lot of heaving, we managed to get the fellow out of the hole as its sides were collapsing back in – and just at that moment the European sergeant-major of my company happened to come around the corner of the marquee.

"What's goin' on here!" he demanded angrily, addressing the *askaris* and ignoring my presence.

He turned to the fellow who had been at the bottom of the hole.

"I told you to dig a hole! What the hell do you think you're doin'? You get yer bloody black arse back down there and start digging, you uppity little bastard!" And he started to push the *askari* towards the pit.

Each company had two sergeants-major, one a European seconded from a regular unit of British Army infantry, the other an *askari* who had risen to that rank through promotion. Both blessed and cursed, my own company had been assigned an extremely intelligent and competent African sergeant-major, and a notably unintelligent racist bigot as our European sergeant-major.

It was this white but now red-faced imbecile who was standing before me at the edge of the hole.

"Why have you told that man to dig a hole?" I demanded of him.

He stopped pushing the *askari* and turned to me as though it was none of my business to enquire. But then he said:

"I've given the impudent little bastard a punishment, sir – somethin' to teach 'im a lesson."

"And just what is the lesson he will learn from digging this hole, sergeant-major?"

"It's punishment, sir, that's all. Sloppy soldier, sir," was his reply.

Then he added:

"I told 'im to dig it, and then fill it in again, sir. Good for 'is discipline ... but you undermine my authority by 'elpin'im, sir! I've ordered 'im to dig it – I've ordered 'im!"

"I understand, sergeant-major. But under no circumstances is that man to get back into that hole, do you hear? Surely you can see it's in danger of collapse."

"Sir!" he expostulated in my face. "You are undermining my authority, sir ...!"

"Whatever the man has done, sergeant-major, this punishment is excessive and it is dangerous. That soldier does not go back into that hole."

Still the sergeant-major faced me, pugnacious, angry, confrontational. I was becoming angry myself.

"Sir ...!" he wanted to continue.

"Sir, nothing!" I cut him off, and I turned to all of the *askaris* standing about and ordered them to go away.

"Away from here ...! Go back to your duties."

The sergeant-major elected to stand his ground.

"I'll not have it, sir ..."

"You'll not have it?" I exploded. "You'll not have it? You'll damned well have it if I say so, sergeant-major ... Here!"

And I pushed the shovel into his hands.

"Any fool could see your so-called punishment is both excessive and endangering that man's life," I told him.

He held the shovel as if he wanted to hit me with it.

"I'm giving you an order, sergeant-major," I told him. "You fill in the hole. You fill it in – right here, right now!"

And I meant it.

The sergeant-major was spluttering with anger – but I made sure he had little choice. He took the shovel, waited a moment for the last of the soldiers to move out of sight, and in a few minutes of energetic shovelling managed to fill in the offending hole while I stood over him and watched.

*

In the end the incident rebounded on top of me. The sergeant-major reported my action to the regimental commander, and I was summoned to give an explanation.

"Wrong action, sir," said the colonel. "He's a senior NCO, and you humiliated him."

"He was humiliating the *askari*, sir, and the *askari*'s life was in danger…" I attempted a defence.

"Young man," came the colonel's response – carefully couched, but nonetheless quite clear. "The sergeant-major is a white man and, no matter the extent of his stupidity – we all know about that – he is in a position of authority. The *askari* is a black man, there to accept whatever abuse comes his way if it does. He himself has no authority whatsoever. He is there to answer to authority."

Dismissed. I felt as though I was at the bottom of a deep hole I'd managed to dig for myself.

☐

6. Tracking

I mentioned bush patrols as being a third category of our military activity, and the one I preferred.

Life in the bush revived me enormously. What we called bush was only sometimes "bush" – the tall ochre grasses, acacia and thorn trees, the dusty savannah that seems to be the favoured visual image of vast tracts of Africa. I loved that landscape, but for us the bush was just as often thick jungle, and this excited me as well. There was a special solitude to the jungle – the light, the heat, the freshness of the green canopy, the special smell of decaying vegetation on the forest floor. I have always favoured life in the outdoors – the more rugged the better – but the Aberdare forest was primal, and it thrilled me. To get into the forest we would have to cross wide stretches of savannah country – and this, also, assaulted my nostrils with a heat and excitement I'd not known before. There would be animals of all kinds, as there had been when I was up in this district before with Gun – rhinos, elephants, gazelle of multiple species. Invariably there would be giraffe. I seldom saw any of the big cats on these patrol forays, though I saw them elsewhere on other occasions and under different circumstances. In all my time in Kenya I saw only two snakes: the black mamba was dead; the fifteen-foot python was asleep. Village raids were a degrading and unpleasant slog for attackers as well as the attacked, but life in the forest was a taste of freedom. While village attacks invariably lasted no longer than the day on which they were mounted, long enough to make sure we had given the villagers good reason to think us a total abomination, forest ops sometimes lasted for several weeks on end. To me, as with most of my fellow officers, this was more like soldiering. As honourable creatures several cuts superior to policemen (we had decided the Kenya Police were corrupt, cruel and inefficient), we considered the raiding of villages to be distastefully nit-picking police work. We saw ourselves as fighters, warriors. What on earth were we doing rummaging about in people's homes, disturbing their private lives? The forest was fairer to us, it was our milieu. The forest was where we could best employ all our acquired soldierly skills.

Mrs. Queen's Chump

Group shot of author with some members of his platoon in the Aberdare forest. WOPC Nyamahanga and author carry troop-trial FN's – a most unsatisfactory weapon in those conditions. The *askari* on author's left is carrying a Bren light machine gun. Askaris at rear are armed with jungle versions of the Lee Enfield .303.

In the months patrolling the forests of the Aberdare Mountains I became passably good at tracking. Several of my *askaris,* Nyamahanga among them, were highly skilled at it, and I was naturally curious to be able to see what they saw. There were so many signs to look for – a scuff mark, a turned leaf or blade of grass could open up a whole new avenue; the sound of animals moving in the near distance, or the sudden flight of a bird, could be an indicator they were being disturbed by others if not by the passing of one of our patrols. Body odour or farts could hang a surprisingly long time in hot, motionless and dusty airs. Anxious to avoid the authorities, the Mau Mau would devise all manner of means to disguise their passage. They would put shoes on backwards, or strap animal hooves to their feet in an effort to confuse anyone following their trail.

"But this is always obvious," Nyamahanga told me. "Those who have passed are easily given away by the depth of the indentations in the earth. An animal places its hoof squarely on the ground; a human has to roll his foot, back-to-front. And as you can smell them, so they can smell you. If you shave, for instance, they can smell the shaving soap, or your aftershave lotion."

It came to be my turn to try my hand at tracking – leading from the point position. There were nine of us in dense forest, and we had discovered a footprint that led us into a steep-sided gully. I had been watching the *askaris* close enough that I reckoned I knew more or less what to do …

I crouched down. "What do you think?" I asked Nyamahanga.

"No shoes," he replied. "Small foot. Woman, or child."

We moved forward in total silence, and kept this up for several hours. The gully widened into a broad area of forest growth that thickened our field of vision but was not difficult to move through. In the end, though, I was forced to turn to my *askaris* and shrug my shoulders. It was towards the end of the afternoon, and dark would be coming on soon. We had to make a decision as to whether we should go on or go back to our camp; by now I was hopelessly lost and had to admit it.

"We've known that for more than an hour," said one of the soldiers, smiling.

"Then why the blazes didn't one of you say something?" I flared.

"Well, you were doing fine, and we thought it best to let you get the practice … But you have not been following Mau Mau."

I scowled. By now, I could see, they were playing with me.

"It was a woman, maybe a small man, moving alone and carrying a large pot of water. She turned away about an hour ago, and you have been following the track of a wart hog ..."

At that I decided we call it quits for the day and head back to our camp. I turned in the direction I thought we ought to go.

"Not that way. This way," I was informed curtly as members of the patrol began to move off in an entirely different direction.

In less than ten minutes we were back at our camp, and I was perplexed. I had had no idea that throughout the day we had moved in a gigantic circle.

Nyamahanga came up to me then.

"That track you found – it wasn't a woman. It was Private Sabiri – see, he's resting over there ..."

Indeed Sabiri, one of those left behind in camp that day, was lying on his back with his bare feet cast up on a log. He was spooning into a mess tin of rice that had been cooked up on an open fire during the afternoon. By far the smallest man in the platoon, apparently he had gone out on his own earlier to see if he could locate fresh water. Now, beside his head, was a gigantic ceramic water pot, a trophy of his excursion that we most definitely had not brought with us when we had entered the forest several days ago.

"He found the water," Nyamahanga was chuckling. "He also found that large water pot. You be sure, some Mau Mau left it at the watering hole. We can use it for now, but we must break it when we leave here – unless Sabiri wants to carry it out ..."

"But when we first saw the track, how did you know it was someone carrying water?" I asked him incredulously.

"That was not difficult," Nyamahanga replied. "Some water had been spilled. The pot is heavy when filled. Tracks showed he had put it down, and then had difficulty lifting it up onto his back by himself in order to carry it. The story was all written in the dust, but we didn't know it was Sabiri ..."

◻

7. Nurses

I had been sent to Nairobi on a Swahili course, and was sharing a room at the Avenue Hotel with Mac, a junior officer in one of the Kenya battalions of the KAR. Like me, he was struggling to make himself understood by his *askaris* and wanted to be able to address them directly instead of going through an interpreter.

We attended rigorous language seminars during the daytime, but in the evenings our time was our own. Usually we would wind up at one bar or another. We had a few favourites, the names of which I can no longer remember. The best ones were those that had a dance floor, and we would pass hours wishfully jangling the few coins we'd been able to assemble in our pockets, ogling the ladies and trying to coax a single beer into lasting a little longer. Ladies were a scarce and competitive commodity in Nairobi, hard to come by in those days. Ladies of whom our mothers might have approved were rarer yet.

Coming from months of operations in the up-country bush and being starved of female companionship, neither of us was in the least aware of how our idiotic licentiousness might have shown itself to others. We were full of ourselves, no idea whatsoever that all the ladies in Kenya left in their wake troops of raunchy men, that it was a silly woman indeed who was not tuned into the fact – as well as the knowledge that she was such a rarity she could really take her pick if so inclined. Yet for some reason we felt certain that if only the local ladies knew of our presence they would be scrabbling energetically among themselves to leap into our laps ...

Mac was an enterprising fellow.

"I know!" he declared one evening when we had agreed between us what it was we both wanted most of all.

"Let's telephone the nurses' residence at the hospital and see if we can persuade a couple of them to do dinner and a movie with us ..."

Good idea, worth a try. I was all for it and needed no convincing. We counted out our shillings. The project was just feasible.

Mac called. Two young officers down from the sharp end were lonely, at loose ends, and didn't know anybody in this big, bustling, heartless city. Were there, perchance, two gracious and understanding young nurses willing to accompany us for the evening ...? Mac managed to sound reasonable – pleading, even.

But both of us were surprised when an obliging female voice at the other end of the line said she would put the word out ... Could we call back in an hour?

Mac and I went into a huddle. Did we actually want to do this? Just what might we be getting ourselves into?

What the heck! Price of two dinners and a show. Couldn't go wrong ...

We called back. Yes, two nurses would be free that evening, Florence and Sandra, and would meet us at five o'clock at the main entrance of Torr's Hotel.

Like two schoolboys on an outing, Mac and I waited on the balcony of the New Stanley Hotel across the street – with a pair of binoculars. Both ladies showed up at precisely five – and the two of us looked at one another, fumbling with the binoculars and feeling stupid. We quickly ran downstairs; Mac asked the receptionist if he could hold onto the binoculars, and the two of us raced outside to cross the street.

We were both nervous and breathless when we approached the two nurses, and the first thing one of them asked:

"Have you been waiting long ... or were you just in hiding across the street with a pair of binoculars?"

"No!" Mac lied.

"No!" I lied.

Florence and Sandra giggled. They had been kibitzing. Had they seen us on the balcony? They stepped forward together, each of them taking us by an arm.

Sandra said: "We thought we might scout you both out first with a pair of binoculars, see what we were getting ... but then we thought we'd already committed ourselves, and what the heck ...! Where are you taking us for dinner?"

And the two of them giggled some more.

Both our guests were qualified nurses, strictly confined to living in residence and discouraged from going about the city unescorted. Dinner conversation tended to consist of questions. Ours to them: What do you do to fill your hours of spare time? – (answer: they didn't have much spare time); How do you manage to do your essential shopping each day? – (answer: they moved about the city in groups of at least four, made use of hospital transport and guards); What do you do about male companionship? – (answer: the men they had met so far were generally jerks with their minds in their underpants).

Both ladies understood quite well neither Mac nor I were at liberty to discuss our work, but they did not show any interest anyway. The words "Mau Mau" and "emergency" entered only the fringes of our conversation. Instead, we told them animal stories, and they listened politely – but it soon became apparent they had already heard their fill of bush adventure from other bush-whacked adventurers.

It was not a particularly comfortable dinner. Two bush-whacked idiots with limited time or funds to prowl the big city, their minds in their underpants; two ladies, both of them discerning, coolly – even cynically – perceptive and (except we were too eager to twig to it) interested mainly in having an entertaining evening for as long as the limited funds of these two particular jerks would stretch. They knew well enough that behind us there were others, all of them with their minds in their underpants.

We decided on a film and walked to the cinema, but Mac thought he had eaten something in the restaurant that did not agree with him. We settled into our row seats. Mac went first, followed by one of the ladies, then me, with the second lady taking up the aisle seat. The lights had only been dimmed for a few minutes when Mac suddenly lurched forward and groaned in pain. He was faint, and slumped over the seat in front of him. This was not part of any plan we had discussed, so I assumed he was genuinely ill.

Hero to the rescue, I leaned across the nurse that separated us and grabbed Mac by his left armpit, hauling him towards me and at the same time ducking my head down between his legs. I was trying to lever him into something like a fireman's lift, a difficult manoeuvre in the narrow confines of theatre seats. I did not have him correctly over my shoulder as I worked his inert corpse into the aisle, and felt a twinge in my back. With Mac slumped over me, and in a completely distorted fashion, I staggered up the aisle and through the doorway into the foyer, then bent my knees in an attempt to lower my burden gently onto the floor.

It was a disaster. He was dead weight and I did not have hold of him correctly; I was bent over sideways and didn't have the strength to prevent him slipping and twisting me even more out of shape. That was when my back gave way. I doubled up in agony, gasping for air and allowing my burden to fall the last two feet. Then I collapsed onto the floor beside him.

Side-by-side, the two of us lay on the dirty foyer carpet. Mac was out cold, the colour of a soiled bed sheet; I was in excruciating pain, gasping for breath and quite unable to get to my feet.

We must have been that way for at least several minutes. The foyer was empty while the show was in play, but a concierge wandered over dressed like a toy soldier with golden stripes on his pants and a red peaked cap. He stared at us. The spacious entranceway was a blaze of light, but he had a flashlight in his hand and he beamed it at us dumbly, unable to figure things out or contribute more than open-mouthed curiosity.

Gradually Mac came to his senses, groaning terribly. He saw me, then turned away and vomited.

"Mac – you okay …?"

"Must have eaten something rotten …" he spluttered.

"I can't move," I told him. "I've buggered my back."

"Jeeze!" Mac said, and we both lay breathless.

Sandra and Florence came out to the foyer. They had emerged from the darkened interior of the cinema and were standing over us. Nurses, I thought; they'll help us.

"What on earth is going on?" they demanded in unison.

"I think I've got food poisoning …" Mac said weakly.

"I've wrecked my back ... can't move," I grimaced bravely through my pain.

The two of them looked at one another in blank surprise. This was supposed to be their evening's entertainment? Then they both giggled.

"Well, you're a fine pair of champions, you are!" Sandra sniffed.

"I'll say!" Florence concurred.

They looked at us again, and in unison they turned and walked straight out the front door of the cinema and into the street.

Minutes passed and it became obvious to the both of us the nurses would not be ministering to our needs that evening. Mac pulled himself to his feet. With the help of the concierge he managed to pull me up and we staggered into the street to hail a cab back to our hotel.

"Nurses!" Mac was both puzzled and outraged. "You'd think they'd have helped …"

"They don't need to know the likes of us," I said. "Those ladies were dressed for a good time this evening, and it's early yet. By now they're probably already hooked up with some other blokes to take them clubbing..."

"Well, fuck 'em!" spat Mac.

"Not these lovelies!"

We both coughed up a laugh.

□

8. My Brother's Tale

I was discharged from the British Army in 1956 and returned to Canada in time for my twenty-first birthday in December of that year. Two years later I decided I wanted to write a novel based on my military experiences in Kenya, and I thought it would be useful to draw on stories told me by others. With this in mind, I wrote a letter to my brother. He lived in Kenya following his military service, but had moved back to England by now. He had served in the infantry before me, 1951-53, and had completed his tour in Kenya with the same battalion of the King's African Rifles I myself was destined to join later. Having made up my mind that I was bound to serve, as the options came up I purposefully requested to be permitted to follow my brother's path exactly, from basic training right through to home regiment and colonial secondment. In due time my requests were granted. Roughly speaking and with a few notable gaps, my older brother was present to cover the early part of the Mau Mau insurrection, and I was destined to be on hand for some of the closing portions of it. Together we had the emergency fairly well covered. I thought my brother's input could be useful to the writing project I had in mind.

Mike could spin a good yarn. Talking to all of us at the family dining table on the night following his return from service, his remarks pointedly directed to me on the eve of my own call-up, he launched into how important it was to keep my eyes open intelligently, avoiding naïvetés – where possible. It was a light-hearted and joyful evening, and the off-hand manner in which he delivered his report set us all laughing. He knew I was due to go for my basic training at the same barracks where he had done his, so much of his dinner table conversation revolved around amusing anecdotes of his own time in the Winchester barracks.

In the last weeks of his basic training and with little to keep them occupied, my brother and some of the other fellows from his squad had taken to pub crawling during their evenings off – navigating up, or else down, the old city's main thoroughfare. Mike had already passed his WOSB exam, and would soon be leaving behind his basic training comrades as he headed out for officer training at Eaton Hall.

Each evening's crawl, the group told one another (and anyone else who could be bothered listening), was just practise – training to slay a fearful dragon. It was said, by those who professed to know about these things, the city's main roadway boasted more pubs than any other in the kingdom. The game, they had never tackled it in earnest, was to down a pint in every pub along the way – both sides of the street, starting in one of the houses at the bottom end of town, and climbing all the way up the hill to the barrack gate at the top of the town. Apparently no one had ever completed the course standing. Few, in fact, had even made it halfway.

And so now, on one of his last nights at the Winchester barracks before heading off to face the deadly serious stuff the army was going to throw at him at Officer Training School, he and the usual group of diehards from his unit decided it was time to take a crack at what all had assured them was the impossible – to down a pint in each house that qualified for the Winchester Main Street Pub Crawl. No doubt a grateful British Army would have in store for my brother all manner of honours, promotions, medals and accolades at the conclusion of his two years of service – but tonight there was serious competition to be undertaken.

Marching purposefully through the barrack's main gate, Mike happened to comment to those accompanying him:

"If they'd just place a roadside stand right here at the barrack gate, we wouldn't have to go all the way into town to drink our small beer ... Think of all the chaps who'd use it – beer, hot dogs, what have you. The proprietor of such an establishment would make himself a killing!"

"Hey, Mikey, you sure got it upstairs, man! Yeah! You got it made ...!"

It was Norris, one of the brighter sparks to hail from London's dockside area. He spoke the language of a slow Grade 6, but he was a fine soldier and knew a good idea when he heard it. He liked to walk beside my brother – the charisma thing.

They rolled into town, and when they later rolled back again, singing the loud praises of those who passed their time in Her Majesty's forces, Norris was somewhat louder than all the rest combined. He was proud, he said, to consider himself my brother's good friend. Despite their failure to complete the full mission, at least they had failed together, "as good mates should."

Sure enough, as Norris had so rightly predicted, my brother went on to achieve great things during his time as an officer. After graduating from Eaton Hall he was commissioned into one of the Home Counties regiments –

and promptly seconded to active service in a battalion of the King's African Rifles. He did well, saw action during the Mau Mau rebellion, travelled in Tanganyika, and at one point had been selected to be bodyguard to Kenya's colonial governor, Sir Evelyn Baring.

During that homecoming dinner I did not have access to the detail he was to send me a few years later, but he was able to impart sufficient of his adventures for me to glean an extraordinary story. Bits of it were to filter out in later conversations, tantalizing little snippets that finally prompted me to seek a fuller explanation.

His response to my letter in 1959 was to arrive as a reel-to-reel tape. With both of our periods of military service now behind us, he was living in London and I had relocated to western Canada where I was living close to family. This enabled me to ask my father's office secretary to transcribe the tape Mike had sent me. Poor lady, she could not have realized when she first agreed to it what an immense chore she had taken on, but she knuckled under and over a period of time rattled out a first-draft typescript for me – some thirty pages of close single-line typing.

I never used it. The tape was so long I do not believe I ever listened to the whole thing, or took in its details. My brother's voice would ramble on rather monotonously while I would get out of my chair to put on a pot of coffee, or go to the bathroom. One way or another I know I missed large portions of it, and once it got turned off I know it never got turned back on again. Like many projects I took up in those days with a sense of priority, my enthusiasm for cranking out a novel had waned.

I am likewise sure I never read the entire manuscript once it had been typed up. Like my brother's audio voice, the document was delivered to me absent paragraphing, and with minimal (and inaccurate) punctuation. By the time the rough typescript was ready I had long since abandoned my original book idea and was engrossed in something completely different.

The tape itself disappeared during some upheaval or move across country. Somehow the typescript found its way into a file folder where it was easily forgotten, and where it could remain undisturbed as it yellowed with age. That rigorous process of amnesia was started, as I said, in 1959. The document remained hidden for the next fifty-two years, and came to light again when I happened to be ferreting through some old files looking for something completely unrelated.

Moving forward, now, to a more contemporary setting, and trying to sort out my thoughts concerning my own military service, it occurred to me that maybe I could, after all, make good use of the material Mike sent me so many years previously. I examined it with much greater care than before and found its subject matter relevant to this current narrative; the more so because its story prefaces the story of my own service.

The typescript required considerable editing, and I found certain inconsistencies and even questionable sequences. Some of it was plainly out of sync. Though irritating, these are small points – and in any case it is far too late to query my brother on any of them now. The whole draws a picture of the time, another angle on an historical period already well-documented.

Except for my editing, I offer the tape's story pretty well as is:

My first few days in Nairobi were spent in the Queen's Hotel. I thought the army had forgotten about me, but after a while I found they hadn't ... and I was stationed out at Langata Camp.

I was there about two or three weeks, and was then ordered to take command of two platoons ... one at Government House, the other at the Commander in Chief's house.

That job lasted about two months and was the cushiest one can imagine. All I had to do was to mount the guard each morning and evening, and the rest of the time I spent lounging in the governor's swimming pool and playing squash with his ADC ... or else in civilian clothes out on the town, just generally beating it up.

It was a shock after two months of this luxurious life, during which I had servants all around me and a half-bottle of gin every night, to be whipped out suddenly, up to the Kinangop and into the forest at a thousand feet.

This was the heart of the Mau Mau country and, being up at that altitude, it took quite a bit of training to get used to it.

We would patrol about twenty-five miles each day.

The visibility in this forest is very, very dense ... about ten or twenty yards at the most. We had to watch out for ambushes especially.

Mrs. Queen's Chump

We found there were cases when animals – elephant and buffalo – had been wounded by the bombing ... they became vicious ... on several occasions we rounded corners in the forest and found ourselves face-to-face with ten or twenty elephants ... if any had been wounded they could be extremely nasty.

An elephant, by nature, is a curious animal ... he is short-sighted as well, so maybe won't mean to attack ... he'll come up for a closer look.

We overcame the difficulties (with elephants) by blowing our whistles at them ... the high-pitched whistling would scare them off.

Up in the forest we had one or two skirmishes with gangs there.

The practice, as horrible as it is to imagine, was to cut the hands off (the dead) ... gruesome, but that's what we had to do. It was so long a distance to bring the bodies (of those we might have killed) out of the forest ... one of the *askaris* would collect all the hands in a sack ... these would be taken back to base for thumb printing ...

Any wounded would be taken to the military hospital where they would be kept until they were fit enough to go into one of the detention camps.

While we were up in this forest, we would often wake up in the mornings with frost on the ground. But, after the first month or so, we really began to enjoy life ... it was a physical and healthy life. The *askaris* obviously got a bit frustrated because there weren't any women, but that's one of the penalties to be paid fighting a war – even a war such as ours.

After a few months in the forest we were brought down to Langata again ... two incidents here to relate to you – the Ruck murder, in late January of 1953, and the Lari massacre in March.

We were called out ... to the Ruck farm, a particularly horrible example of the murder of a European family, the results of which I witnessed ... there was Mr. and Mrs. Ruck, Roger and Esmé, and their little boy, Michael. Mrs. Ruck was pregnant.

The gang had got themselves thoroughly drugged on an herb they call *bhang*, which has the effect of making them completely fearless and irresponsible. They'd become temporarily crazed, and if they took this herb as a constant thing, they could become permanently crazy.

But these thugs went up to the Ruck's farm, knocked on the door – and when Mr. Ruck came out to see what they wanted they dragged him onto his own front lawn. A tree had been felled and they beheaded him on its stump. Inside they found Mrs. Ruck in her sitting room. They tied her up, slit her stomach open and removed the embryo of the child. Police found (the embryo) hanging by its neck from the mantelpiece. Mrs. Ruck was chopped up and left to die. Upstairs the gang broke down the locked door of six-year-old Michael's bedroom. Whether he was asleep or whether he was just lying there too terrified to do anything, no one will ever know, but they chopped his little body so far into the mattress and into such minute pieces that the mattress eventually had to be buried with his body. I can't tell you the feeling of nausea I experienced after witnessing all this.

The Lari incident ... you probably remember, the village is located about ten miles beyond Limuru ... a Kikuyu settlement, but its inhabitants were known to be supportive of the government. They wouldn't have anything to do with the Mau Mau.

So the Mau Mau went in and massacred practically the whole of the village. I'm not sure, but I think well over a hundred people were killed.

As we drove up we could smell burning flesh from about three or four miles away, and when we got there it was difficult to try to piece any bodies together. There were bits of leg in one corner of the village, heads in another. People had been hamstrung, some had their legs cut off. It was a ghastly mess, I can tell you. They had not only cut them up, but had set the whole village on fire.

We constituted a small platoon, so there wasn't much we could do about it. The police, and I think it was the 3rd KAR – I'm not sure, it might have been the 23rd – went after the gang responsible, and I believe they captured and killed a fair number of them.

That will give an indication of the horror of Mau Mau. There were many other cases of maltreating animals, hamstringing them, and such ... ghastly little war. Only a little war because it didn't extend to many of the African tribes, although I know in Kenya, now, there is a strong anti-

European feeling ... politics ... but largely because in Kenya there is an element of the wrong kind of settler ... power-happy men who maltreat Africans ... beat them if they don't do exactly as they command. There are fines now and prison sentences for cases of beating ... I think in due time it's bound to swing over to an African government ... (then perhaps) the European and the African will be able to live peacefully in Kenya. I hope so anyway.

We had a series of uneventful times after the Ruck murder ... patrol after patrol in the forest. Nothing much happened, and eventually we were sent to Gilgil to guard the ammunition dump there. It was the dreariest job you can imagine, but it was compensated by the fact that we were in exceptionally lovely country. There were opportunities for game hunting and ... fishing in the Malawa and Terasha rivers.

There was one particular woman, a friend of my Godmother's, who had a lovely farm up there. We used to spend weekends at her place. It was on the banks of the Malawa River, and she couldn't have been kinder to us. We spent many glorious weekends fishing and relaxing in her charming surroundings.

Three months at Gilgil, then by train down to Dar es Salaam. Wonderful experience ... Dar es Salaam, as most of the towns in East Africa, especially on the coast, is multi-racial. On a good day from Observation Hill, where we were camped, you could see Zanzibar forty miles away. It is only a speck on the horizon, but it was quite a thrill to see it. It was hot. We had a pleasant camp on top of the hill, but it was not an eventful time ... interminable internal security duties.

When we had been there for about two months ... the Mau Mau, then quite active, had infiltrated over the border from Kenya into Tanganyika. Apparently the police had already shot two or three of them, so we were ordered up to Arusha to give them a bit of support. We had a good time there ... the police boys accommodated us at their camp ... entertained us pretty well. We had a briefing by the police commandant, and he spread us throughout the Masai country. There were three companies of us ... right along the border, from Longido across to Loliondo – over past Lake Natron ... which we thought the most likely place the Mau Mau might infiltrate.

I was fortunate enough to get to Loliondo, over on the western end of our line. To get there from Arusha, we had to go up to Nairobi, then come south again (via) Narok. You will be able to follow all this on the map ...

It was the rainy period then, and there were patches of black cotton soil – awfully difficult ground after a heavy rain. I had a one-ton truck and four or five jeeps, I forget exact numbers, but we all got bogged down in a particularly bad patch of this black cotton soil. We pushed and pulled to get out of there. Two or three of the jeeps made it out, but that evening we still hadn't got the one-ton truck free. Absolutely nothing would budge it. We decided the best thing would be to remain in the vehicles overnight and hope it would dry out the following day ...

The rain stopped, but it was just as muddy and we couldn't shift the truck.

Over on the horizon there was a column of smoke, so I sent one of the guys over there and we discovered it was a small Masai *manyata* (cluster of dwellings). He managed to get about fifteen or twenty *morani* (warrior youth) to come over and give us a hand.

They got hold of the truck and pushed and heaved and tugged ... nothing would budge the damned thing. So eventually my batman, who is quite a character, suggested we could probably fool the tribesmen by giving them some aspirin tablets and telling them they were health efficiency tablets ... that this would build them into great strong men.

We couldn't lose anything by trying, so I gave each man a tablet ... and sure enough, one heave and the truck was out, no trouble at all. All the *askaris* fell back in the mud killing themselves with laughter. They always do when anything amuses them, and they had a right go of laughter over that. Pleased me no end because I loved to see them laughing.

We got the trucks out and proceeded on a bumpy road through to Loliondo ... spent three weeks there in this little Masai settlement ... and a small population of white people. There was the District Officer and the desert locust man, and that was about it. There were a few European houses, so I stayed in one of them and the *askaris* slept down at the police HQ.

It was there I met a friend of mine, Ronny Crabb. He was the policeman in charge of the detachment, commanding a group of men on this aspect of the emergency, and we used to patrol daily ... alternately sending out the police or *askaris*, as I only had a single platoon with me. We'd range from ten to twenty-five miles in a day. There was one particular occasion when we went out on patrol – in a (district) about twenty-five miles away (from camp), and we had to get there by truck. We patrolled about fifteen miles, and while we were patrolling a little stream we'd crossed earlier in the day had swollen into a river because of the rains. We tried to get the trucks through, but the first Land Rover to go in disappeared under the water. First of all the seat cushion floated to the surface, and then a bewildered looking driver ... we dragged him out, but it was impossible to get the trucks across the river because, as I say, it had swollen so much and there was no likelihood of it going down overnight. There was no other place along the banks where we could cross.

There was no point staying with the trucks for possibly two or three days, so I decided to leave a driver with each vehicle and foot it back to Loliondo. It was about a thirty-mile walk in all ... and believe you me we had some pretty big blisters among us. If it had not been for the knowledge that I was going to get a nice home-cooked dinner from the Indian *duka* owner that night, I don't think we would have made it.

From Loliondo after three pretty futile weeks we went back up to Kenya ... and then back down to Dar es Salaam again.

When we got back to Dar it was just the same old routine of internal security duties again ... we had a native dug-out boat they call a *ngalawa* ... we used this to go out spear-fishing. Weekends were when we had the most time. We made quite a bit of money on weekends ... selling our catch for one shilling a pound. If we were lucky we'd catch a big grouper or rock carp and make quite a bit of money. It paid the petrol bills, because by that time I'd bought a dilapidated old car. I paid about fifty pounds for it, spent about twenty-five pounds on repairs – and sold it for five pounds. As you can see, I'm a pretty astute businessman!

We had some marvelous times ... fascinating sights under water. The coral – it's like going into a different world.

We spent about a month on that second visit to Dar es Salaam, and then we went back up to Kenya ... spending about a week in Kiambu (with) the 6th KAR ... then going from there on to Limuru and Tigoni.

We were told we were to make our headquarters right next door to the police station at Tigoni ... in an old courthouse. It was made of wood. We made it quite comfortable, but it was like living in a barn.

During the course of our stay we had several incidents ... bright and early in the morning we used to have to go and cordon off these Kikuyu villages ... it was a routine sort of thing ... we would search right through all the huts of the whole village for arms and ammunition, any type of weapon that could possibly be dangerous.

(We) had a system of hooded men ... who had been terrorists at one stage but had changed their minds and gone over to the government. They would, in fact, be kept and securely guarded by the police, because if the Mau Mau had got to know they'd changed sides they'd have been bumped off right away. They were kept secure, not allowed to circle amongst their friends or anything. We used to take two or three or more of them from the village we were raiding on that particular morning ... hoods would be placed over their heads so they wouldn't be recognized. You can imagine the atmosphere, early dawn with the mist coming off the ground in amongst all the wattle trees ... possibly a clearing of the wattle trees, with the mud huts of the Kikuyu villages and thousands of Kikuyu people sitting ... men in one compound, women in another with their children ... all of them cordoned off with soldiers and barbed wire.

One-by-one they'd be led in front of the hooded men ... who weren't allowed to talk, incidentally, because that might have been the recognizing factor. If the (hooded men) recognized anybody brought before them, they'd give a tap on the table. If they recognized (someone) as being a particularly bad terrorist, they'd give two taps. If they recognized a number one top terrorist they'd thump the table so hard that you'd stop and interrogate the bloke concerned on the spot. He'd be taken aside and probably questioned more thoroughly by the CID people.

On one occasion we had a queue of people traipsing in front of two of these hooded men ... they tapped on the table and whispered in the policeman's ear that he was a senior Mau Mau. They suggested that we take his coat off, and when we did so he had under his arm one of these long *simis* which, as you know, are double-edged knives used for hacking people up ... razor sharp ... and when his coat was thrown on the ground a snake slithered out of the pocket. Obviously he had put it there, hoping some policeman would put his hand in his pocket to search him.

Fortunately it didn't work. The snake was killed and the fellow was no doubt put inside for a good long stretch. Probably in there now.

I had my second kill there. One night we got a call from a farm run by a Mr. and Mrs. Jolly ... apparently a gang had got into their farm, and one of the gangsters had burst through the kitchen. All the kitchen boys were too terrified to do anything, and this gangster ran into the dining room while they were eating, brandishing a pistol and obviously drugged up to the eyebrows. He couldn't stand up straight, like a drunk. There was a terrific skirmish in there and as Mr. Jolly was grappling with (the intruder), Mrs. Jolly pulled her pistol out and shot the fellow dead. She apparently emptied so many bullets into him ... one went right through the gangster and she shot her husband in the groin ... not too seriously wounded.

We arrived there about two o'clock in the morning having not received the call till quite late ... and we were rather overpowered by the smell of death in the room because this Mau Mau lying on the floor had started to bubble by then. The sight was pretty horrible. He'd been dead for some while.

We were there, but we couldn't do much because it was dark. Obviously the gangsters had failed in their kill or capture, or whatever they had wanted to do, so had pushed off. The only thing we could do was hope it wouldn't rain that night so we could use the army tracking dogs ... which we did (in the) morning.

This lovely long-haired Alsatian came up, specially trained for the job and with a terrific record. He had many arrests to his name ... We had old Rex put on a leash and we took him outside. It hadn't rained that night and the trail was still fresh, so we put him onto the trail ... and followed with him and his handler for miles and miles and miles ...

through the coffee bushes and over hills and down in the valleys ... all over the place ... I can't tell you what a walk it was.

I was in the lead group with the tracker dog and his handler, about seven of my *askaris* were in a line behind me ... and a policeman with his *askaris* behind them ...

Eventually we came to the centre of a coffee plantation ... coffee bushes on either side of us ... we were on one of those little paths that wind their way through the bushes when suddenly the dog stopped and the handler turned to me and said, "The dog won't go any further. This must mean either the end of the trail, or ... there's certainly something peculiar about this ..."

We found breadcrumbs and a few indications on the ground that people had been there recently ... so we gathered it was probably the gang that had been at the Jolly farm the night before.

The police went off to the right through the coffee ... and I went off to the left of the trail with my *askaris* ... the tracker dog stayed on the path. We'd gone about fifty yards into the coffee ... unfortunately my men were in single file behind me, otherwise we probably could have done more. Suddenly I noticed a face looking at me from under one of the bushes ... coffee forms a natural shelter for anybody who wants to lie under (a bush) overnight.

There were several people. I yelled at them to stay where they were, and they all started jumping up and running ... before I had time to deploy the *askaris* on either side ... I had to open up with the Patchette (sub-machine) gun I had.

The visibility was poor ... as you probably know ... because these coffee plantations are thick with bushes ... and I knocked down two of these terrorists before they managed to get away ... a third kept on running ... so I kept on firing. I could see him running through the bushes and I just kept on firing and firing and, when I came to the end of the magazine, I did a quick reload and just carried on shooting ... finally he dropped.

We found he had thirty-eight bullets in his back. How he managed to keep running with all that lead in him we don't know. There was another youngster who we found under the bushes we managed to capture and we took him with us back to Tigoni Police Station for questioning later on. I believe the police found out quite a bit of information about this gang that had pulled the raid. In subsequent days ... the police were able to capture and kill quite a number of them. They found their hideout from the information gathered from this boy.

We followed the rest of the gang for quite a few miles but by that time we'd come out at a Kikuyu village onto the main road, and of course the dog couldn't follow any longer. The gang had split up ... gone to places where trails couldn't be picked up. They must have realized there was a dog on their trail. We had to give up and hand the job over to the police intelligence department.

*

I know a little bit about the oathing ceremonies ... the Mau Mau oaths were designed to be so horrible that no man would want to discuss his involvement with them – with anybody. There was a whole series of oaths, and they were specially designed to make the oath-taker maintain secrecy of the whole business. These oaths also served to debase a man so much that he'd be prepared to do practically anything. Nothing could be worse than the oath, so once having taken it he could go through all these murders and everything knowing that, according to the Kikuyu moral code, he had already committed the worst he could.

During raids in and around Nairobi we recovered a fantastic amount of arms and ammunition that had been stolen from government sources, and also a great quantity of money ... amounting to thousands and thousands of pounds.

To conceal this money ... again a pretty horrible thing to describe to you ... but the women used to wrap it in cellophane paper and conceal it inside their bodies. Whenever we went on one of these raids we used to take a few female Africans along with us in the screening team. They used to search any female prisoners ... with tweezers ... prying into their nether regions.

Always we would try to get hold of one of these Mau Mau cashiers because they usually went around with enormous wads of currency. Of course, if one was knocked off or captured, that was the last you ever heard of it ... (the money) would be pocketed right away.

There was one sergeant in the Kenya Regiment who bought himself a brand new Chevrolet with it ... and also put the down payment on a house ... so you can just imagine how much they used to carry around with them.

There was one occasion when I was up in the forest on patrol. I had about six or seven *askaris* with me ... never more than that in the forest because it created rather a lot of noise. We were about two or three miles from camp on the end of a patrol this one night ... it was dusk and that brought down the visibility in the forest. We stopped for a smoke, and suddenly, all around us, we could hear voices. They were Kikuyu, yelling at my *askaris* to knock me on the head and go and join them ... they'd all be paid a certain amount of money - five or ten pounds, which was about two month's wages to an *askari*. Anyway, I had a lot of loyal Tanganyika boys with me, and they didn't want to do that particularly – so we just opened up in one direction, and ran like hell back to camp. We couldn't see anyone around us, the visibility was so dense.

A friend of mine was sent out with the Black Watch. On his first patrol he walked straight into a hideout and got shot up badly ... one bullet in his chest, which they finally dug out of his stomach ... He was rushed down to hospital for a week, then to the coast for two weeks recuperation ... and in three weeks total he was back up to the forest. Pretty efficient medical system, we had.

Whenever you went for a run around Gilgil, up in the Kinangop or somewhere like that, in the earlier days of the Mau Mau, you could virtually guarantee somebody in the forest would take a pot-shot at you from one of their homemade guns. Fantastic weapons ... made of an old curtain rod slung onto a wooden butt, a door bolt on an elastic acting as the hammer. Amazing there weren't more casualties among them, come to think of it.

All this is pretty grim ... but there were moments of humour ...

There was a European housewife out there who was going to have a big dinner party one night, and so she told her head boy that when she rang the bell at the dinner table, she wanted him to come in looking nice with his red *kanzo* on, and his fez, carrying the boar's head on a tray,

Mrs. Queen's Chump

with an apple in its mouth and parsley in its ears.

At the appointed moment she rang the bell, and in walked the head boy looking just fine. He had the boar's head on the tray - but the apple in his own mouth, and the parsley sticking out of his own ears.

(While we were) in Gilgil we had a new mess boy called Ernest ... we had just taken him on ... he'd never worked in a European kitchen before.

Unfortunately for Ernest he arrived on Christmas Eve (just in time for our mess dinner). There was no time to train him properly, but he was game. We got through the turkey alright ... then the Christmas pudding was brought in ... Ernest dressed up to the eyebrows in all his servant's gear, carrying the Christmas pudding on a ruddy great platter.

The adjutant got up and uncorked the bottle of brandy, poured it over the pudding and set light to it.

This was too much for Ernest. He was standing with his eyes popping out of his head, and when the brandy was set alight he just dropped the Christmas pudding and ran straight out of the mess.

We were left to scrape our pudding off the floor.

*

Indeed, my brother had returned with honours to his home depot. The stories he told us during his homecoming family dinner party had set a happy tone to the evening. We were all laughing.

"And do you know what?" he asked, not waiting for an answer. "As I was entering at our barrack gate, when I got back there a couple of days ago, I noticed this brightly coloured refreshment stand set up on the curb to one side ... hot dogs, coffee, soft drinks. There was probably even a little snifter of something racier for those who knew how to ask for it."

"What's going on here?" he had enquired of one of his colleagues in the officers' mess.

"O-o-oh!" came the sardonic reply, a note of upper-class distaste filtering all the way down an aristocratic nose.

"Those! Bloody things, they are …! Borough Council should ban them. Some blithering nignog from London's east end has set them up outside practically every barracks in the south of England … Must have made himself a millionaire by now!"

Out of curiosity my brother drove down to the Winchester barracks the following morning.

Norris, now freed of his military service and dressed in an apron, busied himself under a gaily-decorated awning. From behind a polished counter he was serving a couple of soldiers who'd stepped outside the barrack gate.

"Hey, Mikey! My friend!" he called out when he caught sight of my brother. "You're my mate! Man, what a great idea you gave me …! What a fantastic idea! I got these things up all over the south of England. Owe it all to you, man! Brain-power, that's what it was! I tell you, man, you got it upstairs. You sure got it upstairs!"

"Here he was – the nemesis of the biggest drunk of my life!" my brother growled to his family across the dinner table.

"I go out to do my bloody duty, ready to put my life on the line … and I come back with a fantastic adventure to relate … but in reality I can hold onto nothing more than the certainty that I'm going to have to work my butt off for the rest of my born days … Norris, on the other hand, God bless his cotton socks, takes my idea – a simple notion floated out into that evening's only moment of sobriety – and makes himself a cool million. There ain't no justice …!"

☐

9. A Very Large Corporal

"He was a good soldier – went bad after we'd taught him everything we knew ..."*

It was shortly after the Lake Naivasha farce and the events that followed at Nyeri's Outspan Hotel that our battalion of the King's African Rifles, which was a Tanganyika unit, teamed up with elements of the KAR battalion from Uganda. It was not for long, a few weeks at most. The Ugandans were moving to a billet near the northern slopes of Mt. Kenya, but the new camp was not yet ready. The battalion's headquarters company, a couple of its infantry companies, and most of its officers, had gone ahead to prepare the new quarters; the remaining elements stayed behind to pitch in with our lot at the Beck Farm just outside Nyeri. It meant our camp had to cope with an extra four hundred men which was not, as it turned out, too onerous an undertaking. Our battalion had pitched camp on a sizeable stretch of farmland, so it was little problem to erect additional tents at one end of a lower field. Each of us as platoon officers took on a surplus ten or fifteen men, administering the resulting enlarged units as part of our normal command and thus spreading the Ugandan overflow throughout our entire battalion. Quite by chance, one of Fate's more sardonic twists, the largest man in the entire regiment was assigned to me, along with his section of nine men. It was in this manner I came to be acquainted with Corporal Idi Amin.

It would have been impossible at that time to have assessed what the man was later to become. The thousands he would kill were yet as unimagined as they were destined to become nameless. The thought of feeding to the crocodiles large numbers of those who displeased him, once he had become president of his country, would have been an unutterable barbarism even for that coarse moment of colonial mayhem. Could anything be more barbarous than the Mau Mau? Hanging a man in public or shooting him was gruesome enough. Using *pangas* to hack him apart was extremely so, though we knew it happened and expressed our distaste for it. But we represented the cricket-playing British; our barbarisms were at least compatible with pink gin sun-

---

* From a conversation, after the fact, between two KAR officers who had known Idi Amin

downers. Or so thought those of us who had yet to learn the finer details of Rule Britannia. The acts of violence Idi Amin was shortly to commit were beyond our wildest imaginings.

Death by crocodile? Ye Gods!

For my own part, I was primarily conscious of the man's extraordinary size. Well above six feet and several inches, and proportionately wide, he would fill any doorway absolutely – even some double doorways. More than that, though, I also quickly became aware of his efficiency as a soldier. One would think, not unnaturally, that someone of such generous dimensions would have a voice to match, but strangely I cannot remember him making a notable vocal mark for himself in that most military of environments, the parade square. He was inclined to be soft-spoken, as a matter of fact – but then some brutes can be most intimidating when their threats are offered on a soft pillow. If I failed to see what he was, so did everybody else. The man's essential brutality was not visible at that time.

Amin's size alone was sufficient to dominate the soldiers of the platoon, I reckoned, both Ugandans and Tanganyikans, so I wasn't too concerned that I heard no thundering voice. On parade, he would move among them swiftly, loftily, a word here, a muffled bark there, as he stepped forward to straighten a belt or correct a cap angle. But suddenly our parades took on an improved polish and efficiency. The men stood taller and straighter, somehow, and moved about with greater precision. Corporal Amin marched them up and down on our dusty square, and they worked better than I had ever seen them work before. I said as much to WOPC Nyamahanga as he stood beside me looking on.

He smiled.

"I think they are rather respectful of their new corporal," he said, enjoying his successful attempt at English understatement.

"The man's a monster!" I was referring to his size without the least realization I could be prophesying.

About that time one of my fellow officers and I were chosen to compete in the inter-regimental boxing tournament. The team of twelve was divided into various weight categories, and the two of us – the only officers on the team – were the lightweights. All the others on the team were *askaris*, and Idi Amin was our prize heavyweight. It was strange that as a corporal in my platoon, even though temporary, I had few dealings with the man, and that it was only when we met in the gymnasium in Nairobi, where the tournament was to be held, that I finally got to speak to him informally.

Once encamped in Nairobi I was able to take a good look at this jolly giant of a man who always smiled more than he glowered – at least when I was looking at him. He glowered across his boxing gloves, true, and that alone must have terrified his opponents. In the ring his oversized feet would be stuffed into a pair of high-sided gym shoes, no socks, and he would leave the top few lace-holes unthreaded so that the canvas uppers would fold back about his heavy ankles. His boxing trunks were black, our team colour, and he wore no shirt so that one could see at a glance the full size of his belly, torso and arms. Above the waistline his body resembled three black refrigerators laid sideways and stacked one on top of the other. He had no neck that you could discern, but a massive head shoved pugnaciously forward on his shoulders. His arms were the girth of sewage pipes, and his fists were packed into gloves that resembled potato sacks. Between the mountainous gluteal muscles that filled his trunks and the shuffling of his sloppy gym shoes, his powerful legs moved back and forth like engine pistons as he stalked about the ring sure-footed as a leopard, hunched to fell whatever object stood defying him.

In my brief career as a boxer, both at school and later in the military, I never went more than three rounds. This was because three was considered the limit for a gentleman's bout, and certainly team fights within the army were intended to be gentlemanly and sportsmanlike affairs. In addition this limitation more or less ensured that anyone with anything else useful to do with his life outside the ring (like soldiering) would not be too severely mauled or battered about to perform his duties. Long fights can be gruesome. After three rounds a boxer tends to get tired, and at that point he adopts an attitude that tends to heavy pounding. A brawling tenacity sets in. The longer the bout, the greater the chance of sustaining severe damage – broken noses, cauliflower ears, hemorrhaging or brain injuries. On the other hand, three-round fights are so short that they tend to become flat-out bids for a decisive win. Unless a boxer is unlucky enough to get knocked out right away, most fighters can maintain their adrenaline at full pump for the duration of a three-rounder. Three-round bouts tend to be fast, hard-hitting, all-out attacks rather than exploratory sorties aimed at drawing out an opponent, which is what one will see most often during the first three rounds of a longer fight. For sheer energy and some of the best boxing I have ever witnessed it is hard to surpass the excitement of a scheduled three-round match. That should be enough to demonstrate skill; longer fights might better serve blood-lusting spectators than the fighters themselves. There is something culturally raw and utterly barren about an indulgent spectacle of guts and gore, even when mollified by quantities of courage and stamina.

In the weeks preceding the inter-regimental tourney in Nairobi I came to know something of the members of our own team. It was difficult for a white officer to "know" the *askaris*, or any of the African personnel in his charge. Mid-fifties Kenya was an "us" and "them" society, overt racism in all aspects. Exceptions to this were immediately noted and criticized. Feelings of superiority were well inculcated into the minds of junior officers just out from the Motherland, the more so as they had a nasty job to do making sure "restless natives" remained in a heap at the bottom of the social and economic ladder. Anything even remotely resembling "fraternization" with Africans was so deeply frowned upon that even a casual conversation in the street or hotel lobby between black and white might be remarked upon at the dinner table. Certain things were "not done" – the "things" being wide open to interpretation depending upon how any given outsider chose to look in. It bespoke an attitude relating directly to the self-imposition and restraint embodying a constitution never actually constituted: the British manner, the British way of doing things. What is, after all (and, of greater relevance, what is not), cricket. Bullshit, and yet one felt constrained by this "norm" to maintain the "good name" of the regiment. I was to buck this attitude in numerous ways, invariably with a hesitant immaturity that, of itself, quickly brought down on my head a measure of opprobrium – several times a lambasting of varied ferocity, and from a variety of sources. I did not by any means always know what to do about it, how I should answer back – or even if I should. I could not bring myself to feel comfortable employing the attitude of a superior white man, yet I lacked sufficient courage and self-confidence to express openly my beliefs. It was a dichotomy for me: I knew what I felt, but at my tender age and in the vulnerable position of a junior I lacked the convincing vocabulary to articulate my feelings and face down the overt racism surrounding me. It took several years to discover, and after an intensive brainwashing, that the British Empire was oiled by such codswallop; that attitudes of superiority existed absolutely in order to create greater comfort for the collective mind and body of the oppressor colonizer, and for no other good reason whatsoever. Oblivious to the concept that foreign administration was humiliation for any and all Africans, such insufferable attitudes of aloofness on the part of the European settlers quickly infected the military and other newcomers to the colony. Both the conscious and unconscious inhumanity created hatred in immeasurable quantities, and this in turn negated a genuinely positive interplay between the various races. In the end the stupidity of such attitude proved the undoing of empire, but in the mid-50's true enlightenment had not quite yet jogged the collective British brain cell.

The environment of the boxing team permitted me some leeway. There was a measure of autonomy largely, I believe, because sweaty workouts and the smelly surroundings of the boxing gym did not greatly appeal to the sensibilities of the British officer class. On fight nights or at workouts numbers of them might show up so they could be seen to cheer us on, and their support was convincingly lusty enough, I suppose. But they tended to leave early, hankies to noses, so that by and large we were left to our own devices. There were twelve of us thrown together for the match, and the team that won the most bouts would walk away with regimental laurels. The team from the King's African Rifles had been pulled from different battalions, and these in turn came from many regions of East Africa. Initially we did not know each other, but as we were all fighting on the same side it soon became obvious we had to pump for one another. And we all pumped for Idi Amin.

We were in awe of the corporal's size. Watching him on the inner side of the ropes was like looking into the cage of a pacing feline. He was a winner for sure. I knew him superficially through our contact at Nyeri, but in Nairobi I came to know him better. His personal appearance, his bulk, actually repulsed me, a bit like feeling nausea at being given a heaped serving on one's dinner plate and knowing that to indulge at all would be to overindulge. But I was drawn, fascinated, by his boxing. To this day I have yet to see another such enormous person move himself with equal speed. He was far and away the fastest man I have ever seen flashing his way around the inside of a boxing ring, more so than fighters of much more streamlined proportions. He was like Saint Elmo's fire crackling along the ropes. He carried his enormous bulk from corner to corner with a dancer's skill and balance. The force of his blows would crash through his opponent's guard, sufficient to stop and stun some wild beasts. Direct hits about the head were devastating. On one occasion in a practice bout I watched from ringside as Amin smashed his sparring partner's gloved fist into the poor fellow's own guarded face with such force that the man in effect knocked himself out.

After a workout one afternoon a few of us went to an inconspicuous back street bar owned by a Portuguese-Seychellois somewhere behind the New

Stanley Hotel. There we could mix and not draw attention. Amin was with us. We ordered soft drinks.

"What do you think of your chances on Thursday night?" I asked our heavyweight.

His laughter rumbled up out of his belly and he showed all of his teeth.

"I don't know who I be fightin' Thursday, but I put him away sure. They other tribes, they just Mau Mau, so I put him away, you see."

"Come on, corporal," I teased him. "You think all other tribes are just Mau Mau?"

"All of them! All but Kakwa, like me!"

He laughed and slapped the sides of his ample stomach, then fluttered his hands womanishly under his face. The gesture registered with me because of the extraordinary size of his mitts and the expressiveness of his movement. For all that, his fists were like great pink and black hams.

"I'm not Kakwa, but I'm sure not Mau Mau either," I told him, curious as to his reaction.

"No! You're of the English tribe. The English, they the worst Mau Mau of all!"

He was still laughing. He liked this play.

"Ah-ha! You are wrong, there, Amin!" I exclaimed. "I am not English at all. Like you, I am a foreigner fighting an Englishman's war."

His smile faded as he looked at me.

"Why?"

He was not amused at my stopping him mid-joke, as it were. For an instant I thought I could see thunder behind his eyes, a moment of confusion in his demand to know why I should be fighting someone else's war. Then he pushed it away, like a toy he did not really want to play with anyway, and his backslapping joviality returned.

"So we be both foreign Mau Mau fightin' the Mau Mau!" he roared jovially. "You good man, sah! Very generous! Mrs. Queen get good mileage outta you! You be Mrs. Queen's prawn!"

" 'Pawn,' is what I think you mean, Corporal Amin – 'pawn,' not 'prawn'…"

But he was having too much fun to want to pay attention to my language lesson, and I didn't pursue the matter.

I recall the exchange because of its undercurrent of danger. At the time I associated it with the up-coming boxing tournament, his zest for a good fight. Years later I better remember the ominous instability and threat I sensed at that moment; not a man whose humours should be interrupted or corrected.

The night of the big match Corporal Amin did indeed "put away" his opponent. He ran at the man the instant he heard the bell signaling the opening round. His opponent had barely risen from his stool when Amin was on top of him and landed three mighty blows that felled the fellow before he had put his guard up, or been able to move out of his corner. He had had no time to throw a punch of his own. The fight was over in seconds – which was a shame, in a way. The rest of us had been waiting all evening for a good heavyweight bout.

Later I saw Amin in the locker room. He was talking and laughing with some of our teammates, and still had his gloves tied firmly onto his hands.

"Corporal," I called to him. "You didn't give the man a chance to show his fighting mettle!"

Idi Amin rose from his bench, good soldier now, to answer his officer. He stood to attention grinning broadly, and flashed a mock salute with his gloved hand.

"Sah! I don'know what that man be doin' here. Boxin' surely not!"

I had won my fight. I smiled back at him and congratulated him for winning his, and our team in the end took the tournament trophy.

I met Corporal Idi Amin only a few times after that evening in Nairobi. Many months later, after I had left Kenya, I heard that he was one of the first of the *askaris* of the East African battalions to be selected for officer training at Sandhurst. The news did not surprise me. I had had a feeling about him, and remembered him for years afterwards. He had been a good and willing soldier, pleasant natured and a lively person to be around. Fun, even. But then I started to read about him in the newspapers, how he had become the leader of his country's military forces, and then staged a *coup d'etat* and not long afterwards anointed himself President of Uganda. But by that time I had returned to my home in Canada, and was making what I thought was an effort to return my life to something like normalcy. No room in all that for anything so whacky as an Idi Amin.

*

People are surprised and bemused when I tell them I had once known Idi Amin. I dare say I would probably feel a bit like that if ever I met someone who told me (with straight face) that they used to play tennis with Pol Pot. Of course most people can only know about any rogue what they have read of him in the newspapers – none of it ever positive or complimentary, or necessarily even true. I seldom attempt to pass serious judgment on Idi Amin not only because it has been so ably accomplished by others, but because what I knew and remember of the man was beyond my personal reproach. That he became something else is evident, but those things were to happen years later when I was well away from the scene.

Even so, I have tried to figure it out, and have wondered many times what it was that transformed the fellow, turning him into such a tyrant. Now and then I have been asked to express an opinion. That he went mad is a fairly simple, if obvious, commentary. But what drove him to his extremities?

From what I have read I do believe he became syphilitic, and that this might have provided the medical trigger for his condition. But I also have another idea, something that might have worked in tandem: from the outset a racist British press went for Idi Amin like a pack of hounds, almost never mentioning his name without throwing in a few jeers and insults. I learned that during an informal press conference shortly after the *coup d'état* propelling him to the presidency of Uganda he had made a rather light comment in his African-English about inviting "Mrs. Queen" to tea. The British press was universally incensed by the comment, but those present laughed politely and their laughter could easily have been misread by Amin – and no doubt was. He thought he had amused the gathering, apparently, and in an effort to continue the raillery of the moment he became even more offensive. He made some remark about taking Queen Elizabeth as one of his wives or concubines, and that her female attributes were such that she might make a fine mother to his offspring. The journalists present said nothing at the time, possibly already aware of his penchant for violence during wrathful outbursts. But they themselves were outraged, and they later tore into him with merciless venom.

Idi Amin was hardly an educated or sophisticated man. He had emerged from a tribal Uganda, and his background would have trained him to think only in terms of leadership using his brute strength. Through his own efforts he had charged ahead to a position of power as the leader of a nation and, in a way, it should have come as no surprise to anyone that he was clueless concerning the "correct" use of his potency. More than that, having arrived, so to speak, he found that he was not respected – internationally – for his new position; that he was instantaneously judged a pariah, the butt of cruel and demeaning jokes. The British press added its insults and jeers, and this I am sure would have helped to push him over the edge. A man who attained this high plateau in the way Idi Amin had, who saw himself as he did, would not easily be able to withstand the ridicule. It was all so personally directed, and the jeering and laughter would have been too much for him to bear. Poke him like a wild animal and he would react as a wild animal.

I genuinely believe that the monstrous Idi Amin we came to know was in large measure a creation of the western free press. We shall never know the complete story, I am sure. But the tyrant the man became had a genesis somewhere. Had he initially been treated with care, attention, and even a measure of kindness and generosity, he might never have become the hideous ogre he became. The syphilis would have had its effect, no doubt, and perhaps there might have been other health issues. But the overt racism with which he was treated from the outset of his presidency added humiliation to the mix, and it is a wise and well-trained statesman who can handle that.

*

For many years I made my home in Almoçageme, in Portugal's magnificent Serra de Sintra, and many people would come to stay with me there as guests. One evening during a get-together over a good meal and a few bottles of outstanding Portuguese wine, I found myself re-telling my friends these unusual aspects of my encounter with Idi Amin. Sasha Motchaloff, the Russian painter staying with me at the time, had himself many extraordinary tales to tell, and I was subsequently able to write a few of them into my notebooks. One of Sasha's stories, which the conversation on this occasion prompted him to recount, concerned a friend of his who had been employed some years before at the Soviet Embassy in Uganda's capital, Kampala. So what follows is hearsay, but a good story nonetheless.

I do not recall all of the background, but at a certain point in the history of Ugandan-Soviet relations Idi Amin had demanded from the super power an increase in arms shipments, but had been turned down.

Infuriated, the Ugandan dictator gave the entire Soviet Embassy twenty-four hours to close up shop and leave the country. To demonstrate he meant what he said, armed soldiers were sent to the embassy to oversee the move, and trucks were provided to cart all personnel and their belongings to the airport. People were herded from the embassy compound so unceremoniously there was barely time to run the accumulated secret files through the shredding machines. With soldiers waving guns under their noses the embassy staff was understandably alarmed and terrified. Wives and children were in tears of fright and despair at having to leave everything behind, particularly when they were being forced at gunpoint to clamber into the backs of the trucks.

Sasha's friend was riding at the open end of the last truck in the convoy as they threaded their way through Kampala's streets to the airport. Then he noticed a motorcycle approaching the rear of the convoy at high speed. As it drew closer, the friend was astonished to see the machine was being ridden by none other than the president himself. With a thunderous burst of speed, Idi Amin overtook the entire line of trucks.

Arriving at the parking lot in front of the airport terminal, Sasha's friend could see the Ugandan president, who had arrived just before the convoy, standing astride his parked motorcycle. His arms were crossed about his massive chest and a gigantic grin split his visage – all savage teeth and flashing, mad eyes. At gunpoint, the Russians were ordered out of the trucks and told to stand with their backs to the terminal building. They were sure they were all about to be shot. Several of the women and children started to wail and cry.

Finally, when the whole embassy party was lined up, some of them sobbing uncontrollably, the dictator ordered one of his officers to offload a box that had been strapped to the pillion of the motorcycle. While the officer followed and held the lid of the box open, Idi Amin walked deliberately down the ragged line. Reaching into the box, he withdrew handfuls of beribboned medals, and draped one about the neck of each person present.

From ambassador to cook, matrons and children, the entire complement of the Soviet Embassy was invested with the Order of Uganda.

When he had finished, and again at gunpoint, everyone was herded aboard a waiting airplane, and the lot of them were peremptorily kicked out of the country. Idi Amin watched as the plane taxied out onto the runway. He pulled a white handkerchief from his trousers pocket and waved farewell.

☐

10. Ambush

The Nyeri forest was an extensive area of exceptionally thick growth where, Brigade suspected, considerable numbers of rebels were hiding out. I had been in and out of the Nyeri forest a dozen times or more, never once coming across so much as a trace of Mau Mau activity. Brigade's nuggets of alarm were issued at regular intervals, and they seldom panned out into anything worth chasing. Several of us junior subalterns were of a mind it was a ruse to keep us on our toes, busy and in fighting trim.

And yet, for a man on the run – and by this time in the emergency most of the rebels were desperate to get away from us – the Nyeri forest provided near perfect shelter.

It was difficult and physically exhausting to patrol this particular segment of highland forest, but several of us had become good at it. Between us we had covered and re-covered the area so well that we had come to know it intimately – the hills within the forest, rock outcroppings, even some of the trees. We knew the place so well, in fact, that had there been significant movement within the forest itself, or any movement crossing the forest edge – in or out – we would have soon spotted it.

It was tedious to be sent in yet again. We'd search and search, but we'd just never find anything there. True, the Mau Mau needed places to hide close to the town, and there were certainly some fine hiding places in the Nyeri forest; but surely by now they would have figured out we knew the place about as well as they did, and that we were constantly poking about in there. Had I been one of them, I would have nixed the Nyeri forest.

Which is why, on the occasion when we did find telltale signs, we were both surprised and instantly alert. Right at the edge of the forest, a zone of dense bush seamed with a few animal tracks and in an area where humans would not normally have ventured, there was a distinct indication of most careful and surreptitious movement. Whether it was intended as an entry or an exit, we simply could not tell – but there was little doubt that we had stumbled upon a secretive and well-camouflaged trail.

It was late afternoon. In an hour or so it would be dark. My first impulse was to prepare an ambush. With hand signals and the faintest of

Mrs. Queen's Chump

whispers, we set it up right away. In utter silence, my men slid on their bellies into the undergrowth and took up positions that would have given each one of them a distinct arc of fire onto the trail we had found.

Once in position, no man made any movement at all. Without a sound, without movement, we waited. Flies buzzed, mosquitoes bit, and thank God there were no snakes – we all knew our ambush drill: no sound, no movement. If one of us needed to urinate or defecate, the necessary movements had to be accomplished in ultra-slow motion – and no standing up. Not easy, but we had learned a way to do it if absolutely necessary. Smells had to be eradicated as quickly and efficiently as possible by covering urine or feces with earth. We had been told numerous times that the Mau Mau were so sensitive to smell that from several yards away they could detect body odours, farts, hair oils, aftershave lotions and toothpaste. We couldn't obliterate all these scents, but by rubbing our bodies and uniforms with dirt and twining fresh-picked flora around our hats and into the button holes of our camouflaged uniforms, we could get rid of a lot of it.

For hours we lay there, straining our ears and eyes for the least sound or movement. The concentration, the tension, was exhausting.

The dark closed in at six o'clock. We couldn't see one another, but still we waited.

My batman was lying beside me with our radio set. At about nine o'clock it crackled into life, and I felt Edouardi's hand on my arm. Putting his mouth right to my ear, he asked:

"Answer?"

"*Hapana!*" – No.

But whoever it was – I presumed it to be our company headquarters – the caller was persistent. It came over several times before we managed to turn it off and in the silence of the ambush sounded loud like a trumpet band tuning up. I was irritated. Just the noise of the radio could blow the ambush; if I answered it, my voice would create even greater noise.

But at last I felt it best to answer.

It was the company's second-in-command. He needed to speak to me, he said. I did not care for our second-in-command, and wished I'd never brought the damned radio on this patrol.

"Sir ...?"

Already we had created so much noise there was no longer any point in continuing with the ambush. Captain Freeman had a whiney voice, all the squeakier when he had to force it past the crackle and static of our radio sets. In the stillness of the trees his voice and the noise of the set itself could be heard for yards around. Had there been any rebels active in the vicinity they would have gone to ground.

"You want to see me ...?" I asked, not bothering to lower my voice.

"Yes. Where are you?"

By now I was on my feet. The night was dark as pitch under the heavy canopy of trees and bushes. The ambush was a washout, and at this time of night there would be no way we could possibly pick our way back through the forest to our platoon encampment. We would have to remain in our present position until there was sufficient daylight to move.

"We're not due back at the Nyeri barracks for another week," I told Freeman.

"Oh! I had no idea you were out for so long ..."

"We're trying to maintain radio silence. Over and out."

I growled, shut him down and turned off the set. I was angry. How was it possible for the second-in-command of my own company to not know where I was with my platoon – some thirty soldiers in total? And how was it possible that this administrative paper-pusher, simply by calling me, could blunder his way into the sphere of our on-site fieldwork?

I was angry at the man, admittedly, because I did not like him – but I was angry with myself as well. Our radio sets in those days were squawky, noisy contraptions; they were quiet enough when there was dead air and no one was talking on them, but just the act of turning the set on created screech and crackling static; if not adjusted correctly, a voice suddenly coming over the air could sound like an alarm – which was the case in this instance.

Normally I would have left such a cumbersome piece of equipment back at our camp, and I cursed myself for having brought it along unnecessarily. Freeman didn't know we were preparing an ambush, nor that I had the radio with me on patrol when I would normally have left it behind. Moreover it happened to be turned on at an hour when, by pre-arrangement, I usually called into base from our bivouac area. At the least I should have made sure it was turned off when we went into ambush. The noise it created destroyed any possibility of surprise.

I had no right to be angry with Freeman, and yet I was – and my terseness in signing off no doubt irritated him. I rationalized. I could only reason that Major Monke would not have called me unless it was for an emergency, nor would he have permitted Freeman to have done so. Precisely because we were all alert to the fact that the radio was a noisy apparatus, Monke would have waited for me to call in to him within a convenient and pre-set bracket of time. Had I not done so, he would have assumed I was busy and would have waited – at least an hour or so before trying to connect with me. So I could only think there was something amiss. I was conscious that for some reason Freeman had bypassed our company commander, but I could not think why – and that worried me.

I called the ambush off. We stretched out for the night where we were as best we could. I gave instructions for the *askaris* to settle in, try to get some rest, and assured them we'd return to our forest base at first light. We fell silent and allowed the night to take over. We could see nothing at all. Occasionally we would hear some animal in the undergrowth, or birds screeching in a faraway canopy – but we were blind to all around us. Even gazing upwards there was nothing to be seen. The forest canopy was so thick the stars were obscured.

We rested through the night, but I did not sleep. I had been disturbed by that stupid call, and knew something was up. My irritation and my imagination, both, kept me awake.

We were all up and moving in the first moments of dawn. It took us about an hour to reach our bivouacs.

Some of us rested. I sent out a number of patrols and made sure the radio remained with us this time. The day passed, as most of them did, without incident of any note. The patrols came back in later in the afternoon, and we all set about cooking our evening meals.

At about nine o'clock I switched on the radio and signalled our Nyeri headquarters. Captain Freeman's voice came on the line and I asked to speak to Major Monke.

"Not possible," squeaked the company Number Two. "He has gone on course for two weeks. Left me in charge."

That explained last night, I thought.

"Well, we have nothing new to report," I informed him.

"I have!" Freeman chimed in his prickly nasal voice.

"This morning two Micks walked out of the forest in your area – gave themselves up to the Kenya Police. They were sick and tired and hungry, and nearly got themselves caught in an ambush last night. After lying on their empty bellies in the bush till dawn, they saw some of our boys leaving an ambush position at first light, and decided they'd had enough. They waited till the coast was clear, then walked out and turned themselves in ..."

I couldn't be bothered explaining anything to him, let alone that it was obvious our fouled-up ambush was the one the rebels had discovered. Too much detail for him to grasp, and I just wanted to get him off the line. Coincidental success, I supposed, but I was still irritated.

A nest of ostrich eggs in the open bush

11. Spurs

We worked hard in the forest, but we made sure we enjoyed ourselves, too. Not a hard thing for me – I loved the natural life we were able to enjoy in the depths of the undergrowth as much as I detested the alternative – a regimented life in the barracks that centred on the officers' mess and was presented as the civilized existence of white men and white authority. Certain individuals I cared for immensely – Gun McGinty being first among my colleagues in the mess. But Nyamahanga was right up there, too. We had become friends, though my fellow officers would not have tolerated my saying so. I also had a great respect for my batman, Edouardi, who most of all enjoyed laughing. I truly believe this spirited and happy fellow got a great kick out of showing me how to live a life under canvas of most simple needs and pleasures. He came into his own in the forest where he demonstrated he was a camp cook of exceptional talents.

Each of these men felt as I did about life in the forest. I think I had a natural affinity for it, but the fact that people so close to me enjoyed the forest so much eased my orientation.

Forest in Kenya can be jungle in fact; but forest was the preferred word used to describe large treed areas. "Forest" for me has a tone of warm acceptance about it, as though you might expect to find there a sympathetic greenery, compatible with an intelligent and enquiring mind that complements a confident and hardy physical disposition. I was to encounter "jungle" later in my service – and though I enjoyed it also, I found it to be a word conveying a most unforgivingly harsh environment, the kind that invariably requires special training to confront with anything other than sheer terror. One may wander in awe through a forest, but a jungle swallows you whole and then expels you from the experience reduced to a wide-eyed catatonia. Utter the word forest at a tea party, and the ladies will sit back in their chairs, indulge your boring story as they look over your shoulder for something more interesting to rustle their attention. Say the word jungle and they'll move forward to the front edges of their seats, open their eyes as wide as the biscuits in their delicate fingers, stir their tea furiously as you spin them the most outrageous of yarns – be it verity or guile.

So the forest became for me, as I think it was also for Gun, a refuge. I could find solace in the cover of the forest, escape there to get away from the emergency – the dreadful expectation that because I was a member of Her Majesty's forces I actually agreed with what we were all doing. I was a second lieutenant – an unsubstantiated commissioned officer, one pip above a senior Boy Scout. The little perks that went with being in the officer class – leading a platoon, giving orders, having a manservant to clean my brass and polish my boots, being addressed as one gifted with the right to assume the reins of Empire (if I behaved myself) – this was all quite heady. Like thousands of others before and after me, I was drilled in the rightness, the justice, of Britain's imperial role, and that all I ever had to do to encourage the light of benevolence to settle over me like a halo, was to pinch the cheeks of my arse together and obey orders.

The trouble was that as an independent, free-spirited and rather sensitive young man, I was beginning to think for myself and to find my own levels of toleration, my own likes and dislikes. I had been something of a loner even as a child. For the most part I had been happy to play by myself, and as I fumbled my way through school I found the only way to avoid bullies and those who promoted themselves by putting others down was to avoid them – to stick, instead, with those few comrades I could trust. I was never a team player – football, rugby, cricket. I was a good boxer, a fair gymnast, I enjoyed swimming and long distance running. These were all highly individual sports, and if I failed at any one of them no one else would necessarily be affected, and there would be no one to chide me for my failure. It was safer to be alone, and when unsolicited my elders and betters took to telling me what was good for me, automatically I began to question why or what was in it for them.

This attitude was noted by my elders and betters, of course, who would then proceed to inform me of my bloody-mindedness, my reluctance to fit in. After long years in school being told such things, I spent hours trying (and often failing) to pull my socks up; I tried hard to see things the way I thought most others saw them – but it didn't work.

This was my confusion as a subaltern in the British Army. It was for me a schizophrenia – my external efforts attempting to drive me one way, my internal feelings another.

I realized the people I cared about the most were the Africans of my platoon, and that what I liked so much about Gun was his love of Africa and the Africans. The senior officers of the mess were the ones who perpetuated the ignorance, the nauseating pomposity and racist mentality of the Raj. I felt about all this as one might feel after realizing one has been made victim of a particularly unkind practical joke. In hindsight I realize I had not yet wriggled my way to spiritual freedom – that I had not yet straightened my back and stood to my full height championing those things in which I could identify true value, that my beliefs were based in the main on juvenile storytelling, and that I had not yet tuned into the fact I was still rather bent over – not quite double – in my efforts to "get it right."

It was good to go with my men into the forest. One could say it was teamwork – a platoon of men pulling together to defeat an enemy. But I don't think I ever thought of it that way. For me, I was off to enjoy the delights of Disneyland with a troupe of like-minded fellows who would, in the unlikely event of danger, help me to knock it sideways. I was incredibly fit. We walked exceptional distances (the army called it patrolling) – twenty-five miles in a day was about normal, up and down ravines, and through sometimes extremely thick bush. I loved the smell of the greenery and the earth of the forest floor; I loved the texture of tree bark and leaves. In the battalion camp I smoked cigarettes; in the forest not at all. For me the forest was a giant maze, and making it back to our bivouacs (the Swahili word *basha* was somehow a more appropriate description) after an outing of several hours was often sufficient to celebrate a triumph. Forest navigation could be tricky.

Early one morning I sent out one of my corporals on patrol. He took five men with him, and was due to return to camp for lunch – at which time another patrol would go out. But by noon they had not returned, nor by suppertime. Our meal that evening was a quickly prepared gruel-like mix of rice and biltong. All of us were worried, so took our tin plates of food back to our individual *bashas* to sit and eat in silence, each of us understanding the gravity of the situation, but each refraining from any talk about it. The sun sets at six o'clock in the tropics and in the forest it gets dark quite a bit sooner. Before long visibility was virtually zero and I was extremely worried. There was nothing anyone could do until dawn when we would send out search parties. It started to rain, so we all huddled down in our banana-leaf bivouacs. Most nights after the *askaris* had bunked down there would be rounds of light banter and laughter between men unwilling to turn in right away. But this night no one felt like it, and there was only the sound of the rain pattering on the broad leaves of our shelters.

After a time, I clambered into my sleeping bag and tried to sleep. I rather fancied the others were doing the same. The rain came in a steady downpour, the noise of it pounding into my head hypnotically and making me feel sleepy. But I thought of the lads caught out in this muck, and my relative comfort made me feel guilty.

It was late when the rain abated. I couldn't judge the hour, but I heard it stop. For a while I lay listening to the silence. Far off (it could have been at the far edge of our camp – I simply couldn't judge) – a voice. I listened again. Was I mistaken? Then again, this time quite distinctly:

"I got spurs, that jingle-jangle-jingle …"

All the *bashas* erupted

"Karibu! Karibu!"

Laughter and excited chatter as friends met again, asked the questions and received the answers. I could hear horseplay, soldiers clomping around in an impromptu dance as they jostled and jumped on one another in their good spirits. One or two voices broke out with an African-ized version of "I've got spurs …," a bit off-key and the words to the verse hopelessly cockeyed, but they got the part they liked best – the "jingle-jangle-jingle" chorus – just about right. They found it outrageously funny.

Nyamahanga came to my bivouac. He had a flashlight. I could barely see him but there was no mistaking his voice.

"They're back," he said.

"So I hear. What happened to them?"

We went together to the corporal's *basha,* an informal de-briefing. It was as we had surmised: they had lost their way in the tangle of undergrowth and ravines and hunkered down for the night, thinking to set out to find camp at first light. However, they became so uncomfortable when the rain started they decided to try to make it back in the dark, taking a chance on being challenged – or shot – by the sentries ringing our bivouacs. None of them could remember the password that as a matter of routine we established each day, but the corporal figured he knew more or less where they were, and he could find his way if they proceeded slowly. To him it was more important to get his patrol back to base than to worry about a password he'd forgotten. It worked.

He was lucky, and his luck rubbed off on all of them. Two or three times on the way back they thought they were near our camp; then they stopped and sang out the few lines of the song I had taught all of them a few months earlier.

"They took a big chance," I commented to Nyamahanga.

He chuckled in the dark.

"Never mind! They were clever, and it worked."

◻

12. White Knees

European newcomers to East Africa are noticeable – especially pallid English schoolboys – because of the whiteness of their skin. The heat and the rays of the sun are so intense newcomers quickly choose to change into tropical kit, which invariably means donning shorts. It is the pallor of their knees that stands out like the polished brass doorknob on a dark oak door – this rather than their moon-like faces – that gives rise to the admonition: "Get your knees brown!"

It was, maybe still is, a definitive expression of tropical inexperience, always uttered with a quantity of cynicism – and invariably when one of these newcomers might be tempted to pontificate about how things ought to be done.

But it served in other instances, too.

We had a new subaltern named Willoughby come on station, a rosy-cheeked fellow just turned nineteen. He wore a camera on a strap around his neck, and a pair of eyes that blinked "Oh! I say!" about everything he saw before he photographed it. Lord knows how many times he was cautioned to "Get your knees brown" – more a kindly warning on account of his astonishing schoolboy naïveté than stern or sneering reprimand.

He had been sent out on patrol one afternoon with one of the more experienced officers, and when he returned to the mess it was to announce to one and all what a jolly good time he had had: "We ran into some elephants, don't you know – and I think I got one or two jolly good shots of them …"

We teased him a bit about it, and the officer who had led the patrol said the fellow had acquitted himself quite well – except that he had appeared more intent on taking a good photo of the elephants than in conducting a patrol.

"It was alright, though. With the elephants hanging around it wasn't about to be a particularly active area for Mau Mau, anyway ... Willoughby wandered off to get a shot or two, but then we had to get out of there pretty quick. The elephants started trumpeting …"

Turning away from the elephants as he walked back to rejoin the patrol, and winding the film roll through his camera, the commander had had to chivvy him along:

"Those elephants mean business, old fellow. Look at the way that bull is flapping his ears. Better get a move on!"

We laughed, and kidded the newcomer about taking risks with animals.

"Particularly elephant, old chap. You can climb a tree to get out of the way of a buff, or a rhino – but an elephant will simply reach up with his trunk and pluck you out of the branches like a ripe plum. And if he can't reach you, he's as likely to wrench out the whole tree by its roots …"

Filling the camera's frame

Willoughby gawked at us, blinking. "Oh! I say!" he said several times.

We thought no more of the incident as we went in to dinner.

But a day or two later Willoughby went into town and had his film developed. He showed the prints around the mess.

Indeed, the elephant shots were outstanding. One of them in particular showed a bull face-on, its ears extended to the extreme margins of the print.

"Was this one blown up …? Did you have a telephoto lens …?"

"No! No!" said Willoughby, rubbing his white knees nervously. "I was trying to get the glint in his eye, so had to approach till the animal's head filled my frame …"

"But good Lord, man! You couldn't have been more than ten yards in front of him!"

"About that," replied Willoughby, admiring his photograph.

☐

13. Amulet

Not far outside Nyeri there was a rifle range where we would take the *askaris* for much needed fire practice. Teaching them to shoot properly – emphasis on safety and accuracy – was a regular activity in those hours when we were not chasing Mau Mau through the local forests or in the Aberdare Mountains.

I was not a particularly outstanding shot myself. I was good, but others were much better. My favoured weapon was the Patchett sub-machine gun. It was a wide-splatter weapon, good for quick reaction and close-in fighting – precisely the conditions we were likely to find in Kenya's forests. But the jungle version of the Lee Enfield .303 rifle was the weapon of general issue to all the *askaris*, and the one with which they were required to show a degree of proficiency.

The battalion had also been given the new high velocity FN semi-automatic rifle to take out on troop trials. We did not like it at all. It had a tremendous muzzle velocity (I had once seen a demonstration in which an FN round pierced tank armour), and had far too many knobs and protrusions to catch on bush and vine to be of much use to us in a jungle setting.

But all of us had to learn these weapons, to practice and become familiar with them – which meant many trips to the firing range.

The range crossed a long and shallow valley, about four hundred metres at its widest. Firing points were set up at three hundred metres and one hundred and fifty metres for the rifles – the longer distance suitable for FN targeting (though the weapon had a range far superior to that), the shorter for the jungle .303. There was also a firing point at fifty metres to give the lads a bit of practice with hip-firing the Patchett. They carried their rifles, but needed to know the Patchett as well – in case I dropped mine, I told them.

At the target end of the range, set against a steep escarpment of the valley, were what was known as "the butts" – a deep and wide trench dug the full width of the range. This trench was partially roofed with heavy timbers, as was the back wall set against incoming fire. The roof was to ensure protection from sun or rain, and also from the spurts of dirt or rock kicked up when a shooter fired too low and hit the embankment that had been heaped

Mrs. Queen's Chump

The small arms we used

FN 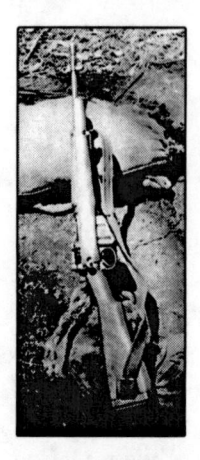   Jungle .303   Pachette
           Lee Enfield   sub-machine gun

up against the (hopefully!) bulletproof back wall. Earth had also been piled on top of the narrow roof. The targets had been mounted on retractable easels so they could be pulled down and mended by the detail that worked the butts. Signalling with long pointers, butts could notify the officer of the firing point (he had binoculars) precisely if and where each shot had hit the target.

The butt detail consisted of two *askaris* for each of ten targets under the command of a single officer who, early one warm morning when it would have been preferable to be doing practically anything else, was me.

In training in Britain the trench structure had been built in concrete and there was no doubt concerning safety. But in Nyeri there had been no question of concrete in the structure of the butts; the whole thing had been built of wood – mostly eucalyptus logs. It was solid enough, but I was never entirely convinced the wood at my back was entirely impenetrable.

On this particular morning I sat somewhere about the middle of the long bench that ran the full length of the trench. Leaning my back against the log wall, I radioed back to the firing line that we were ready for the morning's shoot. Clean targets were run up, and the barrage commenced – crack-and-thump. *Crack* – as the bullet slammed into the side of the escarpment close behind the targets; *thump* – as the bullet exploded from the muzzle of the rifle one hundred and fifty metres behind me. That was the order of things – you'd hear the bullet hitting the target area above your head before you'd hear it exit the spout of the rifle. This morning's practice was with the Lee Enfields.

The sun rose quickly in a dreamy blue sky and by mid-morning the heat within the confines of the butts, for all that the space was fairly open, was stifling. I took off my felt slouch hat and set it on the bench beside me. I had a tune on the brain, and was humming it to myself. An Old Etonian with whom I had been drinking in the mess into the wee hours of the morning had sung for me one of his raunchier rugby "hymns," as he had called them – to the tune of the old English folksong, The Ash Grove:

> She married an Italian, with balls like a bloody stallion
>
> And the hairs on her dickie-di-do hung down to her knees ...
>
> One black one, one white one, and one with a bit of shite on,
>
> And one with a little light on to show us the way.

I was daydreaming, chuckling to myself as I hummed, when there was a sudden and audible *s-m-a-c-k* at my side, and a lump of dirt was flung into my hair and down my shirt.

It was as if Someone up there was admonishing me: "WAKE-UP, you silly bugger!"

This was followed by a distinct fizzing sound – and I looked onto the top of my hat. There in the crown, spinning like some frantic bumble bee, and sounding rather like one too, an almost spent .303 bullet ...

I tried to pick it up, but it burned my fingers. It had not been battered out of shape; its original form was virtually perfect. There was the tiniest nick at the point of it, and the scoring of the rifling was well marked, but otherwise the contour of the missile was intact. It had been discoloured by heat but not distorted by impact. At first it spun frantically in the felt saucer of the hat and I could see a trace of burning phosphorus at the rump end of it – indication it had been a tracer bullet. It was the remnants of this phosphorus, like the outboard engine on a boat, that caused the thing to hiss and spin.

How it came there is a mystery. My own theory is that the shooter fired

Mrs. Queen's Chump

too low and hit the embankment in front of the butts at the precise point where the wall against which I was leaning was joined by the timbers of the roof over my head. It ricocheted straight down and into the hat at my side. It did not penetrate the fabric of the hat, but even so it was probably a good thing I was not sitting in the position where I had placed it.

Waiting until it had cooled, I popped the spent bullet into my shirt pocket – and I have kept it to this day. I have been thinking to have it drilled so it can be hung from a neck string. My grandson has a birthday coming up – a curious amulet ...

☐

14. Horseback Golf

Following his time with the military, my brother returned to Kenya to work for a film company that had made its headquarters in the Brackenhurst Hotel – an establishment that was more akin to a country club than a hostelry. It was located in the Highlands, just outside Nairobi. He was there when my own transfer to Kenya came through, by which time my battalion of the KAR had moved its base to Nyeri, one hundred miles north of Nairobi. Mike and I both had busy work schedules so we could get together only infrequently.

But one weekend I was able to arrange transport to the capital, and so went to stay at the hotel to be on hand whenever my brother and his friends could be free.

The Brackenhurst was laid out in languorous opulence, a sprawling acreage with the lodge, its surrounding cabins and a stable complex set jewel-like in the midst of carefully tended lawns and flower gardens. The place boasted the finest golf course in all of East Africa, but the same could not be said for the attention paid to the upkeep of the stables. They were clean enough, but the horses were unkempt and clearly had been ridden and abused by hotel guests and staff alike over a considerable period of time. Knowing nothing of these details except that we wanted to take an early morning ride, Mike and I selected two mounts to spend an hour scouting out the countryside along the western edge of the hotel's golf course. With the fellows from the film crew still abed in their rooms it was about the only occasion we'd be able to find to spend a little private time together.

On the way out both of our horses plodded along like reluctant cart animals obliged to pull heavy loads of turnips. Nothing we tried would coerce them into picking up their feet, so that by the end of an hour we were barely into the trees on the far edge of the fairway. We did, however, have a chance to talk and exchange a bit of personal news. But then my brother announced:

"This is no bloody fun. It'd be easier to have this conversation over a cup of coffee. Besides, our time's nearly up. Let's head back ..."

So saying, he turned his horse around, nose to the stables – and suddenly there was animation.

"Whoa!"

His mount would have none of it. It took off at a full gallop, like a bargain hunter on market day.

"See you at the stable door!" he shouted over his shoulder, but by that time we were already separated by fifty metres, the gap widening with each word he cried.

My own horse spun around so quickly I nearly fell off. Then she, too, leaped forward as if loosed from a canon. As we had been sauntering out I had removed my feet from the stirrups and allowed them to dangle while Mike and I chatted back and forth. Now suddenly my balance was knocked sideways and there was no time to reset my feet. Instinctively the horse twigged there nothing there to control her. I tugged on the reins, but she pulled against me, her head thrust forward as she settled into an earnest gallop.

Now I have discovered that a horse at full gallop is generally an easy ride. For a moment I began to enjoy myself, to think something like "Hurrah! This is more like it!" But to my horror, as I struggled to reset the tips of my toes into the stirrups, I became aware I had no control whatsoever and that my morning ride, although I was intimately involved with it, no longer had anything to do with me. I was just there.

Looking ahead I could see my brother's horse carrying him down the hill and skirting the eighth green as the two of them headed for the stables.

My own nag was not to be so easily outdone.

Ignoring whatever restraint I attempted, the brute pulled against the bit in her teeth and cut diagonally across the fairway – straight towards the green where a party of early-morning sportsmen was lined up for their final strokes of the hole.

My elbows were rigid as I tugged with all my strength on the reins. My feet now miraculously having found the stirrups, I jammed them forward to the heels of my boots. My legs were locked at the knees so my buttocks were pushed up and out of the saddle. With a spasm of quite hysterical amusement I realized I could do nothing – that my Nelly at that moment could have galloped me all the way to Nairobi City Hall.

Instead, in a desperate bid to catch up with her mate my huffing, sweating nag headed directly for the pin, her pounding hooves digging deep divots into the finest and most expensive Cumberland turf.

The group of early morning players gesticulated frantically, waving their arms and shouting at me in their outrage. Some even raised their clubs over their shoulders as if to swipe me from my saddle as I flashed past them.

What could I do?

At the top of my lungs I shouted out the only thing I could think of to suit the occasion:

"F – O – R – E !!"

□

15. The Rhino Cull

Some years after leaving Kenya I painted a watercolour of a rhinoceros cull in which I once participated. I had not been able to wipe the image of that event from my mind – not then, not later, nor even now, as I write. The entirety of that day remains with me. It was something I might have written about in my notebook but never did, and so the watercolour became the sole notation. The painting was a simple and stylized diagram, hardly a full and accurate rendering of either the event itself or its effect upon me. Referring to it at all is to draw attention to a time and a place and a way of thinking and acting indicative of my surroundings – and, by extension, the dichotomies in which I was enveloped. I long ago lost track of the painting and have no idea where it is, but I took a slide photo of it.

In highland Kenya in the 1950's rhino were considered a pest, especially each seven-year cycle when the herds would grow particularly large and would forage for their food on the lands of the local farmers.

Acres of good coffee were trampled this way, so the farmers would call in the boys from the Game Department to set up a cull. In those days there were no tranquilizer darts to knock animals out prior to transporting them to alternate areas. Sharp shooters would come up and peck them off, leaving the carcasses for the Africans who would eat what they could of the meat, and make handicrafts and trinkets out of the hard skin and bone.

The year I was in the Nyeri district, Mrs. Beck, the local owner and farmer of the land upon which my battalion was bivouacked had just such a problem. She was a single lady and much harried by having to contend with a full unit of soldiers encamped on her property; their mere presence interfered with the efficient running of her farm. She told me later that had she had a larger staff to assist in controlling the invasion of rhinos that year – by building barriers or sending out beaters to chase the animals back into the forest – she might not have resorted to calling in the Game Department. As it was, the animals trampled a significant portion of her year's coffee crop. It represented a huge financial loss, and she felt she had no option but to summon help.

"I don't agree with killing them," she said. "All these animals are so beautiful, living the freedoms we have destroyed for ourselves. But I'm supposed to be a farmer. I don't know for how long ..."

I liked Mrs. Beck. She was an unlikely settler. I would visit her from time-to-time. She was a watercolourist, and the only person in whom I confided my own penchant for painting.

The Game Department didn't have enough available marksmen, so they asked if the battalion could supply a number of officers to participate in the cull. I wasn't particularly interested but Gun had signed on and I was curious. The peer thing more than anything else, I think. Game officers gave us a pep talk beforehand, let us know more or less what to expect. I did not like the sound of it, but neither did I have the balls to back out once I had put forward my name.

We were set up on a rock bluff with a thick stretch of the Nyeri forest right below us. African beaters with sticks then chased the rhinos out of the coffee into and through the trees – and then into a clearing at our feet right below where we were perched like assassins on a low rock bluff. It was a ghastly trap for the animals. All we had to do was sit above them and take our time knocking them off. We were told each marksman was to shoot no more than two animals.

We could hear the beginning of the operation as the Africans, each carrying two stout sticks, started chasing the animals out of the coffee into the trees. Then for half an hour there was one hell of a commotion in the forest, the sound of the beaters' smacking their sticks together or against trees – *clack-clack-clack-clack* – carrying for miles over the canopy of green.

Then right below us but still out of sight there came the sound of crashing and an alarmed huffing ever louder from the animals. Suddenly they broke cover, scores of them, charging up and down the narrow space between the forest edge and the rock escarpment.

What a magnificent sight it was! But, oh my god – they were like sitting ducks!

The shooting began, and the smell of cordite in the air mingled with the smell of the rising dust and greenery of the forest. In the background still hidden from our view and muffled by the blaze of firing, the excited "halloos" of the Africans.

I picked out one rhino, the king of all the beasts, just below my perch.

Mrs. Queen's Chump

Watercolour illustration of the rhino cull: the coffee bushes top left are being trampled by rhinos who are then chased by African beaters through the forest (centre right) and out into the open below a bluff where officers of the Game Department and KAR cull – approximately twenty of them on this occasion. It was several years before culling in similar manner to this was substituted by tranquilizing and removal to a distant safe area.

He was a gigantic animal with a curved horn longer than my leg. He ran up and down like a mountain in motion – snorting, crying, alarm in his eyes as he charged first one way, then the other. I do not think he was trying to get away; he must have sensed it was a trap, though, and I had the notion he was calling for his mate.

He could have been no more than twenty paces from me when I knocked him down with a single heart shot. I was using an FN service rifle with enough muzzle velocity to stop a train. He fell to earth with a crash I can still hear in my subconscious, other beasts toppling all around and near him.

In all I believe the cull totalled some twenty rhinos that morning.

I had thought I might feel like a champion. Instead I felt empty, sick.

In the instant of squeezing the trigger I had an overwhelming sense of remorse. This noble living creature – now reduced to a hunk of flesh and bone by a thrill-seeker who didn't know what else to do with himself on the sunny morning of that sad day, and who lacked the moral courage to speak up when I should have said no.

Now I could only look at the dead animal and feel my emptiness. Useless. I had no pocket knife to skin him. I couldn't turn his horn into an aphrodisiac. I couldn't drag him off to my cave and eat him.

There was nothing to do but gaze upon his death and sense my impotence, for all the power of the rifle I held in my hands.

There was a smallness in my belly in realizing the inanity and stupidity of what we had done. Someone had said it was necessary, and it would be fun for me to join in …

I refrained from taking my second animal, and was glad of that.

Years later in the heavy bush outside my home on Vancouver Island I was obliged to shoot a feral feline terrorist the size of a small lynx. It had been carting its forest vermin into the house through the cat-hatch to attack my defenceless pets, scaring the willies out of them and eating their dinners. Cat fights and caterwauling in the living room at dead of night; a rack of dishes by the kitchen sink knocked over, its contents smashed. It had tramped into our lives and was trashing the house; suddenly it was an "us-or-him" situation. Necessity ... for there was no possibility of tranquilizing the beast and transporting it to some remote part of the bush far from the house; it was so mean-spirited it would have found its way back ...

It is hard to say how closely the pest quotient it lumbered into our household may be equated to the pest quotient of the rhinos that destroyed Mrs. Beck's coffee, but in my head the two killings have about equal resonance. The slaughter of the rhino has always stuck in my mind – a first and last, I had always told myself, a caution and a stern forbidding.

I am no hunter, but then there was that skulking and disreputable invader...

□

16. Watercolours, Animals and Sixth Sense

I was granted a few days leave after the heavy rains. I didn't have a lot of money, so packed my watercolours into my kitbag and bummed a ride in a military truck heading south to Nairobi. For me at that time a camera was simply a recording device. However, a set of watercolours, I've been informed in the years since I thought they, too, were just an alternate and pleasurable recording device, represent a form of therapy. Camera, that was okay for keeping tabs on where I had been, the day-to-day … Watercolours, though, had I the temerity to wield them in front of my comrades, were borderline weird and I was far too self-conscious to argue the point. Though for me they represented a relaxation that lifted me above the moment and allowed me the pleasure to indulge myself without a thought or care for anything or anyone else, my watercolours remained tucked away in my kitbag until the moment I knew I was absolutely alone.

Not just young, but painfully self-conscious …

In Nairobi I met up with my brother, working now as assistant cameraman with an American film company – and the whole crew, as it happened, was heading out the following morning for Rumuruti, northwest of Mount Kenya. It meant travelling back the way I had come just the day before, but I had never been to that area of the Rift Valley before so happily tagged along. There was a former big game hunter at Rumuruti by the name of Carr Hartley who, as it was explained to me, now made his living by capturing animals instead of shooting them. He would sell them to zoos all around the world – and for astronomical prices. The crew was going up to film some of the animals he was holding in captivity ready for shipment. These I might photograph – and did; but I was absolutely certain I would not pull out my watercolours on this stretch of my leave.

Demographics in those days in East Africa were notably different from what they are today. The population of Kenya in 1956 was just a little over seven million; today as I write it is well over forty-two million, and rising fast. The pressing urgencies of housing and feeding such growth is necessarily reflected on the land – and Kenya's land in the mid-1950's, unlike today, was a wide-open paradise for all sorts of animals. As had been the case when I'd been on operations in the Aberdares, the animals on the one hundred-mile stretch of road between Nyeri and Nairobi, for instance, were about as profuse as they might have been in a game park. Rarely did we fail to see giraffe or at least several species of gazelle. Ostriches and wart hogs were common; so, too, were both black and white rhino, though we wouldn't necessarily see these on every trip. It was not unusual to spot buffalo, cheetah, lion, elephant. There was always something magic to these sightings, and the magic never ceased to delight.

The Hartley establishment at Rumuruti had specimens of all these creatures and more. The animals were penned, but it was no less a privilege to see them up close. There was a black rhino and a baby white rhino, a giraffe, several ostriches and wart hogs, and an orphaned baby elephant. There was a sampling of most of the cats, and an abundance of snakes in specially-built hutches.

We were having sandwiches and beer in an open area behind the main house when some of Hartley's assistants ran up excitedly. They had spotted a python.

"Big! Big! ..."

Hartley picked up a pole with a noose on the end of it and, dressed only in shirt, shorts (he had brown knees) and sandals, stomped off through the grass to a depression over to one side of his property where the assistants indicated the serpent was at rest. Film crew followed, shooting footage.

We came to something that looked like a length of mottled green seventeen-centimetre drain pipe on the ground. Hartley examined it. Lying fairly well concealed in the grass it was impossible to tell which end was which.

"Where's its head?" he asked, walking towards one end of the snake.

"Nope!" he called back. "That's not it. Must be the other end ...!" He retraced his steps and walked off in the opposite direction

The snake must have had a meal within some recent hours. It was sleeping, and there was a bulge in its mid-section. I recall my alarm at Hartley walking up to the thing in his bare legs and sandals and slipping the noose over its head. He and his assistants then calmly proceeded to stuff it into what I thought was a far-too-small gunny sack. The creature folded up nicely; two men tied the sack to the noose pole and it took four men to carry it to an area behind the house, leaving the rest of us to resume our lunch.

Mrs. Queen's Chump

"That one must be over fifteen feet …" Hartley announced.

I had no reason to disbelieve him. Except for the mamba I had seen chopped into little pieces by one of my *askaris*, I had encountered no snakes at all in Kenya. This one, I reckoned, was big enough to make up for all the ones I might have missed.

The film crew shot the footage they needed in the afternoon, and we left before nightfall – back to Nyeri. It was late when we arrived. The crew arranged to stay over at the Outspan Hotel, but as my barracks was only just down the road I decided I would sleep in my own tent for the night, and travel to Nairobi with my brother and his friends in the morning.

The night before departing on leave, I had summoned Edouardi, my batman, to my tent.

"I'll be away a few days, Edouardi," I had instructed him. "Make sure my tent space is kept clean, air it out, and be sure to look after my kit …"

Edouardi had understood well.

It was late when I arrived from Rumuruti. The mess was closed for the night, and all the officers had long since gone to bed. I headed straight for my tent. But as I approached, I saw my hurricane lamp was lighting up the canvas interior. Not unnaturally, I wondered what was going on, and I quickened my step. Edouardi stepped out of my tent just as I came up.

"Edouardi …!" I exclaimed, swiftly moving past him and into my quarters.

I had been good to Edouardi, and now I felt a sickening sensation of disappointment. In the moment I was fully expecting to find gear missing – sold, probably! – and I was about to raise an alarm. For what other reason could he possibly be here at this hour? I thought his actions suspect, and my first instinct was to query his honesty …

But before I said anything, I noticed my bed was not just made but had been turned down ready for me to climb in. My pajamas had been pressed and laid out on my pillow. My billy can held fresh boiled tea, and the enamel basin in my washstand was filled with warm water – clean towel hanging on the bed rail.

I couldn't figure it out …

"What's going on, Edouardi …?"

The whole confrontation till now had lasted mere seconds. Realizing the instantaneous anger I had felt at finding Edouardi among my belongings, I now felt a deep shame at the coarseness of my assumptions – and a fear that this man for whom I truly felt a deep affection and respect might have seen and understood my suspicion.

If that was the case he was far too clever to show it.

"Bed ready … pajamas … wash … mug of tea," he replied, smiling and waving his hands at each item in turn.

"Yes, but how did you know I was coming in …?"

"*Efendi* not want?" His voice sounded hurt.

"Yes I want, but how did you know …?"

"Edouardi know …! Edouardi know …!" he laughed. "Good night, *efendi*!"

My batman vanished into the night, presumably to sleep in his own tent. Although I later questioned him several times I was never able to learn how he could possibly have divined my return.

"Sixth sense," said my friend Gun. "They've all got it."

To this day the incident remains a mystery to me.

*

I returned to Nairobi with the film crew and decided to head from there to the coast; on my limited funds the easiest way to get there was by hitchhiking. A single small bag flung over my shoulder contained my toothbrush, swimming trunks – and my watercolour equipment. I took a bus to the southeastern outskirts of Nairobi, then stood beside the main road and stuck my thumb out. Within minutes a car stopped.

It was a large white Peugeot station wagon. The driver wore a turban and I assumed was of Indian origin. His car was full; there were several Indian ladies in voluminous dresses, and a small horde of their children.

I bent down to ask through the window how far he would be going.

"Mombassa," he replied. "Get in! Get in!"

There was a large well-perfumed lady next to him and he ordered her to move closer to make way for me on the front seat.

As we pulled away from the curb I noted all the passengers were speaking a language I could not understand, and assumed it was one of the Indian dialects. I tried to address the lady next to me, but she only smiled and made no reply. So I turned to the driver, asking him how long it would take to get to Mombassa. It was already mid-afternoon, and I calculated we'd be driving through the night to arrive at the coast in the early hours of the morning.

"Mombassa, yes! Mombassa," he replied, and I could tell his English also was practically non-existent.

We crossed a portion of the Nairobi game park and headed southeast over a wide open stretch of countryside. Not all the southern game parks were well defined in the mid-fifties, and it was sometimes difficult to know when one entered or left a preservation area. Not being able to converse easily, I busied myself counting herds of gazelle and zebra when, at Athi River, the driver pulled over to let one of his passengers alight. She came around to the driver's window and gave him some money.

Continuing on our way, we were probably more than halfway to Machakos before I thought to ask the driver how much he expected me to donate for gasoline expenses. Being as broke as I was, I explained, it would not be possible for me to give him much ...

"This is taxi!" he said explosively, slamming on the brakes.

"No, no," I replied. "You don't understand. I was hitchhiking ..."

"You pay me fare ...!"

"I haven't enough money to pay you a fare. I was hitchhiking. I have no money ..."

"You go out of car!" he said, reaching across me and opening the passenger door.

I had no choice. I was embarrassed in front of all the ladies and their children, and had no wish to make a scene. On the spot he obliged me to step out onto the side of the road, then he put the vehicle in gear and pulled away.

I was in the middle of nowhere, with wild animals all around me and night coming on. For a time I remained beside the road, hoping a car would come by – it didn't matter which way it was going.

Nothing.

Dusk is the hour for hunting. As darkness closed around me, and with no trees in sight, I decided to take what precautions I could by lying flat on the ground and wriggling myself backwards under a thick thorn bush. Snakes? I wasn't so fearful of finding one of them as I was of a hungry lion picking up my scent. I had a cigarette lighter with me, so I kept it close to hand, my thinking being that if any predator came too close, I'd set fire to the bunch of dry grasses I'd gathered and was holding in my hand – or if necessary the entire bush surrounding me. Not being much of a chess player, I didn't bother to figure out my following move in the event I survived self-immolation and required yet further cover. Optimist by nature I even began to feel quite secure.

However, my optimism did not survive the entire night; I lay awake the entire night. I was as watchful and alert as any wild animal out there on the grasslands in front of me.

Thankfully the grasses were not high during that period of the year. At least in daylight, and on my feet, my range of vision would have been sufficient to spot even a crouching lion at considerable distance. But now, from my eye-level position twenty centimetres off the ground, the horizon was painfully close. There was a moon, and stars, so their faint light provided enough visibility for me to mistake the movement of shadows and see in them all manner of ferocious feline shapes.

Ferocious in daylight,
invisible and terrifying at night

Mrs. Queen's Chump

It was a long night. At one point I heard a snuffling around my bush – several animals in concert which, I decided, were probably hyenas. I knew they could be as dangerous as lions, more so if they were hunting in a pack. Pulling my knees up to my chest, I set fire to the small clump of grass I was clutching, managing at the same time not to allow the sudden flames to fire the bush covering me. When a minute or so had passed, I extinguished the flame and lay listening. No sound at all, and I assumed the sudden flame and smell of smoke scared the animals off. But because of the few moments of bright firelight, my vision was impaired and I could not be sure in which direction the creatures might have fled – or how far. Would they return?

Gradually dawn broke – another hour when predators roamed. I lay still until the sun was up and I had a good view of the wide countryside around me. Then I scrambled out. There was nothing anywhere, no animals of any type whatsoever. Under the cover of darkness they had all moved away.

I moved up to the edge of the road and sat down to wait for the first car to come along. Either direction, I didn't care which. If headed for Nairobi, I'd return there and reassess my travel plans; if for Mombassa, well and good – I'd continue as I'd originally decided.

At the moment there was no sign of anything – no people, no animals, no vehicles. For a while I sat quietly as the sun rose higher in the sky and shadows receded. In the far distance, towards the north, a long line of purple hills formed my horizon, the ground in between a range of blazing hot colours from strong yellows and ochres close-up in front of me to stripes of orange and dark reds lying parallel to the higher ground. The lower edges of the purple hills took on a mysterious green tint, the tops of them now a distinctive thin line of black. Above that the hues of the earth, somewhat muted, were reproduced in the morning sky.

Fishing my pad of paper from my sack, I splashed a little water from my water bottle into a small tin container attached to my palette. It took minutes and a few quick brush strokes to capture the scene before me, so I did two of them, swinging a little to the east for the second sketch. Well satisfied with them, I turned about just in time to see the bright rays illuminate the rounded snowy cap of Mount Kilimanjaro.

And I had just finished a rendering of that third scene, rather pleased with my before-breakfast accomplishments, when I heard still some way off the sound of a vehicle on the road headed in the direction of Nairobi. As it approached I leaped out and ran to the edge of the roadway. At first I thought it was a police jeep, but when the vehicle stopped at my frantic waving the driver turned out to be the local District Officer.

"You need a ride," he told me before I asked.

"Yes, I've been out here all night."

"Why?" he asked, and I told him my story.

He furrowed his brow angrily.

"Describe the taxi to me," he said, which I was able to do. I could even furnish the licence plate number.

"Well, you should have been more careful about thumbing a ride, but that driver had no business leaving you out here in the open. God, man! You're lucky to be here this morning."

As we drove back towards Nairobi the District Officer told me he was pretty certain who the driver of the taxi was, and that he was "going to have a word with him." Whether or not he ever did, I don't know. I left Nairobi that same day and headed back – hitching – towards Nyeri. I remained living at the barracks for the following few days of my leave, venturing out a couple of times into bush areas of the Aberdares, and some of the Kikuyu villages in the vicinity. This was one of the few occasions in my life I have ever had the time and freedom to wander any countryside at will and devote my creative energies to watercolouring.

I became reacquainted with Mrs. Beck. We spent time painting together at the farm's main house, which was set in an attractive compound on its own section of farmland about two kilometres from the officers' mess. On occasion we would take ourselves off to other remote sections of the spread, or even venture further out into the countryside. Maybe I couldn't pinpoint precisely how I felt, but I knew I did not like the work I was being obliged to do in Kenya; it was a brutal realization, and right then I wanted more than anything to push all things army aside and concentrate instead on something that gave me pleasure, a sense of liberty and exhilaration. I could talk to Mrs. Beck about how I felt, and found she had a sympathetic ear. She was considerably older than I was, and I discovered in these purposeful and directed encounters a sense of equilibrium quite absent from my military round. I began to learn from her the courage to express myself – in watercolour before the words came.

Though we ventured into the midst of so-called Mau Mau country we encountered no problems whatsoever on these outings. No distractions. Both of us were able to concentrate on our painting and immensely enjoyed one another's company. Mrs. Beck, I know, would not have ventured into the bush areas unaccompanied, and by being with her I was able to provide her a sense of protection. Conversely, she recognized I was timid and self-conscious about admitting my artistic bent in front of my army colleagues, and by going with me she gave me the incentive to do some alternate and earnest work.

I thought it wise to travel armed, however. Waiting under a thorn bush to be attacked by lions or hyenas, I had had no weapon at all – and had wished otherwise more than once during that long night. In the countryside of the Aberdares there were animals, and maybe even hostile people, so I was prepared if necessary. But in the ways that really counted the climate was perfect for watercolouring excursions. I remember this as a productive and happy time, and for a few hours each day was able to put aside all thought of the primary reason Her Majesty had summoned me to Kenya.

I managed to produce some twenty watercolours I liked. I later gave away a few as gifts, but in 1976 I held a retrospective of my work at the University of Lisbon and was able to hang about a dozen of them in a cluster. They looked delightful like that, and I managed to sell them all. A strong visual memory, and not a bad perk for an enjoyable few days spent twenty years earlier.

One rather crude pencil sketch from that time has survived – a silhouette of the Aberdare Mountains. It is not a good drawing by any means, but the outline is accurate and for that reason it pleases me.

*

I kept a wild animal notebook throughout my time in Kenya. I was a skimpy note-taker in those days, but there is sufficient detail in its pages to bring back a host of memories that can excite me even now.

Impala and thomson's gazelle (tommies) were so common a sight in those days I barely made note of them in the journal, and the same was the case with the herds of bushbuck and zebra. These animals were in abundance where people weren't, which meant that the vast stretches of land

J. J. Hespeler-Boultbee

Aberdare range in silhouette

swept of its population by the British (during the emergency the British wanted to see all of Kikuyuland in villages – if not in prison) was wide open for grazing. Rhinos were also numerous – both varieties, white and black.

It makes me shudder to think of it today, but there was a game the soldiers would occasionally like to play with rhinos, and they challenged me to join them on a couple of occasions, which I did simply because it was a challenge. In hindsight, I must have been mad.

The game depended a lot on the animal's initial position; it was best to come to it head-on. Conditions being right, it was considered great sport to dance about in front of the beast and make it charge – but only after a line of soldiers had prepared themselves for its onslaught.

As many as four, five or six soldiers would form a line directly in front of the rhino, positioning themselves in such a way that the front man was at a distance of some fifty feet from the animal's snout. His comrades would line up behind him with maybe ten feet between each of them.

Seeing only with difficulty and without benefit of perspective, the rhino would actually perceive only one person. Then, antagonized by our movement, its head would go down and it would charge.

The trick was to watch carefully the left-right swing of the tip of the horn and, as the animal came on, each soldier would leap just off centre to one side – and then do a hand vault over the animal's back, from one side of it to the other. In truth, some soldiers jumped out of the way in the nick of time as the rhino thundered by. The game worked well when the rhino's impetus would carry it forward in a straight line deep into whatever scrub was behind the soldiers; usually it would be so confused it would just snort and trot off. Once or twice, though, it would surprise us by veering mid-charge, or by turning around and coming back. In such cases we would have to be pretty nimble-footed to get out of its way.

Many years later I was to see a close approximation of this extraordinary game when the *forcados* of the Portuguese bullfight presented themselves – on foot and in line – before a charging bull during the *corrida*. It is the closing feature of the Portuguese bullfight. Because the game with the rhino is peculiarly African, and because of Portugal's centuries-old association with Africa, I have noted the curious similarity and often wondered whether the defining move of the *forcados*, in which they use their bare hands to bring the charging bull to a full stop, might not have had its origin in Africa.

I am aware of the macho sport of bull-leaping in ancient Crete, which sets me to musing: young men find it necessary to prove their manhood from time-to-time, and there is probably little to choose between facing a charging rhino or facing a charging bull. I have to admit, it would seem both acts have more to do with bravado than brains.

*

One day I visited the Nairobi Game Park with a small group of friends. We had had a thrilling experience watching a variety of animals, and thought we had seen something all of us would remember for the rest of our lives.

Indeed, if we hadn't we were about to. The park closed at sundown, and we were driving towards the main entrance, the road running along the top edge of a long but fairly shallow valley.

Someone said, "Look at the tommies down there, the way the low sun is shining on their backs ..."

And then someone else said, "Yes – but look at that cheetah just up the valley. He's stalking them."

We stopped the car and the four of us got out carefully and quietly, without slamming any car doors.

There was tall grass on the valley floor between large boulders, and some of these were extremely large. We watched, all of us caught in this vertiginous moment of life and imminent death, entranced by the ancient scene being enacted just below us. The cheetah raised his head to scout out his dinner, then ducked and crept forward, down wind and unseen by his prey.

The thomson's gazelle, a herd of maybe forty of them, grazed in brazen nonchalance as the cheetah moved closer and closer.

Surely they can see him, I thought. He was so close – and at my thought he leapt forward, his superlative dash for dinner.

In the same instant the tommie herd bounded into flight down the valley. Some sprang over gigantic boulders, others over each other as they criss-crossed the valley, never once even one of them stumbling or running into one another. In the angled sunbeams of that hour it was a show that could have been staged, so perfect was the light – and for all of us high on the valley's rim it was a once-only performance.

The cheetah bounded by the stragglers of the fleeing herd, and by now we could tell which gazelle he had picked for his dinner; but the gazelle, too, was aware he'd been selected, and he began a flamboyant series of evasive swerves and leaps in order to escape.

The cheetah was just drawing level with an enormous boulder, when an ostrich – full grown and in full charge, its legs flailing like pistons, its wings angrily thrashing the air like the bellows of a giant's furnace, raced out from behind the rock and ran at the cheetah. Decisively ambushed, the cheetah somersaulted out of the way of the attack and fled back up the valley as his prospective dinner made off the other way.

Back in the car we congratulated ourselves on our good luck at being witness to such an event. Dusk was on us quickly, and we were following about one hundred metres behind the red lights of another car when it turned a corner. As we approached the same corner our driver had to slam on his breaks to avoid rear-ending the car we'd been following. It had also had to break hard in order to avoid hitting a cow giraffe that was with her calf, both of them caught and bewildered by headlights.

We were waiting patiently for the animals to move off when the cow suddenly turned, reared up on her hind legs and came smashing down with her front hooves on the engine hood of the car that had disturbed her. An eight hundred kilo pummeling of infuriated motherhood, and now she and her baby wandered off as though they had just won an argument.

The occupants of the car leapt out to inspect the damage – which was considerable. The metal work had been crumpled like the silver paper of a chocolate bar, the hood popped crazily open and steam escaped from the damaged radiator. That vehicle was going to stay where it was for the night. We had a full car, but we moved over to make way for the driver and gave him a ride out to the park gate.

The game warden was a veteran. Breathlessly we told him about the cheetah, and then we told him about the giraffe.

He shook his head.

"You are lucky people!" he told us, though our passenger from the other car was sceptical. Ostriches were known to be defensive birds, he said, and could be dangerous when riled ...

"I've never heard of one attacking a cheetah like that, but I can't say I'm entirely surprised. She probably had her chicks behind that rock, and I wouldn't want to confront a mother ostrich defending her nest. They can indeed be dangerous ..."

But the giraffe incident – that was just astonishing, he said.

"I've never before encountered an angry giraffe ... they're such a docile animal. But mothers and their young ... I suppose it's possible ..."

And then he commented:

"I've never had two separate groups of visitors coming out of the park with two such weird stories to tell ..."

He bundled our extra passenger into the park Land Rover and the two of them set off along the dark trail to collect those we had had to leave behind.

*

Wild animals are difficult to photograph; even though in front of my lens by their thousands they would seldom stick around long enough to oblige an amateur photographer the likes of me. They tended to turn and present me their rump-ends just as my shutter clicked. Yet in a country like Kenya the challenge was always the perfect animal shot. In those days the countryside had such an abundance of all varieties you'd think the odds would eventually click in your favour. Some people had the knack; not me, even though the decimation of the animals didn't get up a full head of steam until the 1960's, and from then on was unrelenting, I seldom managed a good animal shot.

But the vistas, that was different. Landscapes are stunning and much more obliging. You have to be in the right spot at the right moment – that precise instant when the light is just so. Landscapes change each moment of the day – but they are always there. Cities expand, villages spring up where there were none before; but the shapes across the land remain the same – varying only with the subtlety of light at the rising and setting of each day's sun. The sun has special resonance in all parts of Africa.

Lesson: do not travel through any part of the continent without a camera hung permanently about your neck.

Often I would see people or faces I wanted to capture on film, but this was a different thing. Photographing faces was invasive. Asking permission, which was always appreciated, rather killed the idea of spontaneity.

*

During one of our numerous village raids, and when I had become acutely aware of the glares of hatred and sheer contempt of a local Kikuyu population disrupted and maltreated by raiding British and African soldiery, I spotted an old man seated on a dirt hummock in front of some houses. Barely moving at all, he looked at me with solemnity as if studying me as I stood nearby. I was uncomfortable, awkward under the steady gaze of this old man. I couldn't easily move away; I was part of a search group working in that section of the village, and was standing where I was because the precise spot permitted me a view across the area where my soldiers were rifling through peoples' belongings, searching for illegal weapons.

Perhaps because he looked to be so frail the old man had not been moved into the hot and crowded pens set up for the rest of the village population. But for some reason I had the feeling he was seated there for a purpose. Was he a lookout? I became suspicious. Seated in that spot it occurred to me he might have been able to give hand signals indicating our movements to someone I couldn't see.

I turned and looked directly at him, but he looked right back – and I am sure I blinked first. For a long while we looked at one another. I wanted to say something to him, to give him an order to move, to quit looking at me with such an air of insolence ...

There was no proof he was stationed on the hummock for any special reason whatsoever. It was merely my imagining. And so what if he was giving hand signals? No harm in that. Anyway, I could hardly ask him if that was why he was there.

Then I thought: I cannot prove any of my suspicions about this man, but in case he is being used as a Mau Mau scout it might be useful to have a mug shot of him. By this time I was numb and he was enemy.

The camera was in my pouch. I fished it out, calculated the right setting, deliberately aimed it at him and clicked.

The old man barely moved a muscle. He sat there like Methuselah himself. He didn't attempt to wave me off, nor did he turn his head. He just looked at me, and I felt small – and invasive. A rash of thoughts entered my head at that moment, all of them at once: because I was a soldier, a member of the conquering team, I had licence to be so rude, so ill-mannered? The man was neutral, he posed no threat – just sat there and did not take his eyes off me. He was a living, thinking being, someone's father or grandfather, and I had just photographed him as I might have photographed a bushbuck or an elephant, shoved the intrusion of my camera lens at him using my half-baked notions of his motives as an excuse to treat him with the utmost disrespect.

But the deed was done once the shutter had clicked – like pulling the trigger on a rhino and having instant regrets about it.

I straightened up and put the camera back in its pouch. Still the old man did not move, and I said to him – ridiculously:

"*Asante sana* – thank you."

I kept the photograph. It was quite a good one, I thought. More than that, it served as a reminder of yet another instant in my life (from start to finish it could have extended no more than three minutes) when I had made some form of transformation of idiocies within myself, clicked an internal switch and maybe grown just a little bit as a result. Many years later I used the photograph of this old man – I tried to portray his features in a painting. Bad painting, as it turned out, though I thought at the time it was pretty good.

What I had failed to see among the lines of the old man's face, in his eyes and in the ever so slight pout of his lower lip – what I had failed to see in my photograph and what I had failed to capture in my inadequate painting of him – was the desperate look of a wise old man who recognizes only too well the savagery of invasion. The hurt, the contempt, the dull subjugation that accompanies defeat – all of it was written on that old face when I clicked my camera. I saw none of it until much later – when I had become old enough to see these same emotions in another context and to know them at first hand.

Youthful soldiers all fired up to go – they don't see these things. They are too quick to pull the triggers of their guns; quick as I was to trigger the shutter of my camera.

A soldier may be well-trained, but he is a poor fellow who fails to permit himself an introspective moment to consider such things.

It is unlikely our generals would concur with such sentiment. They need to know when their subordinates can smell blood.

The old Kikuyu villager was no spy ...

☐

17. Christmas Up A Tree

By Christmas 1955, I had been in Kenya long enough to have acquired a handsome pair of brown knees. I was ordered with my platoon to patrol a large section of the Aberdare Mountains – the idea being either to flush the Mau Mau out of the bush or to force them into keeping their heads down and remaining out of sight till they gave up in desperation.

From the Mau Mau perspective, flushing risked being shot at, while remaining out of sight meant risking starvation.

Most of the *askaris* patrolling with me that Christmas Eve were pagan, so did not know about feeling nostalgic when asked to work over Christmas. That was something left to me alone as we coursed the dense high ground above the forests. The area was mostly grassland spreading for miles before us, the height of the growth and the massive outcrops of rock ensuring poor visibility. Here and there were copses of thorn bush and acacias, the type of country greatly preferred by some of East Africa's larger animals – buffalo, elephant, lion. And rhino, as it turned out.

I had decided to lead the patrol. But I had allowed my mind to wander, wondering about where friends and family were just now. I was quite content doing what I was doing; I liked this high country. But I suppose there was a part of me that wanted to be somewhere else. And, not unnaturally in that frame of mind, I had led my patrol hopelessly off course – directly into the midst of a herd of rhino.

The *askaris* – I had nine of them with me – had become aware of the danger considerably before I did. One would think it virtually impossible not to see a rhino directly in one's path, let alone a whole posse of them, but I had not seen anything at all. When at last the precariousness of my situation dawned on me I felt alone and not a little vulnerable.

There were four rhinos – north, south, east and west of me. I counted them. And I had a hunch there were even more out of sight in the bushes, deciding among themselves which of them would bowl me over. Aware of the rules of preservation in such cases, and without so much as a word, the *askaris* had disappeared like shadows. I caught glimpses of one or two of them. Like gymnasts performing on high bars, they had swung themselves up onto the skimpy branches of nearby acacias and thorn trees. There they clung in breathless silence, some of them frantically trying to signal me the danger.

I am not quite sure how I managed to get into one of the trees, but quite miraculously I discovered myself cradled none too securely among branches some twenty feet off the ground.

No doubt realizing he had responsibilities, one of the rhinos – the biggest – had trotted forward and was snorting angrily at the base of my tree. It was not a sturdy tree, and I hoped he would not tamper with it by charging or using it to scratch his hide. He failed to find me, and loitered off to nose about under the trunk of another tree a few yards away. I watched him, trying at the same time to keep an eye on his rhino companions. I had visions of being condemned to remain on my roost till at least nightfall, my *askaris* sitting safely in some clearing and chuckling to themselves as they ran a sweepstake on the duration of my discomfort.

There was an unnatural movement of the branches of a nearby tree and, peering at it, I recognized the face of my batman, Edouardi – always a jolly fellow who would invariably find humour in any situation. He saw me at the same time. He called out something that sounded like "Watcha!" – and simultaneously raised an arm to wave.

Then the whole scene changed, everything happening in quick succession.

Losing both his grip and his balance, and with a screech more of surprise than terror, he toppled headlong from the branch upon which he was sitting – landing on and bouncing off the back of the animal that had just been pestering me, but was now right below him.

With a snort of fury the rhino turned on my batman to grind him into the landscape, but the plucky fellow used his rifle butt to club his adversary across the snout. It had precious little effect, but for an instant the brute turned his head slightly to one side, giving Edouardi just enough time to bolt for my tree and swing himself up.

"Hello, sah!" he greeted me, sitting like a dandy astride the bough to which I also clung.

"Hello, Edouardi," I rejoined, feeling a little like Pooh caught with his head in the honey pot.

Undaunted, Edouardi smiled broadly. He flashed his bright white teeth, and with a gleam in his eye leaned forward and clasped me by the hand.

"Merry Christmas, sah!"

A delightful and sincere pagan salutation, I thought, and we both laughed heartily. Under the duress of the moment we were not so much officer and batman as just two quite athletic fellows attempting to save our skins.

☐

18. The Mountain

Several days before the New Year, battalion headquarters received more "red hot info" that even greater numbers of Mau Mau than the "Naivasha ninety" were skulking about on the forested slopes of Mount Kenya. Once again four battalions raced up into position, encircling the mountain to do battle.

On the flat of the map stretched out before us, we could see the mountain was quartered pie-wise in heavy red pencil, each of the four sections designated for one of the battalions. In the centre of this contoured "pie" was an expansive area that contained the mountain's multiple peaks, all of these clustered like cherries plonked into lashings of thick white cream – white patches on the map being left blank because they had not been surveyed (the result of cloud cover the day the survey plane had flown overhead). Austere and snow-covered, the highest of the peaks rose to a little over seventeen thousand feet. They were marked, though there were white patches around them, and at various points further down the mountain. Some were marked "cloud."

The Kikuyu, who lived at lower levels and never ventured so high, called this mountain Kirinyaga, the throne on earth of their god Ngai, who rested here unmoved under a cloak of white ostrich feathers.

This central area of the mountain's peaks constituted a high no-man's-land – snows and rocks and defiles it would take a well-equipped team of mountaineers to negotiate efficiently. Looking over the large-scale sheets showing the mass of the mountain, each of the four pie slices was marked with tight contour lines indicating the inclination of climb. With the base of the mountain somewhere about two thousand feet above sea level, this would mean a climb of something near ten thousand feet from the edge of the pie to the highest point of each slice – the boundary of the peak cluster, the border of the central area marking the highest point of each slice of the pie perhaps only four thousand feet below the level of the highest peak. Our battalion had drawn the south-west section of the mountain. As I was in command of No. 1 platoon A company, I would be obliged to scramble my men up to somewhere above twelve thousand feet, a point just a little shy of the snow line.

In addition to the thirty-or-so men of my own platoon, all of whom were excited and looking forward to a break from the routines of local patrolling and barrack life, the colonel had assigned to me a further ninety Kikuyu spearmen. My own men were well armed, carried their own food, and were generally prepared for a three-week excursion into the Mt. Kenya forest. This new lot, though, materialized just as we were about to leave the barracks. As if by magic they stepped out of the grey early morning mist that shrouded the motor transport yard just inside the barrack perimeter. In a brief that could have lasted no more than two minutes the battalion commander assured me they were "a loyal bunch ... volunteers ... take 'em with you and make the blighters work ..." This was a total surprise to say nothing of a hefty responsibility. I had not the faintest idea what I was going to do with an additional ninety men who were, apart from the spear that each of them carried, as unarmed as they were undressed.

Loyal Kikuyu volunteers. I had no idea how I was expected to make them work. Sloshing this new information about in my head, playing for an idea that just might occur with a mite of extra time, I did the military thing: I lined them up and counted them before hustling them onto the trucks that were going to take all of us to the mountain. My sergeant wrote down their names.

Yep – ninety and every last one of them barefoot, all in ragged second-hand clothing, only a few of them in military overcoats – without buttons. They all brandished long wooden-shafted spears with hammered iron tips, and sported "Best Birmingham" steel *pangas*. I was alarmed to learn I was expected to lead these semi-naked men to a zone just shy of the snow line and had visions of them freezing to death.

"... And what are they going to eat ...?" I enquired bleakly.

"Oh," the marshalling major explained confidently, "there will be some sacks of rice for them at the foot of the mountain. And you can probably let them do a bit of hunting ..."

It was a fair convoy that set out – six trucks just for my bunch, and there must have been at least another four hundred men in the companies that followed behind us. No great secret about the approach to this op, I reckoned. Roaring engines and grinding gears, the whole lot of us laboured over a tortuously twisted route to the staging area at the south west quarter of Mount Kenya's base. By the time we arrived our presence would have been well-advertised to more than just a sizeable portion of the countryside round about, thus most assuredly eliminating even the remotest chance of encountering a group of Mau Mau picnicking by the side of the road.

There was the usual milling about before we started the climb on foot. Bags of rice were distributed among the Kikuyu, and each member of my platoon was issued an extra blanket; nothing of the kind for the spearmen. I folded the map I had been given so that it would fit snugly into my long thigh pocket, and then we were ready for the hike. Up.

We followed a rough path into the forest, two sections comprising nine soldiers in each with my sergeant in the lead, the ninety spearmen straggling out in a long line behind them. The third section, WOPC Nyamahanga and myself brought up the rear. The column must have stretched nearly a mile from front to rear; there was no way it could fail to be noticed, not just by all the Mau Mau in the forest, but also by all the beasts a skilled huntsman might consider carrying back on the point of his spear for a dinner offering to his friends. In place of roaring engines and grinding gears, the men now puffed audibly. The air was rarefied, oxygen short, and they laboured at the climb. Our tracker dog panted like a locomotive, occasionally barking on the end of his handler's leash, and even though exhausted the Kikuyu chattered and laughed among themselves, smacking the hafts of their spears on the stony ground as they used them as hiking sticks.

No danger of uncomfortable silences on this leg of the excursion.

The lower reaches of the mountain did not present a particularly difficult climb, except that it was a constant and exhausting slog – always up. For the most part we were able to follow a clear-cut path. At first it ran in long straight stretches, sometimes for several hundred metres between the forest on either side, then it would kink at an angle and run for another long section. But as the incline increased, these straightaways shortened, and we were forced to reduce our speed, increase our effort – and climb. Around what might have been considered a lunch hour, shortly after we had taken a break for a gulp of water and something to eat, the path turned itself directly into the mountain, and it was not hard to notice how the men were beginning to flag, their pace becoming measurably slower as the angle of ascent increased.

I was not so worried by the faltering Kikuyu. They would follow the troops in their own time, and I had no doubt that by nightfall all of them would meet us at whatever point we selected to camp. It was the soldiers that worried me. They were fit and hardened, I knew that, but the heat was withering through the late morning and early afternoon hours, and the air was becoming noticeably thinner. As exhaustion set in, the line became longer and opened up. It was increasingly difficult to breathe, our pace slowing appreciably to little more than a crawl, and we had to stop for rest every few metres. It remained hot until mid-afternoon, and we sweated heavily. Then as the sun began its fall into the west our stops became ever more frequent, and we were buffeted by cold mountain winds that blew up from beneath us. By late afternoon we were well above the forest trees and bamboo and were negotiating unforgiving rock outcrops and defiles, scrubland with copses of what looked to be a pigmy cedar. I had been told to expect to find wildlife – gazelle, elephant, buffalo, rhino, even leopard – but I am sure if there had been anything of the kind near us the racket we were making would have put it to flight long before we might have clapped eyes on it.

The regular commander of A company, Major Monke, had gone on leave and was being replaced by his second-in-command, our administrative officer – Captain Freeman. I had never made a conscious effort to get up the Number Two's nose, but I confess the possibility that my general demeanour irked him in some calamitous way. As he informed me on several occasions, I was just a colonial – perhaps that was it. I never divined a single reason as to why he detested me the way he did, but he certainly made no secret of it. No doubt it was an accumulation of small events – combined with the load of pepper he bore in his bowel by the shovelful. It might have concerned me more had it not been so obvious that he bore a grudge against the world at large, a chip the size of a snow-capped peak on his shoulder manifested by a cynical red-faced temper. He seemed to think his humour aced (at least it provoked him to laughter) when employed in the demeaning of others. A sure superiority and its incumbent airs, the theatre of one-upmanship (he once confided to a group of juniors he was able to corner in the mess) was the hallmark of an English officer and gentleman. We were silent but not terribly impressed. To us his views flagged him as an untrustworthy prig. He made no attempt to conceal his racism. His belittling of the African troops was constant, all the more abhorrent when it was so obvious they understood much of what he was saying. They may not have understood the words, but they could have had few doubts about his tone, though they dared not respond in any way.

We were his juniors but in matters that counted we also knew we were his superiors. He must have known we found him contemptible. The sneer in his voice, the haughty manner in which he spoke to and of others and, for those of us who could understand his words, his asides and half-spoken commentaries concerning what he thought about those he was addressing, made it extremely difficult for us to respond to him. We could neither agree nor disagree with him to his face, so we just detested him. Had any of us given the man the responses he deserved, he would have pulled rank to make life miserable. So we turned our backs on him, avoiding anything more than minimal and necessary contact.

By contrast, Major Monke, who was universally liked, was an active participant in all of his company's responsibilities and patrols. He showed concern for his junior officers and knew how to draw from each of us a high level of co-operation. He took the trouble to get to know the soldiers in our individual platoons, and to him they responded, as did the subalterns, with respect and humour, great efficiency – and even a level of affection.

Captain Freeman, was the polar opposite of the major. The man was not stupid. He noticed how we shunned him, and it curled his lip a little more. No doubt to be ostracized in this way pushed him even further back into his anti-social misery, but a man like that digs his own cesspit; it is hardly surprising others refrained from willingly climbing into it with him. He was not shy of toadyism in his dealings with the major, but when, as happened from time to time, he thought he was not getting what he wanted, he would turn to us junior officers and give voice to the spitefulness he actually felt for pretty well all around him, his immediate superior not excluded. It was clear to those of us operating so close to him that he thought himself socially above the rest of us, and a better commander than the major for whom he held such contempt, and whom we so revered.

Major Monke was blind to all this animosity. His treatment of his Number Two was always totally even-handed – at least as best as the rest of us could make out. While we found it difficult to conceal our loathing for the captain, our major remained effortlessly disconnected, scrupulously fair-minded. To my knowledge none of us ever spoke to our company commander about his miserable Number Two; and I am sure I never heard the major speak negatively about the captain, either. The major was above in-fighting, preferred to discard what would have been distasteful to him and instead to zero-in on essentials.

Our major was sadly missed on the occasion we climbed Mount Kenya, his command passed on to the captain. And it was Freeman, not Monke, who ordered me to march my men to the summit of my slice of the mountain's pie. Pointing at the map over my shoulder, he stuck his finger on a bunch of contour lines running close to a blank white patch marked "cloud."

"Make your camp there!" Freeman had said to me at the base of the mountain. Like me, he could have had not the slightest idea what was "there" under the cloud patch.

As it turned out "there" was just under the thirteen thousand-foot level, a place of serene beauty well above the tree line in such pure and rarefied air we could only breathe it in delicious short gasps. I remember standing on a rock outcrop, looking down and south to where the vast expanse of Kenya spread itself out towards the Tanganyika border. A small private airplane flew by far below me, yet so close that I could pick out through my binoculars the identity number painted in black lettering on the upper side of its wing, and the shadow form of the pilot in the cockpit.

Long before we arrived "there" one of the soldiers folded. He sat at the side of the track.

"I go no further, *efendi*," he told me. "Shoot me here."

He was not just tired. He was done in, and he felt shame. We still had a long climb in front of us.

"Come on!" I bullied him.

"No, *efendi*!"

I could not leave him there. If Mau Mau were present in the area he would have had his throat slit before breakfast.

"I'll get some of the Kikuyu to walk with you when you are ready," I told him. "Keep your weapon, but give me your pack ... try to make it to camp before dark ..."

In taking his pack, I was taking his food. I reckoned if he wanted to eat a meal that night he would have to make a special effort. As it turned out, though, my motivation was outmanoeuvred. The friendly Kikuyu spearmen who stayed with him cooked up a pot of rice, and none of them made the least effort to move on up to the platoon camp until early the following morning. It was cold. There was ice on the tea billy. The group arrived at first light and huddled about one of the fires we had kept burning through the night; the soldier had pulled his blanket tight around his shoulders, but could barely contain his shivering. The three Kikuyu who arrived with him, all of them dark-skinned plainsmen, had turned a ghastly grey-blue colour. Their eyes were wide, their teeth chattered.

This was a major concern. The snow line was only a few hundred metres above our heads. Pumping and puffing our way up the mountain during the daylight hours we had managed to stay warm enough, but after the sun went down the mountain air attacked, relentlessly gouging at us like a wild animal we could not escape. All the men, even the soldiers who had been given an extra blanket apiece, were suffering terribly from the cold. That first night we failed to make it to "there" on my map, and I allowed the men to light as many fires as they felt they needed to keep themselves warm. I ordered the climb to continue just as the first rays of the morning sun were marking the horizon. I thought it the best way to fight the temperature.

I checked the map. Our path led us to a saddle of ground that lay between the bulk of the mountain and a high spur that jutted out towards the west. We had been going about an hour, and we needed to call a halt in order to cook up a morning meal. Between the point of the spur and the rise of the mountain's mass towards the snow line was a wide open area of what at first looked like an alpine meadow. It was about a kilometre across and two kilometres from the tip of the spur to a point at approximately the same height on the main slope. It nestled right under the thumb-sized white patch marked "cloud" on the map. It was a massive bog, headwater of a substantial mountain stream that ran away to the west.

This was the "there" Captain Freeman had indicated. It was a totally unsuitable place to stop, let alone pitch a permanent base camp. It took me all of two minutes to decide exactly where we were and to move around the bog towards the east. By now we were well above the level of the main forest. What trees existed were stumpy and spread out, but about two kilometres further on we found a copse that occupied a large piece of level ground between huge boulders. It was fairly sheltered from the freezing winds that were a constant at that altitude, so I ordered the men to pitch camp and make themselves something to eat.

From here, as the day opened up, I sent out half-a-dozen fan patrols. There were three or four soldiers in each, plus an equal number of spearmen. I myself set off with six soldiers and three spearmen. Our objective was to discover the precise lay of the land. I had the only map, so I was relying on these patrols to give me an accurate assessment of the ground they covered so I could match their descriptions with what I had in hand. There were too many "clouds" marked on my map for me to consider it at all accurate – or even particularly useful. The men were told to take more or less three hours and then to report back to camp.

Several coincidences came into play at this point; I had sent the patrols out in six different directions, and the patrol I chose to lead myself could have gone any which way.

I chose to take my group eastwards, and we climbed two hundred metres to follow a narrow animal track that led off across the face of a steep slope, many boulders and rocks lining each side of it. Normally the commander of such patrols does not walk out in front. It is a safety and control measure. If there happens to be an ambush, it is usually the lead man who is hit first. Putting the commander further back in the line of the patrol maximizes his chances of survival, with the hope that he will be able to take firm hold of any situation and fight back. But on this occasion for some reason I cannot now fathom, I had taken the point position.

We were approaching the eastern edge of our slice of the pie, and for obvious reasons I did not want to bulldoze into the area next to us where there could be another unit patrolling. The wind had dropped during the night so that the early air was still and quiet. A heavy morning mist shrouded large parts of the slopes blanketing sound – so much so that I turned and signalled the men to step carefully and make no noise themselves.

It was at this precise moment we all heard, and distinctly, the sounds of muted chatter and a sharp burst or two of laughter. The voices were coming towards us, and on the same track.

The rules of engagement under which we were operating were clear: in our own area of patrol, we were to open fire and shoot to kill.

I spun about; my men were ready and knew what to do. I made a quick hand signal, and in a flash the entire patrol was concealed among the rocks on the upper side of our track in a perfect ambush position. Strewn with large boulders, the lay of the land was such that it gave itself, completely, to our trap. It took no more than a few seconds for us to be ready.

The voices continued their sporadic conversation; we waited in silence.

I was still in the point position, so I was the first one to see the leader of a line of men that now emerged from the mist, unaware of our presence.

Instantly I recognized other soldiers. More than that, I also recognized the man who was leading them. Michael Barker had made the same tactical error as myself, for he was also leading the line at the head of his patrol of *askaris*. If he had been in his correct position, I would have most likely allowed the entire group to come within the bracket of our kill zone, and there is no doubt in my mind we would have shot all of them.

I had less than seconds.

"Do NOT fire!" I called out at the top of my lungs – and instantly Michael's patrol swung their weapons towards us.

"DON'T SHOOT!" I called again frantically. "DO – NOT – SHOOT!"

For an instant we all looked at one another, wide-eyed and terrified. Nobody dared to breathe. Then the moment was past. No one opened up. Not a shot fired.

"Michael!" I called out. "My God! We nearly shot the whole lot of you!"

Michael Barker stepped out of his line of troops and came towards me, squinting slightly and rubbing the mist off the lenses of his spectacles.

"Good heavens! Is that you Jeremy? Fancy running into you up here!"

"But, Michael, you've bulldozed into my area ..."

"Oh, I don't know about that," he said. "Perhaps you lot have bulldozed into mine ..."

The two patrols mingled then with a deal of nervous laughter, and my friend suggested we take a break and brew up some tea.

We did that. We sat down and compared our maps and location to check which of us had bulldozed (he had), and for another two hours filled in the months since we had last seen one another in England. Michael had also been posted to the King's African Rifles, serving out his time in a Kenya battalion. Quite by chance his unit had been assigned the slice of mountain pie next to mine.

"Close call!" I told him several times, and he agreed.

But then he said:

"Do you know what day it is?"

I had no idea.

"It's January the first. I don't think we should talk of killing anyone on New Year's Day. Much better to just sit a few moments and enjoy our tea..."

New Year's Day 1956. It was an occasion to remember.

An hour or two later I bade farewell to Michael Barker as he led his patrol back along the narrow path upon which he had been ambushed. He waved cheerily, once again wiping the mist off the lenses of his spectacles. He got in touch with me by telephone a few weeks later when the operation had wound up and I was in Nairobi. He was coming down to the capital and we made arrangements to get together.

Those days on the mountain were pleasant. I couldn't have been more content, clambering about like a high altitude goat. I managed to look on my time up there as a singular form of meditative repose. What the military handbook and those who had written it preferred to consider a patrol – an element of warfare – was, in my other and more imaginative reality, a magnificent opportunity to wander a precious natural environment so rare it was unseen by most of the rest of mankind. I felt myself to be a thousand miles away from my captain commander and his dyspeptic notions of strata, even though I knew he was only a few hundred metres lower down the track I had ascended. For the time being I was quite certain I was far higher up the mountain than he was – spiritually as well as physically high enough that it was only those for whom life's miracles were in clear definition that so much was given as passed through my mind, day or night. There was not the slightest sign of Mau Mau, and even if I had encountered them my happy frame of mind was such I was convinced they would prove to be reasonable men if only I could get to sit down with them, billy up some tea ...

In the evenings I would squat around one of the campfires with my soldiers and the Kikuyu spearmen. Nyamahanga would act as translator, and I spent many hours listening to stories, learning about the people that accompanied me each day – the Kikuyu from the plains below us, the soldiers who hailed from central and western Tanganyika. High on Kiranyaga we huddled around the fires in the cold of the nights and tried to keep each other warm with companionship and laughter, sharing what few blankets we had between us. The spearmen did not complain. They laughed. Why had they been selected to come up here? they asked me. Why, indeed, I asked them back; it was the will of the commanders. But then, not wishing to prove too critical of my superiors, I told them that for me the more important reason they had come was in order that I might learn the amazing stories of their homeland, their people – and what they thought of the foreign white people who had come to their land and obliged them to trudge barefoot up the mountain with me. There was always laughter, and as the evening wore on they would peel away and huddle in groups, spoon-like together for warmth and whatever sleep they could get. Some would stay awake to tend the fires and keep watch.

Constantly, no matter from what point on this holy mountain's surface one gazed, there was a spectacular vista that spread to the haze hiding a distant horizon. Even with a sub-machine gun in my hand, and orders to kill whatever dared intrude itself onto the surface of my slice of the pie, the world around me felt pretty darned perfect. My nemesis was my youth; had I not had the hoot-headed mind of a twenty-year-old at fourteen thousand feet, I might have guessed that a large chunk of this mountain Paradise was about to crumble under my feet.

The camp quickly developed its routines. Guards, lookouts, chores, water and firewood collection – all of these things evolved into their twenty-four hour symmetry. Fanwise, and in rotation, I sent out eight- or nine-man patrols daily right after we'd taken our early meal. There was a job to be done, after all, and by doing what we were doing we were ensuring that our upper regions of Mt. Kenya were totally absent of so much as a sniff of enemy activity. We were some one hundred and twenty men all told, and it did not take long before we had looked into every crevasse, under every bush, and behind every rock. We were continually performing this kind of search, so before long we had become quite familiar with all corners of the territory assigned to us.

Finishing up a patrol, I returned to camp at about eleven o'clock one morning to be greeted by my sergeant with the news that I was to report immediately to Captain Freeman at his camp further down the mountain.

"He was here," my sergeant told me. "Very angry."

Suddenly, a sense of foreboding. I had no wish to see the captain, especially if he was angry. We made a delicious rice for lunch, took time eating it – and only then was I ready to set off with the sergeant and one of the soldiers to see what was itching *bwana* captain's evil temper. It took nearly two hours to get down to him.

"Damn you, sir!" he screeched at me as soon as I set foot in front of his bivouac.

"This is supposed to be a secret mission. You've set enough bonfires up there to light the whole damned peak like a Belisha beacon! Any terrorists could see you from a hundred miles away ..."

"I have one hundred and twenty men, sir. Our camp is spread over a wide area, and so I have permitted them to light ten fires. They are ill-equipped. They are all bare foot, they have inadequate clothing, no blankets – and they are cold all the time, but particularly at night. There is little natural shelter, and the temperature drops well below freezing ..."

There was no point in trying to talk to him. All my reasonings meant nothing to him as he sat there on a log in front of me, one boot off. He had been drinking. I could smell it.

"Don't answer me back, you impudent scoundrel!" he shouted, belching the last word.

So I stood silently in front of him.

Captain Freeman had pitched his headquarters among the forest growth to one side of the main track leading up the mountain. It was not a bad location for its purpose – good cover, a nearby stream of mountain water. From a military standpoint it was a much better situation than the openness of the one I had been obliged to select higher up beyond the tree line. I looked around. My sergeant and the *askari* were standing at ease behind me, a little embarrassed and discomfited by my predicament – their senior officer being roasted by his senior officer.

"What are you standing there for?" the captain demanded to know.

"You wanted to see me."

"I don't want to see you. I don't want to see you again. You disobeyed my specific order ..."

"I don't understand ..." I began to tell him, and in fact I did not.

"I indicated to you exactly where you were to make your camp. You did not do so."

I pulled my map from where I kept it in the long pocket of my trouser leg and showed it to him, pointing to the patch of white – the "cloud" that lay in the saddle between the mountain's shoulder and the high south-westerly bluff.

"You told me to make camp there, and when I got to this precise location

I discovered it was a bog. There was no way I could make my camp there..."

"Damn you! Damn you!" he shouted, red faced and spitting. He had a towel in his hand, and flung it at my head.

"Don't answer me back ...! I was up at your camp just this morning. I saw what a shambles it was."

By now I was angry myself, but rather anxious not to make matters worse. So I stood and said nothing. He pulled on his boot and rose from the log, then he came up and stood right in front of me. He was shorter than me. His eyes were burning as he looked at my face. He tried to look into my eyes, but he couldn't; my own gaze out-thundered his, and his eyes constantly flitted off-focus in his drunken discomfort. His moist lips parted in a sneer allowing me a glimpse of his yellowed teeth. His stubbled chin was in need of a shave. Again he caught his breath, another disguised burp.

"Just who the hell do you think you are ...?"

"I'm sober," I told him calmly – and in hindsight I have to admit the comment did indeed make matters worse.

"You are under arrest," he told me. "I'm relieving you of your command. Have your men return to your camp and collect your gear. You will stay here until they get back with it, and then you will report in to battalion headquarters at the base of the mountain ... I'll give you a letter to deliver to the colonel."

By now I was numb. I moved off to one side and wrote out a quick message for Nyamahanga – my companion, my friend, my rock for nearly a year. Now I was having to tell him to take command in my absence. I did not know when I might be seeing him again, truly had no idea what would happen next. I gave him instructions to pack up my kit and send it back down to me as quickly as possible, for I did not wish to have to remain overnight at company headquarters to hear more of the captain's invective.

By now I wished nothing more than to waste no time getting down the mountain so I could report in to the battalion commander. He was a reasonable man, I thought.

My biggest regret about that whole incident was that I was never to see Nyamahanga Boke again. For about a year I wrote letters to him, and he always replied in his gentle manner. He was a good soldier, a kind and thoughtful man. In his letters he wrote about his family back in Tabora, how he would retire from the army and look after those he loved by turning his attention to his farm, his cattle and his church. As more boy than soldier, it was hard for me to accept that I could not now turn to this man, this most astute old soldier, for the trust and affection I think we both felt for one another. Now, as I write these words, I know that my association with Nyamahanga during those months of our working together in Kenya was a major passage in my life, far more important to me for the man I became than the work I was obliged to perform as a soldier.

At the base of the mountain the colonel read over the report I handed to him from the captain, and announced that he had no option but to accept the critical words of my senior officer.

I was not to be trusted, he said. I had proven this when I had broken my "covenant" with him weeks ago, and continued my fraternization with the troops at their nightly *ngomas*. Oh yes, he had noted my disobedience, he said. He had said nothing till now because he had hoped that I would come to my senses and see things his way. Obviously a young man with such a wayward colonial mind – "like some American know-all" – had little concept of how the Empire was held together; that it could only be held together if its separate parts could be held apart – for the better maintenance of order and discipline ... Of course, could I not comprehend that? Us, them ...

It would be better by far if I were to be on my way.

"I shall have to write a report about this to the War Office – an Adverse Report, you understand, not a great mark of distinction to go on your record. It will come up for review in six months. If you pull your socks up there's a chance you can redeem yourself. You're well-trained in jungle warfare, so perhaps someone can find a use for you. For now, I've got a job to do here, and I can't be bothered with chasing after people who just don't fit in ..."

That was the end of it. In hindsight I probably could have said something in my defence, but I didn't. The argument against my behaviour (in my case the word "behaviour" had loaded meaning) was clear enough. Indeed, I could hardly deny having committed the "crimes" of which I was accused; possibly my greater crime was in not understanding that this "behaviour" was such a monstrous crime ... I began to feel guilty of something I did not quite comprehend. The colonel and that wretched captain, they were my seniors; in my hurt and confusion I thought they might have a handle on some deep and mysterious knowledge about the secret me that till now had been totally obscured to my youthful mind. It was a bit like being sent into Coventry and not understanding why. No one would talk to me or explain ...

Though resolving to "try harder," for some reason I could not quite pinpoint where or how I was supposed to do that – or to feel shame about something ...?

A truck took me back to the barracks at Nyeri. For a week before being posted to Buller Camp in Nairobi I was left pretty much alone at the mess, so had plenty of time to shuffle events around in my mind and become even more paranoid. And then suddenly I was gone, before the battalion had returned from the mountain.

*

At the Nairobi headquarters my temporary commandant informed me all battalions of the KAR were starting to shift onto "lower establishment" – reducing their officer quotas as the British were gaining the upper hand and the emergency was starting to wind down. Never mind that I'd got myself into a bit of hot water, he told me. That could happen to anybody ... Being sent down from the battalion was no big deal – a convenience for military planners that just happened to coincide with the current personnel requirements. I would have to remain until such time as passage could be found for me to join my parent Home Counties unit – which happened to be in Malaya.

"Good thing you're trained in jungle warfare ... you'll be useful in Malaya ... if you pull your socks up ..."

But Nairobi was a fog, and a confused and painful one at that. Michael Barker called. He and some friends from the Gloucester and Kenya Regiments had decided to come down to the big city to visit with me before I left the country. A car full of young officers set off for the south. It crashed near Thika. Of the six aboard, five were killed outright – Michael among them. The sixth was flown home to Britain before I had received my Malaya posting.

I was shattered. By the time my posting came through I was ready to leave.

*

Mrs. Queen's Chump

A troopship would pick me up in Aden to take me to Malaya. In the meantime I was instructed to fly north a few days early via Aden Air, escorting a troop of sixteen soldiers being assigned as reinforcement to the small and beleaguered city garrison just then plagued by internal strife – an uprising of citizen malcontents unhappy, of all things, with their status as a British protectorate.

"Oh, before you go, old chappie," a day to go, and my Headquarters commander caught me as I was going out the door for lunch.

"Seems to me you should be rather well acquainted with dead bodies these days – used to it, wot? I mean, what with your friends wiping out in that car accident the other day …"

I turned, hardly able to believe the chatty, nonchalant tone of his words.

"Well, you see there is to be a military hanging of those three Micks the court found guilty last week, and we need to supply a witness. I thought maybe you could just take a whip round over to headquarters detention centre – simple matter. Just see the deed done and put your "John Henry" to the death certificates … I'd go myself, but it's an unpleasant business, and I'm supposed to meet a bunch of HQ chappies for a golf tourney later this afternoon … Might put me off my game. Be a good chap, there, would you … You'd be doing me a big favour …"

Leaving Nairobi

☐

19. Aden and On

Waiting in Nairobi had become boring. I had been counting too heavily on that visit with Michael Barker and the others, and right after their deaths I thought I'd go mad. I was like a zombie walking between my quarters, my office and the mess hall. I didn't go into the city for anything pleasurable at all; my brother had returned to Britain; I had no friends in the city, nor among the other officers in the camp. It was a desperately lonely time.

Nairobi had become a trap of my own construction, a by-product of my diminishing and questionable enthusiasm for the military and what I was doing in it. But the scene was beginning to change for me. Orders had come through that I was to be transferred back to my original Home Counties infantry unit – which at that time happened to be fighting against the Chinese communists in Malaya. "Communist Terrorists," they were called, or "CT's;" some people in Nairobi seemed to know all about them. When they heard I was headed that way they became adamant – it was quite alright to kill them, they said. The tag "terrorist" was the key. Once a man is designated "terrorist" you cannot talk to him, only about him. They'd be different than the Mau Mau. The word was that the Chinese were better organized than the Africans; they didn't turn and run but faced the Brits and fought. Good soldiers, but "terrorists" just the same.

All who learned of my posting assured me it would be better than the static routine of Buller Camp. My troubles in Kenya irked me not a little. I didn't talk about them to anyone; I knew within myself that what had happened on the mountain was not entirely my fault, that I had been singled out by a senior officer who was drunk and had had it in for me. That rationale I could explain to myself satisfactorily. But deep down I knew I bore a sense of failure – that I might not have failed, at least in my own eyes, had I battled for myself a little more courageously, stood my ground and fought back. I had not done that. My lower lip had quivered, and that was what had shamed me. So the prospect of a new chance in Malaya came as something of a relief. It would be a new opportunity in an entirely new location. A new beginning where no one would know me or what had happened and I wouldn't have to explain myself or make excuses.

Besides, I had been trained in jungle warfare. I would be required to do more of what I had been taught to do, so it was not as if I was about to be tested on some untried new syllabus. I had learned my arrival in Malaya was anticipated – if not eagerly, at least with something like curiosity. Other junior officers in the regiment had not had a year's prior experience in Africa.

I was ordered to pick up a British troop ship at Aden and travel with it to Singapore. I would fly to Aden, making myself useful by escorting a troop of sixteen British soldiers north to the protectorate. Some anti-British rioting was going on in the streets up there, and my consignees were to be the initial batch of a reinforcement. Something like that. I did not quite understand the background, knew no details – only that the fellows needed an officer for their successful delivery.

We boarded a contracted Aden Air DC-3 in Nairobi, and headed north – first to Mogadishu in Italian Somaliland. It was blisteringly hot when we arrived and we stood about on the tarmac waiting for the plane to be refuelled. Eventually an Italian officer took pity on us, and invited us into the shade of an airport building. It was still hot, but at least we were not exposed to the direct afternoon sunlight.

Then we boarded again. The queer thing about a DC-3 is that when they are standing on the ground they rest at an angle of about twenty-five degrees. You mount through a side door towards the rear, and then have to clamber uphill to your seat. Leaning back into your seat you are looking upwards at a steep angle. It's not until you have left the ground and are flying level that you begin to feel your position about normal. The wings flap.

We headed for British Somaliland and its capital Hargeisa, flying over what I later learned was a part of the Ogaden – sparse scrubland cut across here and there by dry riverbeds. We were not flying high, probably little more than two thousand feet. The windows of the plane were poorly synchronized with the seating arrangement in the plane's interior, so it was not easy to crane over and see all that was going on down below. Occasionally there would be the glimpse of a camel train headed out across the desert. But no colour other than what one might produce out of an ochre loaded paint box. Even the sky, where it wasn't blazing sun, was ochre.

Being Aden Air, the pilot and co-pilot spoke Arabic, and there was a stewardess in a scruffy grey smock, cigarette burn in the middle of it, and grease stains down the sides of her two hips where she rubbed her sweaty hands. The pilots teased her, which got her giggling; she was also tantalized by the presence of the soldiers – who were happy to while away the time by flirting, pulling at her skirt and pinching her butt. She giggled pretty well all the way from Nairobi to Aden.

I am sure it was a joke of sorts, but at one point the co-pilot ambled back to where I was seated and asked me if I had a piece of string. I did not, but one of the soldiers produced a length of bootlace. The smirking co-pilot, cap angled onto the back of his head, kicked back a piece of carpeting in the aisle between the seats. He then lifted out a length of metal sheeting, bent down and attached the bootlace – to something. Replacing the floor sheet and then the carpet, he turned to me and tipped the peak of his cap to acknowledge my co-operation. He then ambled back to his place beside the pilot. I had no idea what he was attaching the bootlace to; I think he was just having me on – and I have to admit to his success. I was both baffled and alarmed. I didn't feel too secure riding in an old aircraft that needed any part of it to be held together (mid-air) by a length of bootlace.

In England a year earlier I had met a fellow candidate at OTC – another Michael "Somebody" – who declared his romantic interest in joining the Camel Corps, a unit known more formally as the Somaliland Scouts. I never saw him again in the rush of my own embarkation, but remembered him now as we circled Hargeisa and came fluttering down beside a single corrugated iron hut which served as the airport terminal building. A black Humber limousine was parked next to it sporting the colourful pennant of the colony's Governor General – a piece of bunting attached to a little mast on the forward wing, limp in the breathless air. As we stepped off the plane (it had to be refuelled again) the governor came forward, hand outstretched, to greet me – Sir Theodore Ouseley Pike.

"Jolly good show to see you coming through," he said affably. "We don't often get to see our boys out here, y'know … Thought I'd come out and say hello …"

His aide-de-camps stood silently behind him.

"Michael!" said the governor, turning over his shoulder. "Come and meet this gentleman …"

Michael Somebody, whom I had last glimpsed at OTC, stepped forward. He was a remarkably tall fellow, well over six-foot-four at a guess. On his head he wore, as part of his uniform, a stylized cap-cum-turban which added about a foot to his impressive overall size. He was burned such a deep hue of chocolate brown that I could hardly recognize him – but the rest, including his boots, was ochre.

"Good heavens!" I exclaimed. "But I thought you were headed for the Camel Corps ...?"

"Correct!" said Michael. "I am in what used to be the Camel Corps – now more correctly the Somaliland Scouts – but I can tell you I have barely seen a camel since I came out. And I've barely ridden one, either ..."

Sir Theodore had moved off to talk to the soldiers now standing in a clump in the shade of the airport terminal. Michael looked over to see that he was out of earshot, then tipped himself forward at the waist and whispered in my ear.

"Occasionally we went out on desert patrols when I first arrived here last year but truthfully, old boy, that was by jeep, and it wasn't quite my cup of tea. Tried the camel once and got quite sick, so I've been old Sir Top's aide for about a year now. My main job is to ride next to him in the Humber, and otherwise I try to take care of the garden he's attempting to grow at the residence ... The romance has eluded the Camel Corps in this little corner of Briarpatch."

The poor bastard had another six months of service to go.

"Good grief, can't you scratch up a cricket team or something ...?"

"We tried that, old boy, but the finer points of the game are a bit lost on the fellows we can field out here ... They don't quite understand what it's all about, do you see? I mean, the philosophy thing ..."

Our plane left Hargeisa for Aden within minutes, and I have neither seen nor heard anything of Michael Somebody from that day to this.

*

Aden was surreal. I was to pass there four of the strangest days I have ever spent anywhere.

If my memory dims in this section of my memoir it is because I cannot readily recall drawing sober breath while I was in Aden. Free port, and I have this feeling the faucets in the bathrooms of my accommodation were charged with whisky in a diabolical plot to fog my mind. But I was as yet sober and well recall our arrival at one of the settlement's smaller airports, Bir Fahfl at Sheikh Othman, not far from the Royal Air Force base at Khormaksar.

We were just levelling off to land when somebody with a small calibre machine gun perched at the approach end of the runway opened up on us. The seventeen of us were strapped into single seats down each side of the hull when suddenly about three bullets zipped up through the floor of the aisle between us and out through the ceiling. No one was hit, and we landed without further incident. But as soon as we were up at the far end of the runway I clambered forward and told the pilot what had happened, that on no account should he taxi back. Instead he let us all out right there, and I had the sixteen fellows belly up on the tarmac and give the far end of the runway a burst of small arms fire. I had no idea what we were shooting at. Meantime the pilot radioed for a truck to collect us, and eventually we all wound up at what I believe was a police barracks in the old city centre.

There was one British Army officer there, a lieutenant who accepted my detail of sixteen men and declared he was delighted to see me.

"Your orders are to report to the Royal Air Force base over at Khormaksar. You'll be billeted there," he told me. "Your ship won't be able to pick you up for several days, so perhaps you wouldn't mind giving me a bit of a hand here ... We're a little short-staffed. I'll have a driver take you to the Khormaksar mess right now, but I could send a jeep over to collect you tomorrow morning, if you'd like ...?"

Would I like?

"By all means ..." I replied.

*

A young Pilot Officer showed me to my room; a local mess employee wearing a turban and bare feet lumping along my kitbag. The RAF mess was a large airy building with a colonnaded veranda running the full length of its sunny south side, French windows along its northern face opening directly onto sand dunes that, for all I could tell, stretched all the way to the central wastelands of the Arabian Desert.

Mrs. Queen's Chump

The PO told me I would have to share accommodation.

"But he's a good chap. You'll like him. Navigator. He's flying right now, but he'll be back about supper time ..."

He told me to clean myself up and he would meet me in the bar.

"Most of us get together in the bar at this hour. I'll buy you a drink. It's on this same level, near where we entered the building. You can't miss it."

He left me to take a shower, and afterwards as I was toweling myself down I opened the lattice door to the room's full-length clothes closet which turned out to be, in fact, a small dressing room. In it were suspended a row of my roommate's uniforms. The first thing I noticed were the shoulder tags of his jackets, each one marked "Poland," indicating he was one of the few men still serving who had joined the Polish section of the Royal Air Force during the Second World War. Such men were famous; hardy and committed warriors, all of them, and notorious patriots. Sewn to the chest of each of the jackets was the half-wing and encircled "N" of a flight navigator. Most impressive of all were his rows of medals, the three senior positions being taken up by decorations I could not recognize – followed by a Distinguished Flying Cross. This was surmounted by an oak leaf, indicating he had won the medal more than once.

"What's senior to a DFC?" I asked my Pilot Officer friend when we got together.

"Not much," he laughed.

It amused him that I should be billeted with someone he thought eccentric.

He did not know what the medals were named, but the three that piqued my curiosity were senior Polish awards for his actions during the Second World War.

"Ask him when he comes in later ..."

The PO bought me my first drink in Aden, and we sauntered out past the veranda to where a group of pilots were standing encircling a small patch of grass.

"Cheers!" I greeted my host, and raised my glass in salute.

"Oh! Don't drink it. No, no! You mustn't drink it. First drink of the evening always goes to the grass ...!"

He escorted me over to the circle of officers and pointed to the verge of the grass.

"Pour it here," he said.

I did not understand him.

"This is the only patch of grass in Aden," he explained patiently. "For this reason, and because we've all gone a bit barmy out here, we always toast our lawn with the first drink of the evening ... Just pour it at your feet, and we'll go back to the bar and get another one."

And with that he did precisely what he had asked me to do – pouring a full bottle of beer over the grass edge at our feet. So I did the same, and couldn't help but notice how the outer rim of the lawn, as he called it (in reality it was a wretched patch of shabby crab-grass the size of a squash court), had been irreparably singed brown for a metre all around – burned by liberal quantities of alcohol.

I also noticed no one actually set foot on it. Holy ground.

A small group of air force personnel filed past carrying placards:

> *"Don't stamp out our one link with civilization!"*

> *"Reminder of home!"*

> *"Save our grass!"*

"What's that all about?" I asked my escort.

"Oh, we have a new base commander. He thinks the officers are being childish in their treatment of this patch of grass. Today he ordered it to be taken up, and for concrete slabs to be laid down instead ... I guess they're going to do it tomorrow ..."

There was a mite of logic, so I thought, if this was indeed the only patch of grass in Aden. The ritual made less sense to me later when I learned there were, in fact, several pleasant gardens in the city – Tawahi Park and Sheikh Othman – where there were extensive areas of grass that did not receive the same libations as the one at Khormaksar.

Before going in for supper I headed back to my shared quarters to use the bathroom and wash my hands. As I walked in I was greeted by my roommate, effervescent fellow in singlet and jockey shorts who had just stepped out of the shower and was himself getting ready for supper. He had a drink in his hand, and poured one for me as I entered.

He was close to forty years old, I guessed, spoke excellent English with a strong Polish accent. He shook my hand enthusiastically, beaming a broad smile with a gold tooth in it.

"What do you think of our accommodation?" he asked, waving his arms into the four corners of what was, in fact, quite a large room.

I thanked him for the hospitable way he shared his room.

"Look! And we have this magnificent panoramic view … of the eternal sands!"

He stepped to the semi-closed shutters of the French windows, and cast them open to reveal a wide vista of dune – and nothing else that I could make out.

"Magnificent, no?"

I smiled.

"Like a picture on your wall," I said. "Never changes."

"Only one problem," he informed me, pulling on his trousers.

"Look carefully at that dune on the right and you will see something of a track that comes down and passes close by this window. A camel train comes through regularly at four o'clock in the morning – wooden wagons with squeaky wheels, the drivers all slouched over asleep. The camels themselves wear wooden bells that clonk-clonk-clonk me awake at that un-godly hour!

"But only today I determined the perfect solution. When I heard them approaching, I crept out there in the dark and my bare feet, and I turned the lead camel around. None of the drivers woke up, and so the whole train followed the lead. Instead of waking up in the market place over in Little Aden, they'll have all woken up in the middle of the desert, Arabia Felix all around them …! Ha! Wasn't that clever?"

I laughed.

"Yes, but they'll be coming by again tomorrow."

"Well, that's tomorrow! How's your drink? Come on now – let's go find something to eat."

*

"What do you actually do?" I asked the Polish navigator. He and I, and my host, the Pilot Officer, sat together over dinner.

"Well, I'm still in flight training," the PO replied. "Cazyk, here, is doing something quite different …"

I turned to the Pole, awaiting his explanation, and he smiled his gold at me.

"We don't accomplish a lot," he replied. "I go up with a team of six or seven, depending who gets out of bed in the morning. Shackletons. We flew Lincolns and Lancasters during the war, so I'm quite used to these big fellows. Great planes …

"We'll fly out on one bearing or other, and come back on the back bearing. We're over desert the whole time, y'see, so I have to get it right, or we might run out of fuel and we'd stay there till a dune covered us. Occasionally we get to drop a bomb or two …"

"What are you dropping bombs on?" I was curious.

"Well, you know, there are lots of nomadic tribes out there. If we see them, we'll fly over them quite low, just to show the flag. Let 'em know we're there, scare the hell out of 'em. If we see two war parties converging on one another, we'll drop a few bombs on top of one or the other; doesn't matter which. We just keep them from chewing each other up, let them know we don't want that kind of thing – not from either of them."

"What on earth for? I mean, do you even know who they are?"

I was astounded at his matter-of-factness.

"Excuse me," he said, climbing out of his chair. He walked to the bar, bought a bottle of beer, then purposely stepped outside and poured it over the edge of the grass. He returned to the bar, bought himself a whisky, then came back to the table and sat down. His conversation did not miss a beat.

"Well, it's what we're here for. Doesn't matter who they are. Good practice – for all of us: pilot, navigator, bombardier. It's not our concern who we bomb, or why. We're few in number out here, y'know, so we have to stay ready for whatever happens. You'll go into the city tomorrow, so you'll see. The Arabs don't like us much, and we have to stay on top – at least until we decide it's time to leave them alone for good. If you ask me, that's just what we should be doing ... In the meantime, we have to let 'em know who's boss."

We moved outside to nurse our drinks under the stars at the verge of the grass patch. Many of the base officers were there – most of them pilots, and most of the talk was about flying. After a while I noticed that one flyer was particularly quiet – and when I observed him a little closer I could see he was sobbing.

I was alarmed, and caught the PO's eye. He pulled me to one side by my sleeve, at the same time sinking his voice to conspiracy low.

"He was due to go home this month, but has just got word today his posting has been extended. Another year on the rock, poor blighter!"

*

A car arrived for me a little before seven o'clock the following morning to take me to the local army establishment. I was met by the same harried lieutenant who, just the day before, had spoken to me about being understaffed.

There was unrest in the city. Groups of local Arab residents, cognizant of independence extended to India just a few years before, and of movements towards independence in other areas of the colonies, were now agitating to have the British leave the protectorate. It was early days yet. The real troubles were not to manifest themselves for another decade, but even in the mid-1950's voices were raised calling for some form of self-government.

"We've been ordered to patrol the streets of the city, but really I don't have enough men to do the job properly, and certainly not enough officers or

NCO's to take it on. You could help enormously just by leading a patrol for a few hours ..."

Showing the flag, as with my navigator roommate out at Khormaksar; only in the city, though, with its alleyways and narrow deeply shaded streets, it occurred to me it was more like waving a red rag under the nose of a bull.

So I took eight of the fellows who had flown up with me the previous day. We spread out on either side of a waterfront thoroughfare, staggering the distance between each man over a spread of eighty metres; we would walk slowly to the end of each street's significant built-up area, then take a turning and see where the new street led us. Over a period of a couple of hours we managed to criss-cross a fairly large section of the city. Each man carried at the ready a fully loaded Lee-Enfield service rifle, with two or three extra magazines in his pouches; I slung a Patchett sub-machine gun on my shoulder with quite enough ammo to hold my own for a morning's outing. None of us had the least idea whether or not we would run into any trouble, or if we did what that trouble might be.

"If anybody throws anything at you – and they might – chase 'em off with a few shots over their heads," the lieutenant had told me.

"Try not to kill anybody; it would cause the devil of a stink, and things are bad enough as they are. They don't like us, you know. Can't blame 'em, actually, but neither can we have 'em blocking roads and hurling garbage at us. We just have to try and keep the lid on ... We can't expect anything in the way of reinforcements until your ship arrives in a few days. Right now we'd have a hell of a time holding 'em back if something really blew."

Nobody bothered us. It was incredibly hot, and I couldn't help but feel those opposed to the British presence would far rather remain indoors nursing a cool drink; I envied the comfort of their status. Outside in the glaring sun was no place for a mad dog, and I was quite conscious, as I hummed the tune under my breath, that I was no Englishman. Kenya I could understand; at least there was something there to fight over, a defined purpose even if it was perverse. But Aden – a rock with filthy streets, ugly buildings and a population, if I was correctly informed, that was universally prepared to slit my throat. I felt intimidated. The air base was essential for controlling empire, but Aden was not the place in which I wanted to die. I felt great sympathy for the weeping pilot at the verge of last night's grass.

At four o'clock the car delivered me back to Khormaksar, and I went straight to the bar – one for the grass, and three sheets to the wind before one of the eager fly-boys came racing through, dressed in whites and carrying a shiny new red cricket ball.

"We're short a man to field at silly-mid-on. Care to join us?"

There was a locker room where someone found me a white shirt, a pair of ducks, and white shoes that helped me look the part. We played on a sand pitch so that by supper time the bright red cricket ball had lost its sheen, its formerly highly-polished surface now resembling the texture of my morning jowls.

"Good thing I flew in. Everyone's short a man," I thought.

Banker's hours for a little warring on Aden days two and three: off to war at 8 AM. Pack that up for an innings of cricket at 4 PM. Blotto by supper at 7 PM.

Happily, as it turned out, I was not required to make war on Aden day four.

*

The trooper upon which I had a reservation had docked, and there were now fresh personnel to work things out with the beleaguered officer in the downtown barracks.

Jimmy Edwards, the well-known music hall comedian from London had arrived at Khormaksar to put on a show for the servicemen. His performance was to be in the evening, so on that fourth morning I accompanied him to the beach at Tarshyne. He lay his corpulent white self in the fiery sun from 9AM till noon, so that by the time I tried to ease him into the car to return him to the air base for his show he was broiled bright red – the colour of the shiny new cricket ball we'd played with the day before. He was in pain. We headed for the bar where I bought him two bottles of beer (one for the grass) and a bottle of lotion to dollop over the worst of his sunburn.

In the afternoon there was an innings of cricket to be completed from the previous evening, the hatted umpire permitting a liberal number of calls for timeout to refresh ourselves. Without these, clearly, no one would have been able to summon whatever whumph was necessary to complete what was, in all drunken determination, a most serious round of England's national sport.

I shall never quite understand how Jimmy Edwards made it onto the stage that evening. Powdered and looking as chipper as a canary, ever the consummate showman, he and his troupe gave us a rousing evening of songs and humour that kept all of us laughing and boisterously shouting for more. The man must have been in agony, but he was a pro and he never let on.

It was during that show I first heard the song *Love and Marriage* ("go together like a horse and carriage"). Now and again the catchy tune and lyrics of that song – its essential banality – flick across my mind, and I try to shut them out before I'm forced to conjure images of that rock, the patch of grass, the idiocy of those street patrols in glaring sunlight and the impenetrable blackness of deep shadow, the Pole, the weeping pilot, the sand, that bloody rasping cricket pitch and the ball that was like an inverted carrot-grater – and the most colourful Jimmy Edwards

If I let myself go I think I could get drunk on the mere thought of it all without pouring the first bottle of beer onto the ground at my feet.

*

The troop ship stopped for a day at Colombo and then continued right through to Singapore. The journey might have proved rather dull had it not been for Maggy. In addition to troops, service families were also being transported – in this case to such far-flung areas of British military activity as Singapore, Hong Kong, Korea and Japan. Maggy, whose husband was a captain in the Royal Engineers, was on her way to join him in Korea – but when the ship docked at Singapore there was a telegram: he had contracted tuberculosis and was currently recuperating in hospital in Japan. Maggy was instructed to disembark in Singapore where quarters had been booked for her at the Mountbatten Club. She was to remain lodged there until the ship had made its way to Japan and back. Her invalid husband would be collected in Japan – and remain confined to the shipboard infirmary all the way back to Britain. She was to re-board as the ship came through Singapore on its return journey – three weeks or more ...

"When are you expected to report to your regiment?" Maggy asked me as we stood at the ship's rail prior to landing.

Mrs. Queen's Chump

"I don't know if they know anything about me," I replied.

"In that case you'd better move into the Mountbatten Club, too ..." she advised, slipping her arm through mine.

So I did.

Making discreet enquiries, in the following days I learned that my regiment was in garrison at Nee Soon, the barracks at the north end of the island, close to the causeway. I could not imagine the presence there of one more lowly subaltern would be so all-fired imperative, so managed to hold off for the best part of a week before reporting in.

It turned out no one at Nee Soon had noticed.

I was prepared with some unbelievable story about meeting with old family friends in the city, and having some shopping to do for tropical kit, but in the end no such idiotic lie was necessary.

"Jolly good show, old boy! Glad to have you aboard!" the commanding officer greeted me. "Saw your name on orders when they came through, so we've prepared quarters for you. I think you'll find them quite comfortable. Take a day or two to acclimatize yourself to this heat, and then we'll fix you up with a platoon ..."

Um-m-m – thank you.

My quarters were pleasant enough. They were not quite as accommodating as those I had had at the Mountbatten Club, but spacious and airy, with the delicious tropic scents of Malay frangipani and jasmine wafting up from the undergrowth that surrounded the officers' mess.

□

MALAYA

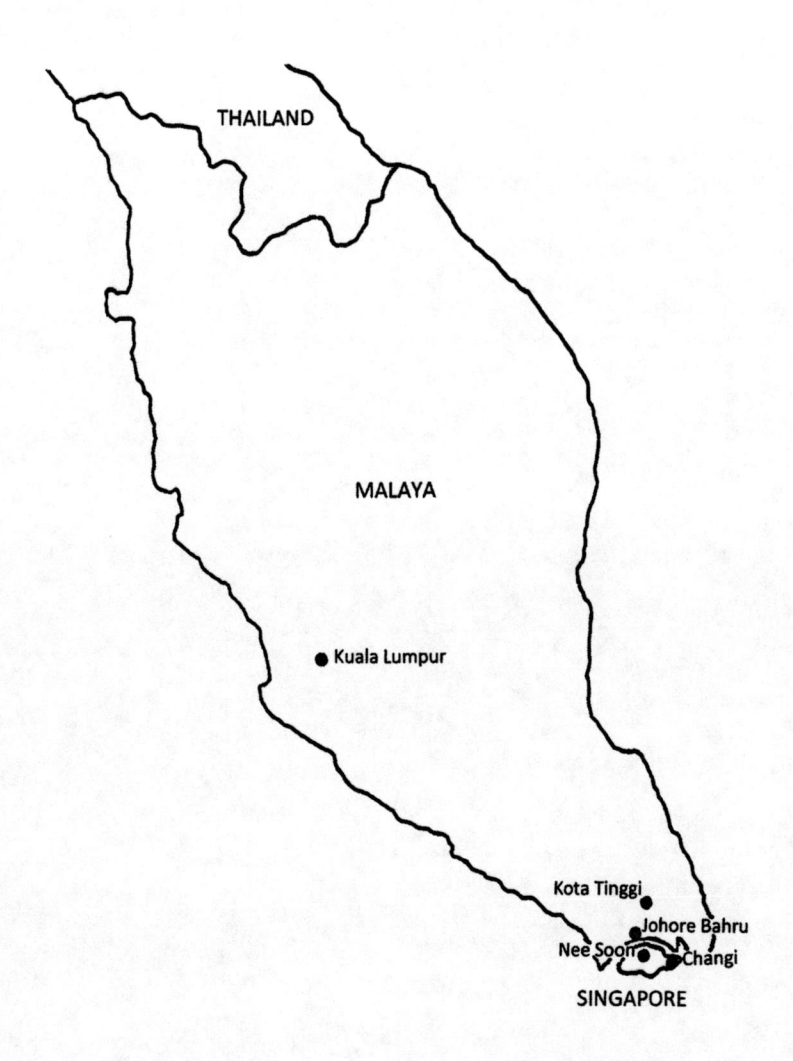

20. Malay Jungle

The war in Malaya had been going on forever – since I was in grade school. So many of my school chums ended up fighting out there that "Malaya" (one did not have to mention fighting or war) was virtually considered a rite-of-passage. In my schoolboy head I reckoned there was something like romance in Africa; when the Mau Mau came along I found the expanses of Africa loomed large and I fancied I could smell the place. "I could be on home turf, there ..." I thought. But there was something grotty and altogether too sweaty about the steam jungles of Malaya. *Passé*, in a way. Everyone had done time out there.

However, as things turned out I was to sample both theatres.

The emergency (there's that euphemistic word again!) in Malaya is dated by the victors to 1948, but its true beginnings were quite a bit earlier.

Today we talk of the geographical entity of Malaysia, which includes the peninsula that juts south from the Thai border all the way to the island state of Singapore as well as the former protectorates of Sabah and Sarawak, on the island of Borneo. In the mid-1950's "Malaya" referred to only the various kingdoms extant on the peninsula that had become part of the British Empire in the eighteenth century. Singapore, separated from the peninsula by a narrow strip of water (a causeway linking them), was a separate colony – as were Sabah and Sarawak.

Japan launched its attack on the Straits Settlements of Malaya in December 1941 – just about simultaneously with its attack on Pearl Harbour. Marching rapidly, or bicycling, south through the jungles, it took the Japanese imperial forces just two months to subdue the peninsula – and a further week to defeat the combined forces of Malaya, Britain, India and Australia at the other end of the causeway in Singapore. Japanese forces were out-numbered three-to-one by the British, but succeeded largely because of prior experience in China and Indochina, and their superior organization and tactics. The Japanese were greatly assisted by British confusion, lack of co-ordination and planning and the general inexperience of their enemy. In the two portions of the campaign, on the peninsula and on Singapore Island, allied killed and wounded amounted to over fifteen

Mrs. Queen's Chump

thousand; one hundred and thirty thousand allied personnel were made prisoners of war by the Japanese. It was described by Winston Churchill as the worst military disaster in British history.

That was about the sum total of my knowledge of the area when I landed in Singapore. This memoir is in no way intended to be a history of the demise of that segment of the British Empire, yet a brief historical survey might be helpful to explain background, and my own small part in a colonial war that ran from 1948 until 1957 – and beyond. The emergency was not declared over until 1960. I was there for the six month period ending in September 1956.

What I did not know then and have been most intrigued to learn in the years since, is the monumental effect that Malaya's (and subsequently Malaysia's) demographics has played in the region, and how the insufferable weight of Britain's racist colonialism ultimately brought about its own collapse there, as it did in other regions of the Empire. The peninsula is presently a mix of three major ethnic groups, each with its own powerful dynamic: descendants of sub-continent Indians amount to approximately eight percent; Chinese, approximately twenty-three percent; Malay, the majority balance of close to seventy percent. A fourth very small ethnic minority of indigenous aborigines lives deep in the jungles and, throughout the emergency, remained loyal to the British. The island of Singapore, now an independent nation but in the mid-fifties an exceptionally close neighbour colony to Malaya, comprises ethnic Chinese by a large majority. Prior to independence in 1957, the ratio of Chinese on the peninsula was higher than it is today. Over the years Britain administered both the peninsula and the island as virtually a single unit (we used to think in terms of "Singapore-&-Malaya") – and managed to treat both badly.

First, a capsule glimpse of the smallest of the three principal groups, the Indians:

There had been resentment and opposition to British subjugation and control over India since the earliest days of the British East India Company, granted its charter in 1600. Sporadic nationalist turbulence is recorded with increasing frequency following the establishment of direct British governmental control – the Raj – in 1858. By the early twentieth century this nationalist feeling erupted with even greater ferocity which the British met with ever sterner measures of repression. Many Indians migrated to East and South Africa, as well as to the regions of British East Asia, where they formed a strong middle class of merchants and government bureaucrats.

Following the Japanese invasion of Malaya and Singapore in 1941, and the surrender of the British armies, fully forty thousand of the forty-five thousand members of the British Indian Army in Malaya – plus hundreds of Indian civilian settlers (all of them taken prisoner on the peninsula and in Singapore) joined the Indian National Army (INA) to fight alongside the Japanese against the British. It was not an easy switch but, in the end, most who took part in it felt they were genuinely being supported by the Japanese in their bid to rid the sub-continent of detested British imperialism. The INA's ranks swelled through recruitment from the sub-continent, Thailand and Burma. At its peak it numbered over eighty thousand men and women under arms. The leader of the India Independence League (IIL), of which the INA became the martial component, was Subhas Chandra Bose, a patriot much revered today throughout India. Mystery surrounds his death. Initially it was claimed he was killed in an air crash in Formosa in 1945 while on his way to Tokyo.

Although the INA was ultimately defeated along with the Japanese in 1945 (several of its senior officers were later charged as "traitors" in the infamous "Red Fort" treason trials in Delhi), as far as their existence and actions were known they elicited huge sympathy in many sectors of the Indian military establishment. The British desperately tried to maintain secrecy concerning both the existence of the INA and the treason trials. In the end the INA cause, and what was considered the patriotism of its officers facing trial at the Red Fort, was instrumental in promoting the Bombay mutiny of the Royal Indian Navy in 1946, and brought about the distinct threat that India's army and air force would follow suit. To this extent, and after the nimble-quick abandonment of the trials, the INA has since been credited by historians with hastening India's independence the following year.

It is argued that the confrontational challenge the INA presented the British gave fresh impetus to anti-British and anti-colonial sentiment throughout the Far East, and that this in turn re-charged the confidence of the communists of Singapore and Malaya – ultimately leading to the British declaration of the emergency in 1948. The great British colonial machine was not invincible. Sentiments between the Chinese defying the British and the Indians who had fought for much the same cause only a few years before were enhanced. Although there were some units of the British Indian Army that participated in the emergency, notably the Gurkhas, few Indian settlers showed sympathy with the British cause or were prepared to fight against those with whom they would ultimately be sharing a common citizenship.

Linked by proximity to the anti-British reactions of the resident Indian community, the story of the Chinese on the peninsula and on the island of Singapore represents a completely different aspect of the imperial saga and its dénouement.

There had been a large influx of Chinese into the peninsula and its islands during the fifteenth century – most of them drawn from a well-to-do-class of Chinese nobility. They settled both the peninsula and the island, forming an intelligentsia that, over the centuries, lived separately but got along well with the local population. This remained the situation until the commencement of colonialism, when the British required manpower to work the tin mines, rubber plantations and gigantic acreages of palm, pineapple and jute. Taking advantage of accumulated unrest in China resulting first from the British-instigated Opium Wars (1839-42 and 1856-60) and then the Boxer Rebellion at the turn of the twentieth century (Chinese historians refer to "the Century of Humiliation") the British encouraged extensive migration of coolie labourers from China.

These abused and underpaid migrants worked the peninsula's mines, and laboured as farm help and rubber tappers – industries that were to prove highly lucrative to British proprietors, managers and stockholders. The largest influx of these disenfranchised workers tended to move into the peninsula's southern regions so that, by the time the Japanese invaded in 1941, they constituted a substantial cultural segment of the overall population. There were few Malays on Singapore Island itself, and there the Chinese population expanded considerably. Both north and south of the causeway, though, it was ultimately the Chinese civilian population, including women and children, that was forced to bear the brunt of racial aggression and cruelty as a result of the Japanese conquest. An intense hatred one of the other was historical, but had been greatly exacerbated by recent memories of Japanese excesses during the invasion of Manchuria in September 1931. By and large the Japanese treated the Malays better than they did the Chinese.

As the Japanese armies were sweeping south through the peninsula the British, along with the predominantly Chinese members of the Malayan Communist Party (MCP), had time to organize an embryonic resistance, amounting to less than two hundred men. They called themselves the

Malayan Peoples' Anti-Japanese Army (MPAJA) – mostly Chinese, but some Indians and Malays as well.

This group had its genesis in the Special Forces Executive which was formed in Britain in 1940 and was comprised of ethnic infiltrators – initially German and Italian – who were specially trained to operate behind the lines within enemy territories. By 1942 this organization was extended to include areas of the Far East occupied by the Japanese. Code named Force 136 in 1944, its agents operated against the Japanese throughout the Far Eastern theatre.

In the beginning these agents faced considerable difficulties in Malaya, but they were tenacious, and able to recruit others to the cause – chiefly Chinese plantation workers and farmers who had cleared lands at the jungle-rubber edge as well as deep inside the jungle itself. Initially they were supplied by networks of villagers sympathetic to their cause. Towards the end of the war Force 136 and its local agents were maintained by allied airdrops. By the time of the Japanese surrender in 1945 its members were highly-trained jungle fighters who claimed they had launched no fewer than three hundred and forty operations against the invaders. Members of the force claimed they had killed over five thousand enemy, to a loss of about one thousand of their own. Japanese figures differ but are impressive: they acknowledge having lost six hundred Japanese soldiers to the guerrillas, and to have coerced about two thousand local police into siding with them. They claim to have killed close to three thousand operatives of Force 136.

The British had been charitably liberal with their promises to anyone who would help them on the various fronts of their war. The hasty negotiations between themselves and the MCP had left little room for doubt that at war's end the Chinese populations of both the peninsula and the island of Singapore would be able to negotiate their freedom from British colonialism.

As things turned out, though, the war shattered the economic spine of Britain, and she found herself at the end of the war greatly reliant on income provided by her colonies – of which Malaya, with its mines, rubber and agriculture was one of the most important. Back in Britain, Winston Churchill issued dire warnings concerning the "domino effect" of letting the communists assume too much power in areas of Southeast Asia. He liked to claim he had never been elected Prime Minister to "preside over the dismembering of the British Empire," and it was his voice and tenacity that was largely responsible for attempts to maintain the status quo. For three years all discussions of wartime promises were conveniently pushed off the negotiating table. Alarmed, the Malayan Communist Party took careful note of how the British were treating the Indians on the sub-continent, how the French were itching to resume their control of Indochina, and how the Dutch were manoeuvring to reclaim their former colonies in Indonesia. All three colonial powers were entirely prepared to soldier on in order to maintain control over what they perversely considered theirs by right. In addition, the Malays were greatly dismayed by the British plan to amalgamate all of their colonial holdings in the region, stripping the traditional rulers of their powers and, in the process, granting full citizenship to the Chinese settlers on what they considered was their indigenous homeland.

The Malayan Communist Party had been banned prior to the Second Word War, but had been reinstated as a legitimate political entity (under its leader Chin Peng) on account of its leadership of the Malayan Peoples' Anti-Japanese Army during the war. Because Malaya's economy was itself in tatters by 1945, there was high unemployment, food was scarce, and plantation and mine workers were incensed that an undue portion of their industries' profits was being siphoned off to bolster the broken economy of post-war Britain. For two years following the end of the war there were constant worker actions, strikes and civil disobedience – which in turn was met with unduly harsh repression by the ruling British authorities. Trained by the British and Americans, and still with large caches of arms and ammunition hidden in the jungles, the MCP decided they had little to lose, and that in any case they were well positioned to take matters into their own hands. They received enthusiastic support from key elements of the Chinese population on Singapore Island. Within a year after the surrender of Japan the Chinese on the peninsula had decided they would have to resume their guerilla tactics in order to gain the political objectives for which strikes and disruptions were proving insufficient.

An emergency was declared following the assassination of three European plantation managers in the north of the country in June 1948. The term emergency was important because property insurance would not have been paid out for damage to mining or plantation operations and equipment had at any time the word "war" been officially applied to the situation.

But it was a twelve-year war in fact.

The High Commissioner, Sir Henry Gurney, was ambushed and

assassinated in October 1951, to be replaced by Field Marshal Sir Gerald Templer who, almost his first day on the job, introduced extremely harsh measures – including tightening up the already existing "Briggs Plan" that forcibly relocated some five hundred thousand of the peasant population (approximately ten percent of the country's population) into "new villages." (It was precisely this pattern that was later employed in Kenya, and by the Americans in Viet Nam.) An immense hardship for those affected, the resettlements did have a measure of success in severing easy contact between the guerillas and many of their supporters, but they also split families, and farmers from easy access to their fields. This measure was followed by a "hunger drive" aimed at starving guerillas refusing to come out of the jungles.

In a relentless propaganda war the two great bogies of the latter half of the twentieth century – communists and terrorists – were lumped together by clever sloganeering. "We will not talk to terrorists" – and in this way the "Bad Guys" were informed they had no right to an opinion, let alone the right to take a stand and fight for what they considered their legal due. In succeeding years "communism" and "terrorism" have been invoked time and again, until today they have become the overarching shorthand reasoning for the capitalistic-minded world to scorn, lie, bully, interfere, occupy or invade. Talk to terrorists? Never! What's on their minds? Not interested in getting into details …

Troop levels were boosted dramatically under Templer; numerous additional British infantry battalions were called into action and, over time, supported by other Commonwealth forces. A regiment of Malays was augmented. Units were brought in from Australia, New Zealand, East Africa and Fiji, as well as several battalions of Gurkhas from Nepal, Sikhs from India, and even the Thai Police. The Royal Navy intermittently stationed ships off the coast (they bombarded guerilla fighters in Johore and Perak). Flights from the Royal Air Force, the Royal Australian Air Force and the Royal New Zealand Air Force were all brought into play for either air warfare or air transport. At peak some forty thousand Commonwealth troops were summoned in a continuous stream to wage this war from 1948 till 1960. Never were they opposed by more than eight thousand "communist terrorists" (CT's or "bandits" to those of us who fought them). The CT's, in turn, were widely supported with food and information by a secretive civilian organization known as the Min Yuen which, despite the resettlement controls, was able to operate from villages throughout the country.

In addition to effective propaganda, Templer's tactic was a carrot-and-stick approach in an effort to win the "hearts-and-minds" of the local population – which is when the "hearts-and-minds" euphemism first came into popular use. Shrubbery by the sides of roads was defoliated; patrols were reduced in size to self-sustaining units of only a few men at most (much as we had used in Kenya against the Mau Mau). All levels of government in the country – federal, regional, municipal – were comprised of joint groups of both civilian and military specialists in an attempt to co-ordinate the fight in all sectors of the colony. Throughout this period the British co-operated closely with senior Malay figures, notably Tunku Abdul Rahman, an exceptionally popular member of the family of the Sultan of Kedah, who himself had worked tirelessly for his people in many roles long before the war and throughout the period of the Japanese occupation.

Elected Malayan Prime Minister, Rahman was able to enhance his own political good fortune by supporting Templer's methods. He offered the insurgents an amnesty in September 1955, but Chin Peng refused to accept some of its terms and the offer was withdrawn five months later. Full independence was a relatively smooth transition of governing powers which was pushed forward despite the emergency. It was granted to both Singapore and Malaya in August 1957, and thereby effectively cancelled out the *raison d'être* for an insurrection.

However, guerilla fighting dragged on a further three years, the communists being pushed steadily northwards all the way to – and across – the Thailand border. In the end it was a military victory for the British and Malayan forces, but by that time I was long gone …

◻

21. Sebastian's Bicycle

My mother had a number of friends living in Singapore and Malaya. One of them was a Mrs. Cornell who had come to visit with us one weekend at our home near Windsor, about a year before I was called into the army. She and my mother had known one another since their school days, and on this occasion she brought her son, Sebastian, with her. He was about a year older than me. The family lived in Kuala Lumpur where Mrs. Cornell's engineer husband worked with one of the English mining companies operating on the peninsula. As with so many expatriate families Sebastian had been packed off to a boarding school in England similar to the one I had attended, and was currently taking advantage of a few summer months of liberty before reporting for his own military service. He would escort his mother back to Malaya, and return to Britain in the fall. Our house was only a fifteen-minute drive from the international air terminal at Northolt, so it was a good opportunity for our two mothers to get together.

Sebastian was fun. He borrowed my brother's bicycle and the two of us pumped our way out into the countryside around Gerard's Cross and Stoke Poges. In this way, and during some long walks through the Buckinghamshire countryside, we came to know one another quite well. The area in the vicinity of our home has been developed beyond recognition now, but for the two of us then there was no end of field and forest to explore. Sebastian talked quite enthusiastically about his upcoming service.

"I won't make a career of it, but I intend to enjoy myself," he told me.

"Are you going to apply for a commission?" I asked him.

"Of course," he replied. "I'm trying for the Gurkhas ..."

The Gurkhas were widely known and admired. Fierce fighters, brave to a fault, backbone of the jungle warfare waged against the Japanese in the Second World War. I was impressed with Sebastian's choice; he told me how his father had been in the Gurkhas, and so he was pretty sure he would be accepted. The British Army favoured links of that kind – grandfathers, fathers and sons, brothers. From war to war, campaign to campaign, it all made for strong bonding.

Mrs. Queen's Chump

Sebastian and his mother left our home after a few days. In the busy round of my own activities – final year at school, holiday in Greece, my own call-up and all that followed – Sebastian's face faded from my memory. It was only revived when, upon learning of my transfer from Kenya to the Singapore and Malaya theatre, my mother wrote me to suggest I keep an eye open for him. She gave me his parents' address in Kuala Lumpur. So I wrote a letter while I was in barracks at Nee Soon, and within days received a reply from Sebastian himself. He had been on operations with the Gurkhas in the north of the peninsula, but was presently stationed with his unit – rest and recuperation, it was called – at another barracks on Singapore Island. It was barely a half-hour away by car from my own unit. We arranged to meet in town.

Sebastian had signed on for a three-year tour of duty – what was called a short-service commission. He was now a full lieutenant – two "pips" per shoulder – in the Gurkhas. I was new to this theatre of operations and consequently had many questions to ask of him, but no longer was I the blink-eyed schoolboy he had met two years before. We met as pals, equal in all but that single "pip" in rank; I was a second lieutenant stationed with my own platoon at Nee Soon for several weeks prior to our unit shipping out to southern Johore. During this period Sebastian was likewise stationed on the island, so the two of us met often in the evenings – either in town for beer sessions with friends from our individual regiments or else at either of our two barracks.

For a short period the two of us lived rather parallel lives. It was the time of Hari Raya Puasa, the colourful Malay festival marking the end of Ramadan, and one evening he invited me to his mess for supper and, after sundown, for a walk on the football pitch below the officers' mess to watch a display of fireworks being set off in the city. It was an extended and spectacular lightshow. We had a perfect view of the entire performance from the high ground of the pitch; an eerie experience because we were located far enough from the display launch site that we were unable to hear the sound of any explosions – a bit like watching a silent film in brilliant colour.

It was a dark night. Right beside me Sebastian was no more than a shadow, his face only occasionally thrown into view by some sudden burst of aerial illumination. I took out a packet of cigarettes and offered one to him. He had to peer closely at my offering before he took it and placed it between his lips. Immediately there was an additional flash of flame as an arm reached from behind us and offered us both a light. Somehow the action was synchronized with the display over the city, but it was so close and unexpected I was startled.

"Good God! What was that!" I exclaimed.

"Lhakpa. My batman," said Sebastian. "Typical Gurkha. Silent like a cat, always in the shadows – and absolutely always at my elbow. Makes me feel quite safe now that I'm used to him!"

"I had no idea he was there …" I commented.

"Exactly. He wouldn't have wanted you to notice him."

We remained watching the spectacle for an hour, then decided to take a taxi into the city – stop somewhere for a beer, take in a nightclub. Before setting out Sebastian thought it best to speak to his batman and explain the man could relax his vigilance – we wanted to be alone. I watched the batman's face. He understood his instructions perfectly, even bowed, but I had the distinct feeling he had absolutely no intention of allowing Sebastian out of his sight.

Downtown was a twenty-minute taxi ride. Both of us were dressed in civilian clothes, so we opted to have our driver let us off in a district of narrow streets, neon lights, bars, clubs and girls – an area quite clearly marked as out-of-bounds to all military personnel. It was known as a rough area, and I suppose that's the reason we decided to go there. The military police had difficulty patrolling these streets. Many times they had been called into action to rescue soldiers embroiled with the local populace. Booze, broads and unpaid bar bills always figured in the tensions somehow, so in an attempt to dampen things down the military simply marked out entire areas for embargo.

Designating an area "out-of-bounds" is rather like hanging up a shingle reading "This Way, Fellas." A soldier on furlough and with a bit of money in his pocket is looking for action, so it's the first place he's going to head.

Movies had introduced me to places like this, but I had never had the firsthand experience of walking through streets so jammed with tinsel, pimps and long legs – bar signs, bar-barking, hawking and screamingly loud music. It was a phenomenon that could only exist at night. Daylight would see the place shuttered up and sleeping it off. But now, as we walked, Sebastian and I – "officers and gentlemen," tough and well-trained warriors, symbols of all that Britain could flourish and shout about to exercise her authority and intimidation and manifest destiny – were subject to the coarsest propositioning and ridicule. Painted girls would step out of nowhere and hang on our arms or round our necks; their pimps would shout at one another claiming the right to our patronage, then grab at our sleeves and try to haul us into any number of clip joints and bars.

"You want fucky-fucky, honey?"

Neither of us were quite ready for this kind of assault, but suddenly we were in the middle of it. The only way we could deal with it was by staying close together, keeping our hands on the money in our pockets, smiling our broad and good-humoured acceptance of all who surrounded us, making the effort to communicate with those who could speak our language, and by doing our level best to present ourselves as two guys who simply wanted to take our time cruising the area.

I was worried and said so.

"Never mind, old boy. You may be sure we are not alone. My man is back there somewhere."

"But I thought you told him we wanted to be on our own? Anyway, how would he get here?"

Sebastian laughed at my anxiety and surprise.

"I could tell Lhakpa a hundred times, and he'd agree. But as soon as I step away from him you can bet your jungle greens he's going to make a big effort to be with me. He'll probably have come downtown by cab, and he'll remind me tomorrow how much it cost him. I'm not looking for him, but I'm sure he's somewhere close behind us right now ..."

I glanced back over my shoulder. All I could see was a street full of clamouring Oriental nightlife. Some people were hounding after our custom, but most were just going about their business. I saw no sign of Sebastian's manservant.

We passed a gaudily-decorated doorway obviously closing off a houseful of illicit delights. The establishment's bouncer looked like a no-nonsense Sumo wrestler, a rather more aggressive version of Mr. Clean. We approached him and asked if we could step inside. He eyed us slowly over his crossed arms.

"You pay!"

"We pay."

He hissed some directive (or expletive) at the throng of people who had clamoured behind us to his doorway. They melted away, and Mr. Sumo spoke to a face on the other side of a hatch before ushering us inside.

It turned out to be a large club with a gigantic dance floor surrounded by scores of linen-topped tables. The place was packed and conversation loud. As far as we could make out the clientele was comprised of well-to-do Chinese. Cute serving girls in lace stockings flitted from table to table with trays of drinks and tureens of steaming food that I could not identify. A lively band pumped out racy dance music from a stand against a far wall. Sebastian and I were shown to a table beside the dance floor. We ordered drinks and sat back waiting to see what would happen next.

"I don't see that Lhakpa followed us in here …" I commented.

"No," Sebastian replied. "He'll be waiting outside in the street. You can be sure."

Roll of drums. The floor show was about to start.

To the throb of some clever drum work an unusually long-legged Chinese lady dressed in a silk *cheongsam*, a plastic smile – and little else – sashayed barefoot from behind a screen near the kitchen door. The smile was a constant, but the *cheongsam* came off in a trice leaving her totally naked save for a whirling tassel hung from each nipple. To the rhythm of the drum she managed to manipulate the two tassels first clockwise, then counter-clockwise. Then, with an extraordinary grinding motion of her pelvic area which emphasized a magnanimous growth of pubic hair resembling a guardsman's bearskin, she managed to get both tassels rotating in opposite directions. Sebastian and I exchanged a quick glance at one another, but neither one of us could thereafter take our eyes off her.

A few feet away from where we sat a group of four or five businessmen, laughing and drinking together and obviously familiar with the lady's act, had stacked a three-inch column of coins on the corner of their table. Spotting this and with a yelp of glee, the lady tippy-toed at a run, opened her legs astride the table's corner and its stack of coins. Extending her arms out to her sides she delicately lowered herself over the coins – still to the rhythm of the drums – and collected the column inside her vagina.

"Oops!" she exclaimed. One coin remained on the table.

Again she manoeuvred over it, dropped down, and picked it up using nothing more that the dexterity of her sexual muscle.

The room erupted in shouting and clapping – and the lady willingly repeated the performance over and over at tables throughout the club. She even took paper money.

Sebastian roared with laughter. I laughed, too – but I was finding it a little overwhelming, and felt anything but sure of myself. No great quantities of manly bravado or confidence here to assist me through the introductory phases of this particular schooling; a hitherto rigidly conservative – quasi-monastic – upbringing must surely have had something to do with my present coping mechanism. This was a lesson that despite (or because of) the British Army's best efforts was now turning many of my previous social assumptions quite topsy-turvy.

Sebastian dug me in the ribs.

"How'd you like to bed a lady who could do that to you?"

"Well, I'd have to keep a close eye on my money …" I replied.

Till the moment of witnessing it with my own eyes, it was a feat that never I would have contemplated or conceived anyone attempting to perform, and I said so.

The lady deftly played out her part for several minutes, an assistant following behind her with a small sack collecting the contents of the till, so to speak, jangling it visibly and audibly to encourage others to contribute. The enthusiastic audience laughed and clapped, and the lady slipped back into her *cheongsam* to take a bow before running back behind her screen.

Our drinks came. Sebastian and I settled into our chairs to see what raucous act could possibly follow that. Again, we did not have to wait too long.

A group of liveried waiters ran across the dance floor and took hold of a large round table which had been parked in an unlit recess of the room to the side of the kitchen door. It was not on castors, but three men could easily push and lift it into the centre of the dance floor where it was to be used in the act to follow and the entire club audience would be able to see.

Again the drums rattled out an intro, which was quickly taken up by the whole band – a fast and catchy dance number. With a shout of "Hurrah!"

from behind the screen, there suddenly raced out a diminutive athletic couple on roller skates. Both smiling broadly and theatrically animated, they were dressed in stage top hats, tailcoats, spats over the laces of their skates and carrying black canes. Holding hands, they sprint-skated to the round table and leapt on top of it, at the same time doffing their hats to the audience and calling out a loud welcome.

To the rhythm of the music the two of them roller-skated at breakneck speed round and round the table-top, never missing a step and performing the most intricate gymnastics and somersaults. It was a wide table, true – about eight feet in its diameter – but that was not a whole lot of space considering the speed and intricacy of their movements. The precision of their footwork was nothing short of immaculate.

This time it was my turn to nudge Sebastian. His mouth was agog.

"That is a-mazing!" he said.

Had that been the couple's entire act we would have been more than impressed. But this was just the herald. There was more to come.

With a shout of triumph the man hurled his cane to the audience, and followed it with his hat.

His partner did precisely the same.

At this the man whipped off his stage trousers and likewise flung them to the crowd. The lady followed suit – and after the tailcoats were also thrown down the two of them, without setting a foot wrong and still hurtling around the table, were butt naked but for their skates.

"Krikey!" said Sebastian, leaning forward. "I think I know what's going to happen next!"

Still circling the table, the couple fornicated right there in front of us, frenetically keeping pace with the music as it quickened its tempo. After several gyroscopic moments of bone-twisting callisthenics, and with a climactic shout of jubilation, the couple leapt from the table and raced off behind the screen. Show over, and the audience behind them burst with whoops of acclaim, delighted laughter and applause.

To say the least, I was surprised. Floored. Biting my knuckles all the time as I watched, I could barely contain my nervous embarrassment – and hoots of laughter. I had never seen such a thing. Sebastian, laughing and

Mrs. Queen's Chump

slapping his thighs, shook his head.

"Imagine the rigours of training they had to go through to perfect that!" he said.

Other acts followed but they were humdrum and rather sordid by comparison, not at all of the same calibre. We left the club fairly soon after that, the bouncer smiling and nodding his cement-mixer-sized head.

"Likey-likey? You come again!"

Yeah, sure. Some surprises are best experienced just once in a lifetime. I never did return to that place; probably couldn't have found it in that maze of backstreets. At the time I thought there had to be a lesson for me somewhere during the evening, but to this day I am not sure exactly what it was. Jungle-competent by training; maybe even jungle-confident. But the ways of the world are ever a mystery, and all the more so to an extremely youthful fellow who steps into the middle of it. At that, I was able to recognize the experience had been a fairly gritty eye-opener.

*

Several weeks after this excursion Sebastian and I again agreed to meet in the city, this time at the Raffles Hotel. A beer or two in luxurious comfort this time rather than a street prowl; we agreed to meet at eight o'clock. I sipped my first beer slowly, then a second. By nine o'clock I was about ready to head back to Changi when Sebastian showed up. He was subdued somehow but wore a rather silly smirk on his face, caution he was about to tell me something.

"What's going on?" I asked. "Did you bring Lhakpa with you?"

"I'm sure of it," he replied, looking around. "I had to pay up for his taxi that last time we were in town!"

We were seated on spacious wicker chairs, and he had to lean out of his in order to prevent his voice booming among the potted palms.

"I'm not sure, but I may be in for the high jump," he started. He was deep in thought and nervously biting his lower lip. Some hint of trouble brewing. Sebastian was a handsome fellow, a little chunkier than myself, and an inch taller. He wore his hair short back and sides, but the top of his head was an unruly mass of blonde curls. I seldom saw him in uniform, but when I did he was a most striking Gurkha officer. Tonight, though, he was dressed in civvies.

"Appearances, old boy," he told me. "I couldn't wait to muck right into this man's army, and now I can hardly wait to get out. Another year-and-a-half to go."

"I thought you were enjoying it," I commented lamely. "With your father having served in the Gurkhas, an'all, seems to me you have something of a family tradition to uphold ..."

"Yes, there's all that ... I suppose I shouldn't complain too much, but to make a lifetime of the army – no way! I quite enjoy myself when we're on ops up on the peninsula, but down here in garrison – it's so deadly boring. I have a lady in my life at the moment, which makes a bit of a difference, but she's married ... and it's proving difficult. Bit hairy, I'd say ..."

I perked up.

"Married?"

"Yes. Actually, that's why I'm so late arriving here tonight. First of all she was so insistent, I couldn't get away; and then finally I had to – quick like a bunny!"

He was smiling again.

It turned out his girlfriend was his company commander's wife, no less. I remembered encountering this story before ...

"You silly bugger!" I told him. "Your company commander's wife? You're asking for trouble ...!"

The two of them thought they had been clever in arranging their trysts to coincide with the major's work schedule – a logistical point to which they would both be party. When Sebastian knew the coast was clear he would ride a bicycle over to the married quarters and leave it leaning against the wall at the back of his commander's residence – right under the bedroom window. That way, if need be, he could exit like a rabbit and make his getaway.

"Bit of a chance, no? If ever you're caught, ye gods! He'll have you jumping all the way back to Nepal ...!"

I started laughing.

Mrs. Queen's Chump

"He'll challenge you ... a dual! *Kukris* at dawn!"[*]

I was having a high old time.

"Don't laugh!" he hissed. "It might well come to that yet ...!"

As I understood the picture, earlier in the evening when the husband was supposed to be on duty, Sebastian and the man's wife were in their bedroom – when a voice from the area of the house's front doorway boomed out "Hello, darling! I'm home ...!"

In a flash Sebastian sprang from the bed, out the bedroom window and onto his bicycle.

I had visions of that much being accomplished in a single movement because, as he told it, he was halfway back to his own barrack block before realizing he wasn't wearing a stitch of clothing. Dilemma: go back to fetch his clothes, or trust the wife can kick them under the bed and continue to the officers' mess – take a chance on being able to sneak up to his room by the back stairs ...

It was dark. No question of going back for his clothes ...

By staying away from exterior lighting, he was able to make his way around to the kitchen entrance at the back of the mess building. He dismounted from his bicycle and was in the act of approaching the door when it opened abruptly and a beam of light illuminated him, curly head to twinkle toe.

The Gurkha cook sergeant was standing in the doorway and though he recognized the officer right away, he hesitated a moment before throwing Sebastian a snappy salute. For his part, Sebastian was more intent on concealing his altogether behind the spokes of the bicycle's rear wheel.

The sergeant quickly understood the officer's predicament and stood aside so that Lhakpa, who was right there of course, could assist his officer by taking charge of the bicycle. Sebastian fled inside and up the servants' stairway to his room.

And so to his meeting with me at the Raffles.

"I'm not sure if my lady will have had the time ..." Sebastian said, drawing in his breath.

---

[*] The *kukri* is the traditional curved fighting knife for which the Gurkha warrior is famous.

"You'll know for sure at tomorrow morning's company parade," I told him.

My friend raised his beer glass.

"That we will!" he replied, still biting his lower lip.

To my knowledge Sebastian was never cashiered.

*

Singapore changed its ways and reputation following independence. The city state is now known for its discipline and the strictness of its Spartan cleanliness. But in the mid-fifty's under British occupation it was a veritable Sin City – much as Saigon was to become during the time of the American occupation a decade later. The term "Sin City" is not intended here as a criticism, but as a statement of the fact that almost any form of titillating or selfish behaviour (bar what was overtly hurtful or damaging) was considered by a large proportion of society to be acceptable. "Bending the rules" – "getting away with it."

"Vice" is a handy catch-all; it encompasses the whole gamut from a *laissez-aller* mindset through to out-and-out acts of self-interest and neglect of the welfare of society as a whole – from the sex trade and all it entails through to sales and trade in weaponry, or the manipulation of corporate and civic institutions and the illicit movement of gigantic sums of money. One of the features of a Sin City, to my mind, is the visibility of lawlessness and general corruption when it spills out from behind the municipality's walls to permeate all of a society.

Such licence in mores should be seen as a feature signal of decline – not of the individuals within the society, necessarily, for they will scramble for their survival at all costs – but of the forces that control that society, which will have become too cumbersome to right itself due to the interests of its component individuals.

So was Singapore in the mid-fifties.

In all hotel rooms, the five-star luxury suite or the flea-infested doss-house, you would find a pair of thong slippers placed at the edge of the bed. If you wanted a companion, you would place the slippers in the hallway outside the door of your room and ring for the bell hop. In moments he would come to the floor, see slippers outside Room No. 000, and knock at the door.

He would ask: "European, Eurasian, Chinese or Malay?" You would state your preference.

Then: "Short-time or long-time?" Again you would state your preference.

Details of the transaction would be resolved upon checking out of the hotel. Costs would be listed against "room service."

☐

22. Ulu

At the beginning of my posting to the Singapore and Malaya theatre my unit was stationed at Nee Soon barracks, located in the northern quarter of Singapore Island close to the causeway that crossed the narrow neck of water to Johore Bahru at the tip of the peninsula. I found it difficult to take life too seriously here. Having come from Kenya where I had led an active outdoor life almost the whole time I had been there, Nee Soon represented for me the worst aspect of military life: square bashing – a continuous daily round of parade square drilling and spit and polish. The evenings were little better. Other than going into the city, the only activity during off-hours revolved around the sheer boredom of the officers' mess bar. Invariably that would risk being cornered by the blather of some senior officer telling and re-telling the story of his Second World War exploits, and how he had (gloriously) "survived it all" to recount his story. I listened over and over to the re-hashing of so many wartime campaigns that, if I had only been drunk enough, I might have believed I, too, had been present at all the great battles in which this or that particular hero had fought and won. Exhausting!

But eventually, and thankfully, my company was transferred to operations in Johore, the area of thick jungles, swamps and untended rubber plantation on the peninsula west of the city of Johore Bahru. We used the Malay word *ulu* to describe this sort of scrubland and rough country. *Ulu*-bashing, as we called patrolling this terrain, was an activity infinitely preferable to square-bashing. At least I thought so. I couldn't have been happier.

We set up in the ram-shackle row housing that had once been occupied by the plantation rubber tappers. This was to be home base for the three platoons of our company – about one hundred men – for the several months' duration of the operation. We had received word that a cell of CT's was operating in this vicinity and there was some fear they might be attempting to cross the water to infiltrate their way south into Singapore.

This entire region is changed now. The years following the emergency have seen much development of infrastructure: roads, hotels and spas where once we had known nothing but jungle, mango swamp, and the thick stretches of *lalang* grasses that formed a virtually impenetrable barrier along the jungle-rubber edge.

Patrolling this country was not easy. The jungle was dense and grew into and up the sides of countless steep ravines. Streams turned into wild rivers, and they into swamplands through which we would have to wade in waters up to our chests. But the worst of all, the most exhausting, was penetrating the *lalang*. There exist many different types of *lalang*, but the grass with which we had to contend formed a broad corridor – a seven-foot tall spread of unruly growth between an estate of planted rubber (often itself badly overgrown) and the jungle proper. It created an almost impenetrable obstacle that had to be crossed before one could enter the cover of the jungle's trees.

It was impossible to cut *lalang* with our machetes. It grew up thick, knotted and dense much as a handful of wet tea-towels might hang down – and just as impossible to cut no matter how sharp the blade. Nor could we easily push our way through it, for the bunches of grass against which a soldier might be pushing was backed up by just as thick a bunch behind it, so tangled and matted it would only give way with the greatest effort. We found the best and probably only way to get through it was for the lead soldier of the patrol to hold his rifle above his head and, using his full weight, fall forward. At first the resistance of the grasses would hold him up, but gradually his bulk would enable him to force himself forward and down, bending to the ground the grasses just before and under his body. The soldier behind would then walk forward on top of him, and likewise he would fall forward. The third soldier would walk over the tops of the first two, and fall forward in the same manner. Patrols usually consisted of nine soldiers, or thereabouts, so that all nine would have to repeat this process until, at the last, the first soldier would get up and walk over those who had walked over him. As he would do this the grasses upon which he had been lying would spring back up into their original state. Within very little time they would completely disguise the fact that anyone had recently passed that way. It was hellish stuff, and there was just no quick way through it. Bulling our way aggressively through as little as twenty metres of *lalang* could sometimes take us a full hour.

And when we were through it – we faced the trees, the blessed jungle.

I felt about Malaya's jungle much as I had felt about Kenya's: shelter and peace. Most people tend to consider jungle menacing and antagonistic. For those who would feel that way, I can muster a certain sympathy and understanding. The jungle is dense and dark – the stretches of it I came to explore in Malaya probably more so than I had found in Kenya. It hides its dangers – snakes, wild predators and creepy-crawlies. But my own experience was generally positive. I found the snakes, predators and creepy-crawlies (except the leeches) were more likely to be out in the open and semi-open country; in the darkness of the jungle most of these creatures would be just as scared of us as we of them. So my feelings of comfort in the jungle were based on womb-like solitude, the stillness of the floor despite, perhaps, a severe wind storm in the canopy. My eyes would quickly accustom themselves to the half-light, and I became adept at seeing into and beyond whatever ground growth there happened to be. I could read the nuance of shadows and see stateliness, even majesty, in the gnarled trunks of individual trees that in all probability had never been seen by anyone before me. I felt privileged to be accepted into such august company as the jungle presented, and truly "at home." The jungle, at least to me, was a state of mind as much as ever it was a physical entity. In my way I think I attempted to honour it. I found the term *ulu*-bashing a little distasteful, disrespectful – conjuring visions of a wanton destruction brought about largely by fear. I did not fear the jungle.

One platoon would always be kept back at company base in the plantation labour lines; the two others would be trucked out to a drop zone, and from there make their way to individual pre-selected points within the jungle. Getting on site sometimes took days as we made our way across abandoned plantations, and then crossed patches of *lalang* to arrive at the jungle edge. Moving into position within the jungle might also take several days as we hiked up- or downhill, or else skirted a particular hill on a chosen contour. Inevitably there were streams or rivers to cross, and on these occasions, admittedly, we expected to encounter the discomfort of leeches or snakes.

On one occasion when I left the company base, I was asked to introduce the jungle to three Australian infantrymen and two heavily-bearded sailors of the Royal Navy, one of them a colossus of a man in (guessing) size fourteen boots. All of them were inexperienced – curious, for sure, but in need of orientation and not a little coaxing. Eventually the Aussies would be working the *ulu* with their own unit, so it was just a matter of showing them what to do and letting them get at it. They had some natural affinity. But the two navy types were different, as out of place as camels at a dog show and not at all easy to convince, administer or command. They were all part of an inter-service morale booster campaign – a "get-to-know-what-the-others-are-doing" programme – and the sailors were clearly operating beyond their depth. They had all been issued jungle kit for this experiment; the Aussies looked well in theirs, but both sailors looked completely out of place in their greens, as though they had shambled out onto the wrong stage – a couple of buffoons interrupting a performance of high drama. My first problem was trying to teach them how to keep quiet, how to keep their voices down and talk in jungle whispers. Both tended to talk above the level of a diesel engine. Clumsy and heavy-booted, they could swear worse than my troopers, and at any little thing they found in slight variance with a strict shipboard routine. Slippery mud, vines that brushed their cheeks, wading in deep creeks – this was all definitely out of the ordinary for them. They were upset, and said so, complaining that the army was not offering them a tot of rum each sundown.

One day, crossing a stream, the bigger of the two sailors fell into the still and brackish backwater of a tiny mud hole. He went right under the dark muck and, when he surfaced, he not only looked like Adamastor of the Deep with bits of river-growth in his hair but was shouting in some alarm.

"What the fuck are all these creepy-crawlies …?" he bellowed.

We hauled him from the water and stretched him on the bank. He was covered in leeches, thin as pencil leads and about the same colour. In less than an instant they had penetrated to all parts of his body regardless of his clothing, burrowing their suckers beneath the surface of his skin. They were in his beard, there was one in an ear, they were on his arms and face. The thing he was really screaming about was the little sucker that had wiggled itself through his buttoned fly.

Two or three of us went to work on him right away, a great fleshy white whale of a man in acute discomfort. We stripped him naked, including his tightly-laced boots, and the first little critter we had to tackle was the one that lay across the bright cherry-red head of his penis and was burrowing into the orifice at its tip. It actually came away quite easily. As soon as we touched a lighted cigarette to the nether end of its tail, its sucker pulled up and we were able to flick it off. But the poor sailor was mortified and looked on in terror, not at all certain what we intended to do with lighted cigarettes so close to his masculine wherewithal. Getting rid of the remaining leeches was a matter of patience, lifting the thin end of their tails off the surface of his body with the flat of a knife (some looked as though they had suckers at both ends) and trying not to burn his skin with the cigarette tips. The critters were all up and down his arms and legs, on his torso and back, between his toes, in his groin, and through the hair of both his head and beard. We must have pulled at least forty off him. Quite the worst of the experience for him was psychological; the depth of the fellow's horror at these slimy little creatures was profound. When we had calmed him down he swore once back on his ship he'd never again venture into jungle.

"Don't know how you bastards can put up with all this shit ... these little fuckers ...!"

"We don't put up with 'em," chided one infantryman. "We crisp 'em up in the fry pan an' swallow 'em whole for breakfast."

"Bollocks! Get me the hell outta here ...!" was how the by now not so gentle giant rumbled his disgust.

He was obliged to remain with us in the *ulu* for another three weeks and, to give him credit, by the end of his time with us he was managing to acquit himself admirably.

Both sailors did have a most useful talent, however. With basic culinary ingredients and a pinch of pizzazz, either one of them could rustle up a meal fit for the admiral, and in short order. We voted the two of them unit cooks and tried to keep them away from muddy puddles.

By and large our guests settled in quite well and were able to filter themselves into the routine of life in the jungle. One of the visiting Aussies encountered a cobra on an afternoon patrol and gave himself a nasty fright. He stumbled against a small tree, shaking the snake out of its branches and onto his back. It was a toss-up as to whether the soldier or the snake was the more alarmed. Tense moment as the cobra slithered off into the underbrush. Other serpents showed up, sometimes startlingly and in unusual locations – but, as it happens, that one (and the dead black mamba I had seen in Kenya) were the only snakes I actually saw in jungle with my own eyes.

So much for myth and terror.

*

Although I liked the quiet and solitude, the air of mystery about our operations in the jungle, it was never particularly easygoing. But I was

Mrs. Queen's Chump

incredibly fit at that time of my life. No physical exertion was too much, and I know now I possessed what I can only call the self-assurance of my immaturity: the mantle of the Gods that somehow granted me both immortality and superhuman strength.

I well recall the occasion when it took three days of hard slogging to manoeuvre my platoon's thirty men into our jungle position in western Johore. The soldiers complained bitterly in the foul-mouthed vernacular of their Cockney origins: the going was too fucking rough, we should stop for fucking breaks more fucking frequently to enjoy the fucking view or have a fucking smoke. The fucking gods should have created greater space between the fucking trees.

But I was having fun, and the one thing I understood quickly was that the complaints of the men were voiced in reverse proportion to their incredible resolve and resilience. They possessed the most phenomenal inner strengths. I was immensely proud of these Englishmen.

Initially we took trucks to the far side of a rundown pineapple plantation – and then there was the *lalang*, which took most of one entire exhausting day to cross, carrying on our backs equipment and food sufficient for a three-week stay. It was another two days' march into the area of deep jungle assigned to us to patrol. It was a complex matter to maintain silence among thirty men for any sustained period, but we had rehearsed our movements for several days prior to moving out and they well understood the importance of stealth. We split into three sections of ten men each, keeping a respectable distance between each group, but following one another in as close to the rehearsed formation as we were able. The lead group entered first the *lalang* and then the thick jungle in single file; the following two groups also moved in single file through the *lalang*, but then fanned out into arrowheads once in among the trees, thus:

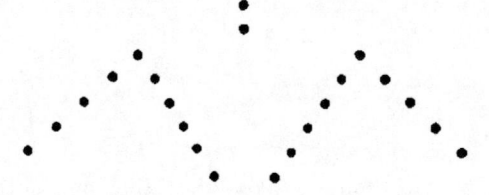

Platoon formation entering "ulu"

It was quite impossible to maintain a precise shape to our formations while in movement through jungle. There was little trouble with the leading single file, but the two arrowheads quickly fell into disarray. The trees and undergrowth tended to get in the way of individuals and disrupt the symmetry of the arrowheads, but in fact the raggedness of the formations worked well. Each soldier making his own way forward, battling against the individual obstacles he encountered before his line of advance, managed to keep a visual link with the man nearest him. The single file was able to maintain the overall direction of movement; the two arrowheads spread out on the flanks, even though broken and uneven, gave width of body to the overall patrol and acted as eyes-and-ears on the flanks of the advance.

We did not assemble at the conclusion of each day's march as we made our way into the jungle. When trying to keep our movements secret it would have run too high a risk of detection if we had gathered each evening as a full platoon. To keep in touch with one another while on the move this way (a part of the manoeuvre we had rehearsed so carefully) the man on the outer edge of each arrowhead would act as "runner." It was his job to make his way to the point of his particular arrow, accounting for each soldier as he passed up to the front. Meeting the point soldier at the tip of his arrow, he would then move ahead and link with the tail man at the end of the single file – who would signal the man in front of him, and so on forward. Having accomplished his task the runner from the flank of the arrowhead would then return to his original starting position. The point man of each arrow was responsible for checking each man on the inner line of his arrowhead. Carried out correctly, all men in the platoon could be accounted for either during the march, or when a halt was called. This exercise would be accomplished by touch or visual communication, in silence and within the space of a couple of minutes. Once the exercise had been completed at the end of a day, the men would hunker down, remaining in position the entire night. Each would eat a dry-ration meal before catching whatever sleep was possible. At dawn we'd all be up, survey the ground in our immediate vicinity, and move forward in the formation we had employed the day before. No breakfast. No prepared meals of any sort until we settled into our target patrol area as a full platoon. Each man would eat the dry food he carried in a pouch – on the move, and for three days if need be.

Getting into position like this invariably involved a measure of discomfort. The emphasis was on stealth above all else so as to avoid broadcasting our intent, or the direction we were headed. Hard to achieve,

Mrs. Queen's Chump

but the idea was that at some point in a time of our own choosing we would appear – ghostlike – in our core position and ready for the three-week roster of smaller fan patrols.

We all knew the CT's were just as clever as we were. Most of them had been living and working in this environment far longer than us, since the days when they had faced off against the Japanese army. It could be intimidating. In jungle, unlike in more open warfare, one would see the enemy only when he (or she) was right in front of you – and sometimes not even then. The first one to see the other – maybe only a few paces away – was usually the victor. Sometimes we felt the CT's might have had eyes high in the trees, the ability to allow us passage – follow us, then follow up with an ambush. By 1956 most of the emergency action was being fought in regions far to the north of where we were, but now and again individual cells were known to filter south – usually in an attempt to make it through to the coast and from there across the narrow strait to Singapore. They were well armed. Unlike the Mau Mau in Kenya, who were poorly equipped and would melt away in order to avoid a confrontation, the Chinese were exceptionally adept in the thickness of the trees and undergrowth. They were prepared to initiate attack if they wanted, and could almost always be counted on to stand their ground and fight back if forced into an encounter.

Our enemies were especially clever at covering their tracks. It was a rare thing indeed to find any trace of CT activity at any time during our operations, and yet we knew (it could only have been our instinct – or paranoia) they could not have been unaware of our presence.

But on this occasion three weeks went by and no contact …

There was a reservoir in our patrol area, the southern end of which ran most of the route out to our company base. I had the bright idea it would be faster to remove the platoon from the jungle by boat rather than spend another three days slogging our way back to base. The men agreed enthusiastically, so we set about building a narrow floating pier of bamboo. It extended from solid shoreline across a patch of gaseous swamp to relatively deep water. On the day we made our move, I radioed to our base for fast outboard inflatables to be sent in, and by the time they arrived the men were lined up on the pier and shoreline ready and eager to make it back to base – and a welcome shower – before sundown.

All aboard for the short ride home – but not quite. The giant bearded sailor who had taken such a tumble for leeches only a couple of weeks earlier, availed himself of this final opportunity to do it all over again. His bulk ensured he was not the steadiest or most sure-footed member of our group and the pier we had built, which served well for those of us of smaller physique, provided indelicate footing for someone of his dimensions, thrust and momentum. Feeling the structure sag under his weight, the fellow attempted a rather awkward run-cum-lunge forward towards the boats – and ran off the pier. He splattered into swamp muck, disappearing into black ooze a few yards short of the safety of the boats or the deeper and clearer leech-free waters of the reservoir.

Unfortunately in this case we could not provide lighted cigarettes while in the inflatables. Salt might have worked but no one in his boat could find any in their kit, so the poor bugger was obliged to wait till our journey was over. By the time we were ready to disembark some of the leeches sucking the blood from his flesh had swelled to the size of his thumbs.

*

Weeks later my unit was sent back into the same stretch of jungle, only this time we were delivered by boat. Nothing had been seen in the area for a long time, and the prevailing thinking was that although it was free of CT activity it was nevertheless necessary we should continue occupying and patrolling the jungle to make sure it remained so. We had to make it difficult for anyone trying to get through to the coast and across the narrow strait to the city. There was some urgency to get boots on the ground, so instead of a three-day hike we dispensed with secrecy and were in position within an hour. But there's a good chance it was just this form of delivery that ensured the trouble we ran into later. The outboard engines of the boats screamed, and must have notified every CT within ten kilometres that we were coming to dust him up. We did not make our camp in precisely the same ravine as the previous time, but the fact we were back in the vicinity at all must have alerted the enemy to be on the lookout for us. It's possible they decided to get to us first – and they damned near did.

We had been in position for nearly a week when, one early morning, a patrol I was commanding stumbled upon a small cadre of CT's – possibly as few as three of them to the nine of us. Each group surprised the other, and I am not entirely sure who pumped out the first shot. I think we had the momentary jump on them, and we should have nailed them – but they had the heavier weaponry and were quick to turn it on us. I was carrying a Patchett sub-machine-gun, a little burper that was great for a close-in fight but had poor range. One other soldier also carried a Patchett, but the rest each had only the bolt-action jungle version of the .303 Lee Enfield. We opened up, firing into the undergrowth; the CT's responded with a wild concentration of automatic fire that forced us to ground.

I think one has to be on the receiving end of machine gun fire in order to learn how to get down on the ground quickly and lie flat. In seconds I had scooped myself a shallow trench and was at one with Mother Earth.

My batman, Watty Watts, lay close beside me. He was rather short. His companions kidded him that because he barely topped the Lee Enfield standard long rifle, he chose to carry the shorter jungle version; it made him look taller. In fact Watts, about as broad as he was tall, was one of the toughest and most tenacious soldiers I have ever encountered. I told people tongue-in-cheek I had made him my batman and radio operator in order to be able to keep an eye on him – but in truth it certainly felt good having a reliable man at my back.

Now he lay beside me, his face speckled with dirt kicked up by the bullets hitting the ground around us, his lower lip jutting in defiance of those who had forced him into this undignified position.

Bullets whistled over the top of us, then suddenly stopped.

Pushing himself up on his arms, Watts raised his head and shouted with a *niah-niah* tone to his voice:

"M-I-S-S-E-D ME!"

"Get down, you stupid bugger!" I shouted, and he ducked just as there came another burst over our heads.

The radio Watts was carrying in a pack on his back was shot to pieces.

Blindly I returned fire, and others of our patrol did the same. We kept it up for a few seconds until we could see we had regained the initiative. Running forward we soon realized how few of them there had been – but we had evidently hit no one. Like shadows, the CT's had vanished and obviously did not wish to continue the scrap that day.

The destruction of the radio set had been our only casualty. A bullet had torn through one man's shirt burning his arm slightly as it passed, but other than that not one of our fellows had been hit.

We fanned out and attempted to follow, but we were approaching unfamiliar ground and ever drawing further away from where the platoon had pitched camp. After an hour I thought it best we rejoin the remainder of our men back at base. They would have heard the shooting and would be on edge till they knew the outcome.

For nearly three weeks we combed backwards, forwards and sideways across the extensive stretch of jungle we had been assigned to patrol. Nothing. Not only were we unable to flush out the CT's who had shot at us, but we were likewise unable to find any trace of them having passed through our neck of the woods. A few cartridge casings from the spot where they had momentarily pinned us down – but nothing more.

Boats were not available to take us out via the reservoir, so in the end I used our auxiliary radio to call up the Royal Air Force and tried to persuade them to come pick us up. They gave me the precise dimensions required for a helicopter landing pad, so I selected a relatively flat spread high above our ravine and set the men to work cutting trees to create the necessary space.

We had only our machetes, and it was hard work for the best part of a day to prepare the pad. When we had finished, I again spoke by radio to the RAF, ordering up a helicopter to take us out. He was overhead in minutes, and radioed to me on the ground. His rotor blades swept too close to the surrounding trees. Broaden the zone by ten feet all around, he demanded – and flew off.

The soldiers complained. They were exhausted.

Without cutting so much as another branch, I called in the Royal Navy. Within minutes another chopper, identical to the first, was over our heads.

"Bit of a squeeze, old boy," the pilot radioed down. "Do you cut keyholes for a living?"

And without palaver he settled his gnat right in the centre of the pad we had cut for him just as gently as he might have placed a kitten on his grandmother's cushion. We loaded ten men, and he lifted off. He was back in twenty minutes and we loaded ten more; another twenty minutes, and he lifted out the rest of us. I sat in the open doorway, my feet dangling out, clutching a canvas strap. It was a short ride. We were all back at our company base in less than an hour instead of the three days it would have taken had we walked out.

*

A Corner of our company HQ

Our company headquarters for several months was to remain this collection of former single-storey worker row-housing – long wooden sheds divided into dozens of rooms, the whole complex possibly dating from before the Second World War. It was set out in the form of a rectangle on the edge of an abandoned rubber plantation. The quarters were bleak to say the least, but over the weeks we occupied them we were able to dandy them up a little bit and make them reasonably comfortable. The large space in the centre of all these buildings (though rectangular we called it "the quad") was our drill and assembly square; in one corner of it we had set up an outdoor badminton court.

The rooms on one long side of the rectangle were occupied by the company's soldiers, and at the far end of the row were a couple of rooms allotted to our Iban trackers – three men from the well-known Borneo tribe noted for its skills in tracking – and (formerly) headhunting. The company's officers and senior non-commissioned officers occupied the rooms along the other long side of this rectangle facing the troops. Stores, the kitchen and dining area, and the company offices took up one of the short lengths, and the fourth length was occupied by our company *char wallah*, Babu, and his staff – mostly an extended family, as far as we could make out. He had a small fleet of battered old trucks decorated like circus wagons; inside these, and lashed on top of them, he transported not only all his personnel but a mountain of belongings. He and his family were camp followers. They took it upon themselves to "provide" for the officers and troops – just about anything and everything we might need. (I am not sure if such service ran to the supply of sexual favours – I had no personal experience – but I would not have been surprised if it had.)

Babu had made himself an essential element of our daily existence. First and foremost, he was our company laundryman and tailor, and in these activities alone his abilities were astounding. He and his cohorts washed the clothing and bedding for the entire company – and we never once received a complaint that anything had gone missing, or that a bundle of laundry had been inadvertently delivered to the wrong person. My own washing was brought back to me impeccably washed and ironed within twenty-four hours without fail, not so much as a sock or handkerchief ever straying. It was not just the officers who commented on this extraordinary feat; the soldiers remarked on it, too. Had Babu been running an established laundry in the city we might have expected something like perfect service and complained bitterly if it wasn't so; it was plain to all, though, that he moved both himself and his family in step with the military company he served, setting himself up and living just as rough as we had to; that he could run a business at all under such conditions was little short of miraculous. His tailoring establishment consisted of an incredible assortment of ancient foot-treadle sewing machines, a nimble-fingered lady or youth on a stool behind each one of them. Despite the fact we were in remote bush next to thick jungle, within twenty-four hours Babu or someone from his family could whip up a perfect suit-to-measure (two pants) and as like as not would produce a pair of stud cufflinks to set off the new shirt you'd be coerced into buying. The inventory of his store (his trucks plus one of the rooms he had been allotted had been turned into a veritable bazaar) contained, without too much exaggeration, a wide assortment of most anything normally sold over the counters of a one-stop department store. His end of the quad was a preview of Exotica: everything he had was for sale, and he had almost anything you could think of. There were all manner of toiletries, things that soldiers buy in all situations – aftershave lotions, toothpaste, soaps, toilet paper, writing materials. There was a selection of civilian clothing – shoes, socks, ties, shirts and even a bowler hat. He sold candy and fresh fruit; sheets, towels

Mrs. Queen's Chump

and gaudy Chinese silk tablecloths; wood carvings, artwork (some of it quite original and of fair quality), knick-knacks, clocks, watches, radios, cameras and camera equipment. Tucked under a pile of records was a portable gramophone which Babu assured me one soldier was negotiating to buy, for he also operated a system of quick loans at low interest – a rather hush-hush operation; the activity was not permitted by the military authorities. He also pinch-hit as our company post office, selling stamps, accepting and delivering mail. Babu, in short, was a master fixer and a most useful person to have at the end of the quad.

One morning I went to him to see if he might be able to sell me a new watchstrap. The leather of my old one had turned green with mildew in the heat and humidity. The metal on the back of the watch was discoloured.

"Leather for watch no good in Malaya, sahib, no good. Give me watch."

He took the watch from me and removed the gungy strap. Taking a pair of scissors, he cut off the buckle, picked up a scrap of white linen from the floor of his hut, and then without getting up from his stool, swung around to his sewing machine. Using the old buckle, in minutes he had made me a double-layered linen watchstrap, complete with intricate buckle holes.

That evening he came to the door of my room with another six straps, all of them with shiny new buckles and fashioned of the same white linen.

"One for each day of week," he grinned. "Change every day."

Tailor-made watchstraps, each a minute and detailed work of art – and now laundered daily (along with my shirts, socks and underwear) by one of Babu's cheerful washerwomen. The sheer luxury contrasted starkly with the surrounds of our location.

On the evenings when the officers dined together Babu would take it upon himself to serve us at table. He was good at it; efficient and not in the least servile. He would bring an assistant from his end of the camp. We enjoyed his chatter as he made his rounds with the soup tureen or platter. Babu, we decided, could do or produce just about anything. One of the officers tested him once:

"Could you fix me a rum and coke, please, Babu?"

"Oh-h-h-h, sahib …" Babu began, as if to chastise the officer for asking the impossible – or the obvious.

He shuffled away shaking his head only to reappear moments later with a bottle of rum and a glass balanced on a tray.

"Three fingers, Babu," the officer ordered, and Babu poured out a generous quantity of dark rum into the glass.

"Mixer ...?"

Without hesitation, Babu fumbled clumsily through the folds of his spacious garment, a rather more-ample-than-normal form of hoodless *djellabah* a shade of dirtier white than the pile of his outsized turban.

"Oh-h-h-h, sahib ..." he exclaimed, dismay on his dark countenance at not finding what he was looking for.

Then smiling broadly once he knew he had drawn our attention, he reached up into the folds of his turban and produced a bottle of Coca Cola. Not bad, for the middle of nowhere.

"Babu! You're a bloody marvel!" the officer clapped his hands in delight, and the rest of us – Babu included, the canny old devil – burst into laughter.

*

Shortly before these events, and while I had been in garrison in Singapore, I had met a beautiful looking lady who I thought had tweaked my fancy, and having nothing more than a rather tedious routine to follow in the company's bush base, I had set my sights on busting out and getting back down to the city. Though lacking civilization's sophisticated amenities and buried in bush, the company's location northwest of the causeway was actually within little more than an hour's drive of central Singapore. I had a long weekend of leave due me, and wanted to make best use of my pass – but without a car I was stuck and facing the prospect of twiddling my thumbs for three days.

Babu patiently listened to my complaints.

"Do you think you could find me a car?" I asked him, explaining why I needed it.

"Oh-h-h-h, sahib – that is a most difficult request. But you have a lady waiting for you, so you must let Babu think about this for a time. It is complex matter ..."

I had convinced myself that getting away would be difficult, for though our position was close to the city we were well tucked into our corner of Johore bush. For some reason best known to young bucks with romantic notions I was, in the case of this particular adventure, pretty cock-sure of myself and convinced the girl in the city would want to see me if I could only get there, all too willing to throw herself passionately into my arms no matter what hour I arrived. I had visions, if not exactly plans, of a three-day leave of sweet delights – yet without transport the vision threatened to fade. Throughout that long day I dreamed of what I was sure could be – if only ... In the company office I was bored out of my skull trying to finish up some paperwork; later in the evening I lay on my bunk in the drab interior of my room. The mosquito net over the bed covered me like a cosy white pup-tent so that the objects within my quarters – table, chairs, my kit – bleached themselves into shapeless things as seen in a fog. For the moment I had isolated myself, dozing off and content to float. I felt an ass for having gone to Babu ... degrading. I wished I had not laid my romantic ruminations so openly before the company *char wallah* ...

There was a soft knock at my door.

"Sahib ...?"

"Yes, Babu – come in ..."

Now I was instantly awake. Pulling the mosquito net aside, I swung my legs off the bed and stood up. Babu still hovered outside my door, hesitant to enter at my bidding.

"Sahib, I have arranged your car for the weekend ..." He dangled a set of keys in front of my face.

"My god, Babu! How the hell did you manage that?"

"In the end, small matter. I have arranged for you to borrow your company commander's car. Full tank of petrol. Better take it and go to Singapore tonight. Tomorrow he may change his mind ..."

I was flabbergasted.

"Babu, I can't do that! I can't take the company commander's car ...!"

Babu looked hurt.

"He's going to need his car. Did he give you the keys?" For a moment I entertained the notion that the wily old *char wallah* had somehow stolen the keys – but Babu was ahead of me, reading my mind.

"I not steal keys for you, sahib. I request keys, and he give …"

"You requested them for me? Or for you …?"

"For you, sahib."

This I had to verify. I would not have dared to ask my company commander for permission to use his car – let alone to jaunt off with it for a three-day weekend. Telling Babu to wait for me in my room, I took the keys from him and walked swiftly along the labour line to Major Montgomery's quarters. He was sitting at his desk under a mosquito net, and looked up as I knocked.

"Oh, it's you Jeremy. Come in … I thought you'd be gone by now …"

"Er-r, no sir." I was surprised. "Not quite yet … Did you give the keys of your car to Babu – to give to me?"

"Yes, I did …"

"Well, I just wanted to say thank you, sir. I'll be off right away."

"Drive carefully …" I heard Major Montgomery warn me as I ducked out of his room and started to run back to my own. I couldn't believe my good fortune. Babu was waiting for me.

"How did you manage to convince him?" I asked.

Babu shrugged, raising the palms of his hands into the air.

"It's easy for Babu to explain youthful officer in love, but not so simple for you, sahib."

The major's car was, in fact, an open military jeep. Wasting no time, I threw a change of clothing and my toothbrush into an overnight bag, raced over to the lot where all the military vehicles were parked and waved my weekend pass under the noses of the guards. An hour later I was taking a shower back in my own quarters at Singapore's Nee Soon barracks.

Bar for a quick one, a chance to jaw it up with a few of my fellow subalterns … telephone to make arrangements with my lady … civvies to sport about town …

Three days of freedom, and I was ready!

*

The lady was not ready.

She had made arrangements to meet with friends at the weekend, and in any case had no wish to be seen riding about the city in an open military jeep. It would play havoc with her hair ...

Could we not at least meet?

No, that would not be convenient. It might have been possible had I telephoned and made arrangements earlier, but as I hadn't there was really nothing to be done ...

"But I was in the jungle on operations ..."

"So sorry, Jeremy. Another time, perhaps ..."

With a click the phone went dead, and with it died my passion for that particular lady – sentiments reinforced a little later that evening by a wild bar crawl through the grungier parts of the city with some of my regimental buddies, and a late-night call at the door of one of the better-known bawdy houses in the district ...

*

Although there were three Iban trackers assigned to our company, we did not always take them with us into the *ulu*. There is no question that they were the finest trackers I had ever encountered. I had worked with them in the toughest conditions, and had also seen them giving field demonstrations of their extraordinary prowess at the Kota Tinggi Jungle Training School. It would have been difficult for me to have believed stories of their tracking abilities had I only been told about them, but seeing them was more than convincing. They could follow the faintest track at a run – and keep it up all day (a patrol of soldiers lumbering behind them). Tracks crossed by both roads and rivers made little difference to them; they would simply throw their heads back, their eyes hooded half-closed, and pick up the pace.

At times, though, I thought the trackers capable of being more of a liability than an asset. By 1956 there were few CT's operating in Johore's southern jungle regions, and often our sorties were little more than an effort to show our continued interest in zones we had previously swept – our presence a reassurance to aboriginals and settlers loyal to the British that we were on top of the situation, and to the enemy that we were ready for them if they dared put their heads up.

The English soldiers did not take too kindly to the Ibans, a sentiment that was oftentimes clearly reciprocated. No matter how I reasoned with the members of my own platoon, few of them had kind words for a people they simply did not trust and whose presence they found both fearsome and repugnant. Morale was somehow threatened; the soldiers were fine if and when we brought along a tracker dog, but when there was an Iban present they became nervous and edgy, as if forced to confront some unsavoury kind of superstition. Moreover, we were good trackers ourselves so leaving my assigned Iban back in base was sometimes the less confrontational choice.

They were a surly lot, the Ibans. I was not the only officer who found it difficult to deal with them. They stuck together in their quarters at the corner of the quad, their communication between one another a minimal series of explosive grunts and silent scowls. They were not in the least sociable with the troops, making it quite plain from the moment they entered the camp that they wanted nothing to do with any of them. On the rare occasion a soldier might stop by to greet them or pass the time of day, the Ibans would wave him off with threatening gestures, pulling ugly faces or even shaking their bush knives under his nose. They wore scant clothing – little more than wrap-arounds covering their privates – and every square inch of their bodies was intricately tattooed with tight swirls of green-black ink that made it difficult for an observer to assess the movements of their limbs. Most chilling of all were their unsmiling faces; here the tattoos broke up their facial features creating disturbing distortions that, on the rare occasion it was necessary, made it difficult to know where to focus when addressing them. One of them had eyes tattooed on his upper eyelids so that, open or closed, a set of eyes would be looking back at you. For hours they would squat outside their quarters sharpening the bush knives they had made from flat automobile springs, honing them like razors. In the simplest of ways they made it plain they did not like to be approached or even looked at by anyone.

So I was taken aback one morning when, just after breakfast, the three of them came to the door of my room, each with a flat-spring knife in hand and looking about to use it. Unnerving.

For a long moment they stood in silence. One of them spoke minimal English and so was used as interpreter when necessary. This man stepped forward to address me:

"Sah! Dewi wishes to make complaint."

Which one was Dewi?

The interpreter indicated the Iban on his left.

"By all means," I said, forcing a smile. "What is Dewi's complaint?"

"Sah! Dewi say one soldier offend him with the eye. Dewi wishes to punish soldier."

"I see," I replied, understanding nothing except that a complication was developing before me. "Tell me more. Just how was this soldier so offensive with his eye?"

The interpreter was attempting a formality to which he was not accustomed.

"Soldier look at Dewi and Dewi not like look. Dewi wants to punish soldier with permission."

"My permission?" I asked. "By all means, but now exactly which soldier are we talking about?"

"Him called Morrison," replied the Iban.

"I see," I said again, more perplexed than ever. "Tell me, just how does Dewi propose to punish Morrison?"

"Take off head," came the reply.

I tried hard not to show agitation. The sun was climbing in the heavens and the heat in my room was already fierce. It was too hot for quick and logical thinking – but the first thing that did enter my mind was that this was a matter for which I might legitimately pass the buck. I scrambled for something to say to fill the moment.

"Does Dewi actually think removing Morrison's head would be a fit punishment?" I asked.

"That's all, sah." Very reasonable.

"In that case, I want you to explain something to Dewi for me, please. It's important. Tell him that I most certainly see his point of view. I mean, soldiers just can't go about offending him with their eyes, can they now? So I want you to tell him ..." and here I started emphasizing with my finger.

"... While I agree Morrison should be punished, there is one small difficulty – and I do hope he will understand.

"You see, while Morrison is a soldier in my platoon, I am not a senior enough officer to make this type of decision. I am not the person to ask. Tell Dewi that he must make application for this to the company commander himself. Major Montgomery is a fair man. He makes decisions like this all the time, and so I am sure Dewi will receive a fair hearing."

The interpreter turned to Dewi and explained the situation. Or so I assumed. For the first time I saw the Ibans in earnest conversation. Dewi frowned at first and my heart raced, but then all three of them came to a decision, and the interpreter turned back to me.

"Dewi agree. When he speak to Major Montgomery?"

I smiled. Relief, but the sweat was streaming down the back of my neck.

"Tell Dewi I understand this is an important matter, so I shall arrange a meeting with the major right away and will send for him."

I waited till the Ibans had left then sprinted over to the company commander's office and laid the full story before him. Major Montgomery agreed to see the Ibans and hear Dewi's formal request right away. Within half-an-hour the three trackers were ushered in, smartly escorted by the sergeant-major and two corporals. I stood to attention behind the major's shoulder. It was, by design, an impressive military ceremony.

Dewi again explained his case through the interpreter, the major in a pose of rapt attention to detail and even taking notes. He shuffled a pile of official-looking papers. When Dewi's story was done, the major turned to the interpreter.

"Would you please explain to Dewi that I most certainly agree with him. Morrison really has committed a terrible crime ..."

All three Ibans nodded their solemn agreement.

"But there's another point I feel I should make here," Major Montgomery continued, nodding his head seriously and sounding totally reasonable as he

Mrs. Queen's Chump

eyeballed each man in turn. It was as though he was trying to draw them all into a conspiracy.

"You know – and I'm sure you will all agree with me – apart from his behaviour towards you, Morrison is actually quite a good soldier, wouldn't you say so?"

The interpreter translated the question for Dewi, and all three of the trackers got a little conversation going. They were warriors. They were not incapable of recognizing another good warrior.

After a moment they began to nod their heads. They were in agreement.

"Even though we know Morrison has done wrong, I'm inclined to think he would be of more service to the British Army with his head than without it ..."

The Ibans were still nodding their general agreement. Major Montgomery's reasoning was sound ...

"... And apart from this, you know, we are rather short of soldiers just now. Losing Morrison would create quite a problem for me ..."

Major Montgomery was warming to his theme, and I suspected he was enjoying himself. He put the tips of his fingers together in a gesture of sincerity as he now addressed the interpreter slowly and carefully.

"So I would ask you to say this to Dewi: he would be helping me very much if he would allow me to administer a more military form of punishment to Morrison – something that would certainly be in keeping with the gravity of his crime, but which would allow me to continue using his warrior abilities. What does he say to that?"

When all had been explained, the three Ibans again put their heads together and (again I am assuming) discussed the major's proposal. Within a minute or so they started nodding their heads, apparently in agreement.

The interpreter faced Major Montgomery:

"Dewi agree, sah."

Suddenly the whole tenor of the meeting changed. The company commander straightened his back, giving a slight nod of head to the sergeant-major who immediately barked the whole assembly to attention.

"Right!" said Major Montgomery. "We are agreed. Sergeant-major –

have these men escorted back to their quarters, and I want an armed guard posted right there to see they do not leave their quarters for one hour."

The Ibans were duly marched out of the company office. When they were gone, the company commander turned to me.

"Have someone fetch Morrison in here – this instant!"

A rather confused soldier was paraded before Major Montgomery within minutes, a corporal rigidly to attention on either side of him.

"Morrison," the major said. "I have an important assignment for you back at the battalion headquarters in Nee Soon. Without delay, go to your room, pack up all your gear – and a car will be waiting for you in the transport yard to take you to Singapore. Do it now. You have half-an-hour."

"But, sir …!" began Morrison, who understood nothing and was hedging for some better explanation. "All me mates, all me friends … I do like it here, sir … Can you tell me more what you got in mind …?"

"NOW, Morrison!" barked Major Montgomery impatiently. "Don't delay! You'll see your friends soon enough when we all move back to the city. Just do as you are told. Get moving, man. There's nothing in all this for you to lose your head over …!"

☐

23. Snakes, Pineapples and Bees

Military Standing Orders were clear: no one in any vehicle was permitted to drive over snakes that had come to sun themselves on roadways. Cobras particularly had a habit of striking upwards at a metal undercarriage passing over them and, even if the rig was moving quite fast, grabbing onto whatever they could. Sometimes the snake could make its way up into the cab and, if it didn't succeed in doing that, there was always a danger that both car and its unwanted passenger could be delivered into the military transport yard. On several occasions the poor mechanic who later had to work on the vehicle received an unpleasant surprise.

We all knew the rules and the reasons for them, and we all broke them from time to time. But one evening just outside Johore Bahru, in a hurry to return to base for the evening meal, I was riding in the turret of a scout car feeling a bit like Rommel in his tank and enjoying the airs blowing about my face. As we rounded a corner I saw a cobra sunning itself on the roadway. We were approaching it at about forty kilometres an hour.

The driver had also seen it. He started to brake, and called up to me:

"Snake in the road, sir! Want me to stop?"

My instincts told me we were travelling a little too fast to be able to stop in time, and that the result if we happened to come to a halt directly over the snake might in fact be far worse. There was not a great deal of time to take stock of the situation.

"Proceed!" I called down to the driver, and we passed over the cobra without appreciably reducing speed.

I looked behind at where the snake should have been. It was gone, and neither could I see where it might have escaped to the verge of the road.

"Stop!" I called urgently. "All out!"

Though intended to carry three, there were four of us packed into the scout car on this occasion. We were squeezed in tight, and it was a bit of a scramble to get us all out and onto the road. Then I tossed a smoke grenade under the vehicle.

The offending snake – around a metre-and-a-half in length – dropped off the undercarriage and slithered away into the bush at roadside.

Not many people have an affinity for snakes, and there was a lesson for me in this brief incident that informed of the lightning speed with which such creatures can move. To be sure I was a little more attentive to that particular standing order from that point forward.

*

One early morning a few days after this incident I led a foot patrol, as usual about nine men, on an exhausting search of a portion of our assigned area's jungle-rubber edge. Again we had received "red hot" information of CT movement. Helicopters had been sent out to scour the zone and saw nothing, but on the off-chance there might have been some activity, ground forces were required to take a closer look. It was a fruitless effort. We combed up and down a strip of abandoned and rugged plantation that ran alongside the *lalang* fringe of the jungle. There was no sign whatsoever that anyone had crossed that way. We were moving light, carrying a minimum of gear – no more than a water bottle on each man's belt – and covering the ground at a run. Had we found telltale tracks, we had a radio with us and were instructed to call for the immediate back-up of a second group which could enter the jungle and give chase for several days if need be.

We covered a lot of ground that morning and by midday we were ready to head back to base. By now we had passed beyond the extent of the old plantation itself and had come out onto a dirt road running off into the distance. For several hours we had heard truck traffic on this road – one vehicle every fifteen minutes, or so. I thought we had better take a closer look at it.

Pretty soon a truck sped down the road so fast that a thick dust cloud was thrown up behind it which hung in the still air for several minutes. All the passing vehicles had been churning by in the same way throughout the morning, so that by the time we arrived the air was thick and visibility much impaired. We were covered with sweat and the fine dust settled on us stuck like the icing on a cake. As we stood by the road several trucks went by, all of them loaded to the brim with pineapples. I could see the Chinese features of the drivers and thought there might have been a chance – slim – that these fellows were somehow complicit in activities we had been sent out to investigate.

I decided we had best stop one of the trucks and search it, so I stepped onto the road and held my hand up to call one of them to a halt. Seeing me, the driver started to slow down, and I moved over to the side so I could speak to him through his window. At that point he slammed the vehicle into a lower gear and tromped on his accelerator, missing me by a short whisker. I had little time to react, save to get out of his way, but one of the fellows in my patrol was quick enough to shoot out one of his front tires. The truck swerved off the road and rolled onto its side, spilling its entire cargo of pineapples.

Hauling a startled driver out of the cab, the soldiers used a bootlace to secure his hands behind his back and around a small tree. That done, another truck came barrelling down the road, its driver showing better sense than to try to outrun a half-dozen weapons pointed at his cab. We stopped a convoy of eight trucks, all of them piled high with pineapples.

It seemed like a genuine movement of produce to warehouse or market, and I would probably have let them all proceed on their way. But the one idiot who thought to take a chance screwed it up for all of them. I reported the incident on the radio and within half-an-hour police and military cars had arrived and the matter was taken out of my hands. I never heard the outcome of the matter, but I think it unlikely there were cadres of CT's buried under all that fruit.

We were exhausted and had a long hike back to base. By now we were sweltering through the hottest part of the day, so I told the men to help themselves to two pineapples each, and ushered them over to the shade of a little grass shack by the side of the road. We could see the police a hundred yards away as they searched the trucks we had stopped, and we were just settling down to cutting open our pineapples when the conversation turned to snakes.

The utility of bootlaces figuring in our minds just then, one of the soldiers diverted the conversation a mite in an attempt to describe what he called a bootlace snake – a notably thin critter, but long like a bootlace and banded by stripes of bright colours. It had a knack, he informed us most knowledgably, for crawling out along the branches of a tree and dropping on unsuspecting victims below – biting at them as it passed. The venom was deadly. Victims would have no more than seconds to contemplate their fate before paralysis would set in and quickly shut down the central nervous system, bringing on death. There was no known antidote, and in any case never enough time to find it in ones kit and apply it ... It was grisly talk. The soldier had an audience, and was enjoying himself.

"Does it look anything like that one up there?" one of the other soldiers asked, pointing to a brilliant but thin black and yellow striped snake slithering its way along one of the poles supporting the grass roof over our heads.

In a flash we had all vacated the shack, and stood about outside looking at each other wide-eyed.

Later, from my description of it, I was told we had seen a krait – a species of snake common to all regions of Southeast Asia. It is indeed extremely venomous, but not with the alarming speed described by the soldier. But then, soldiers love to spin a yarn when they can, and whether or not they know what they are talking about is neither here nor there. In this case he was both exaggerating and confusing his description of several separate species, but none of us was about to hold him to account for that. Even if his spiel was bullshit, we were all thankful it was timely.

At the end of that particular day, it was not the snake incident that stuck in my mind, but rather the pineapples. Thousands of them. And like any old gaffer warbling on about some unusual experience, I occasionally tell my listeners that once upon a time I committed highway robbery in order to refresh the members of my patrol with pineapples ... Gets an audience, rather like our snake charmer.

Platoon mascot

*

Mrs. Queen's Chump

While I'm rabbiting on about creepy crawlies and sundry other give-y'th'-willies beasties, there's a large species of black bee in Malaya renowned for the potency of its sting. Stories abound – one in particular concerning a patrol of British soldiers in Johore jungle who were suddenly beset by them. The beneficiary of prior knowledge, the patrol commander ordered his men to stand absolutely still as the swarm approached and passed close by over their heads. Movement tended to excite them, so he figured if they all stood stock still no one would be hurt. One soldier, according to the account, lost his nerve and attempted to bolt. The cloud of bees ignored the men in the patrol who obeyed their commander, but swarmed on the fleeing soldier. His companions could do nothing for him as he writhed on the ground. He was completely covered by the bees and suffered stings to all parts of his body that even penetrated his bush clothing. In the end the swarm passed on and the soldier died.

Alarming story – one that might have been invented in order to exaggerate the mysteries of the jungle and leave the listener's jaw a-drop, eyes a-bug. Or a fable: "Do as you're told!"

Maybe the story was true, maybe not. But I have seen the bees referred to, and I was suitably impressed.

The manager of a rubber plantation and his family, whose residence featured a swimming pool, invited a number of officers from my company to join them one afternoon for tea and a swim in the heat of the day, sun downers and dinner in the evening. The family lived just west of Johore Bahru, and a few of us drove over there shortly after lunch.

A fairly large party had been invited, fifteen or so in all, and most of us gathered in our bathing suits around the pool. There were deck chairs and a strip of lawn, some umbrellas. It was a blazing hot day, but late in the afternoon the sunlight suddenly dimmed appreciably and a great black cloud loomed over the nearby trees.

"Bees!" shouted our host. "Everyone, quick – get into the water!"

No one hesitated. We all put our drinks down and leapt into the pool – even one or two who had their clothes on.

There was a noise like a steam locomotive hurtling through a tunnel. As though someone had flicked a switch the light from the sun was almost completely obliterated as the bees flew in right over the pool area – millions of them, each one shiny black and about the size of my thumb. No one was hurt or stung, and for a time we all remained in the water to wait for the insects to pass. But they weren't in any hurry; instead they hovered and circled. It was ten minutes before they started to move away and the sunlight was able to break through again.

About fifty metres away there was an enormous tree, its lower branches twenty feet or more off the ground jutting out from its thick trunk. The bees flew to this tree and swarmed on one of the lower branches in a solid body. They were so weighty clinging to the massive bough they forced it down until the bottom-most portion of the swarm was actually in contact with the ground. I doubt if a strong wind would have been able to bend that bough so much. The formation was so dark and dense that it looked as though the tree had sprouted a second trunk. While they were swarming this way there was a notable silence.

Remaining in the pool, we discussed between ourselves whether or not we should attempt to leave and make it back up to the house. It was a dilemma. We felt our movement might disturb them again. In the end we all waited until it was dark, then moved out carefully and in small groups.

All the military officers left much later that night, but one of our number called the following day to thank our hosts, and to learn that the swarm had disappeared by first light.

☐

24. Taking Off

Royal Australian Air Force (RAAF) flyboys were employed as part of an airborne ferry service moving much needed supplies from India and Hong Kong down to Kuala Lumpur and Singapore. They had a reputation for taking risks and cutting corners. A friend of mine, Brian, serving with the Royal Air Force, was attached to the service as a member of its ground crew.

One Tuesday afternoon an Aussie pilot, pressed for time and seeking someone on short notice to give him a hand, collared Brian outside their base hangar.

"I've been detailed to pick up a load of military crud in Hong Kong and wing it down here to Singapore," he explained. "I'm in a bit of a rush, mate ... Can you give me a hand? We'll be back here by tomorrow lunch, honest ..."

The Australian had met a beautiful lady, he said, and she had invited him to meet with her family at their home for a curry dinner the coming Thursday evening.

He was a persuasive fellow. Brian decided he didn't have anything special to do for the next twenty-four hours, so reckoned he could help out a good bloke. However, there wasn't a moment to be wasted, so he popped a toothbrush into his vest pocket and the two of them took off right away – in an empty RAAF transport aircraft assigned for the job. They landed in Hong Kong a few hours later.

The Aussie pilot supervised the loading of the plane for the return journey – a gigantic consignment of armaments and ammunition which the local military types counselled should really only be shifted in two lots.

"Nah – I can't do it like that ..." said the Aussie. "I'll miss me curry dinner on Thursday ..."

So he ordered the loaders to stuff his aircraft floor-to-ceiling and lash it down, figuring he could do the whole lot with just a single run.

Brian told me the loaders' eyebrows were twitching a mite, but that he himself did not feel to be on firm ground in any discussion about overweight.

He did mention to the pilot, hesitatingly:

"I reckon we'll be lucky to get off the ground, no ...?"

"Nah! Dead cinch, mate! We'll be right," the Aussie winked.

Come time to depart, the pilot revved his engines and leaned over to where Brian was sitting beside him, white-knuckled and clasping his knees.

"Here – you sit there right tight, me ol' mucker, and don't take your 'and off of that there lever, okay? That there thingumabob jacks up the wheels, see? So when I says to you 'wheels,' you yank that fuckin' lever back right quick, y'hear?"

Brian nodded, speechless.

"OK, mate? 'Wheels,' ... but not till I tells yer ... Got it?"

Brian nodded his head a second time, and the Australian stood on the brakes as he cranked the engines up to something like full throttle. The plane shuddered convulsively like an angry wombat about to heave itself into battle.

Then the Aussie lifted both feet.

The plane shot forward as if from a catapult. Its engines screamed and the cargo, well-packed in and strapped down, nonetheless lumped itself at least a few centimetres to the rear.

Terrified, Brian could see out of the cockpit's windshield over the Australian's shoulder as the aircraft hurtled the length of the tarmac. Located at sea level, the runway of Hong Kong's old airport ran right into the surf.

Out of the corner of his eye Brian could see the markers signalling the end of the runway. They flicked by – zip-zip-zip – under the craft. The China Sea was next stop ...

"Wheels!" grunted the Aussie when the plane's tires were just about wet.

Brian yanked back on the lever.

The pilot made it in time for his curry dinner, of course – and with time to spare, Brian told me.

But then opening his eyes wide like an owl and cocking his head to one side, he asked:

"Do you know what it's like to become airborne by lifting your bloody wheels off the ground?"

☐

25. The Garrison Welcome

When we came back to Singapore after operations in Johore, my battalion had moved across the city to become the garrison unit at Changi. Shortly, though, we were to be replaced by a freshly-arrived battalion of Australian infantry, and the colonel of our unit, assuming the Australians would be as toffee-nosed about protocol as he was, thought it would be a "jolly good idea" to welcome our Commonwealth brethren with a little pomp and circumstance.

It was a miscalculation that caused all of us considerable discomfort, and cost him a deal of popularity. In order to meet his expectations, for three weeks ahead of the Australians' arrival the battalion was obliged to spend hours each day practicing on Changi's drill square – a blazing sun overhead taking the daytime temperatures way into the high forties Celsius. At the end of three weeks of this crap the entire battalion detested the as yet unseen Australians, and there was barely a man in the unit, officer or other rank, who did not consider our colonel a disillusioned sadist.

When the day arrived for the Australian troop carrier to dock the whole battalion, dressed in their best tropical bib and tucker, was called to assemble on that infernal drill square. We were a magnificent sight, for all our grumbling. Kipling would have been proud of us, dressed as we were in freshly washed and starched khaki shirts and shorts, our brass glinting in the strong light like so many distant semaphored mirror messages. The OR's (other ranks) cooked under their hot blue berets and stood to attention with their rifles at the slope; the officers, aware they were on show that day, donned their natty peaked caps and swung their swagger sticks in spritely style – oodles of pretentious pomposity. (Swagger sticks were designed to exude precisely that loftier-than-thou impression, but were useless for anything else.)

The gates of the garrison were thrown wide and off we went, about 9:30 AM, the drums thumping our stride and the pipes and bugles playing stirring marshal music for the ten-mile trek. Through the streets of Singapore – a thousand men, give or take a few – we snaked our way to the docks to bid welcome to the Aussies.

The sight of us and our band drew crowds of spectators along the sidewalks, but they made not a sound. Not so much as a rustle of paper. Just blazing heat and blazing eyes.

Silence.

No illusion here: we could feel the hatred pulsing from the thousands of people, children and adults alike, who lined the roadways. No smiles. Hunched shoulders and stoic stares. Not a man present in the battalion that day could mistake or ever forget the smoldering power of loathing that emanated from the sullen faces staring at us only a few feet from our flanks throughout the full length of that tortuous march.

We tramped for nearly two hours under that tropic sun without a break. Eventually we reached the port. The Australian ship was already tied up and secured to the dockside, but there was not a soul to be seen anywhere.

We came to a halt and formed up in three lines parallel to the ship's flank right under her rail, the band beside the gangplank at a right angle to the rest of the battalion. Gleefully they played their version of Waltzing Matilda.

When the tune was finished – silence.

No one showed to acknowledge our welcome – not from the area of the warehouses running along the length of the dock behind us, not from shipboard.

Heat. Sun. The men started to collapse.

Fifteen minutes went by – and finally, without a sound, a single Australian soldier stood at the rail looking down at us. From childhood I had always had the impression Australian soldiers rose eight feet tall. This fellow was a nipper – five-foot-and-a-lick at most, his felt slouch hat, its left side turned up to show its brass rising sun badge, looking as though it rested on his ears. He was astonished to see us.

Thrusting his head forward, he peered up and down our ranks, tilted his hat to the back of his head, and mouthed the word "kh-ee-rikey!"

Then with a smile twitching about his lips – the sort of look that sergeants like to interpret as "dumb insolence" – he lumbered his kit bag over one shoulder and ambled aft along the deck to the head of the gangplank, and so down onto our level of the dock.

Now his insolence was truly manifest, for he proceeded (still with his kit

Mrs. Queen's Chump

bag over his shoulder, hat jauntily pushed to the back of his head) to shamble along the front rank of the band – "inspecting" them. Winking and smiling as he greeted one or two of the bandsmen, here and there adjusting a belt or hat angle, he then turned left and proceeded nonchalantly down the unmoving front rank of the battalion behind the backs of their company and platoon officers, "inspecting" them also. He wore a supercilious smile on his face, as if to say, "Thanks fellas! All this just for me?"

The colonel glanced over his shoulder.

"What's that man doing …?" he bellowed.

At the end of the front line of British soldiers, who by now had begun to titter their amusement (none doubted what was about to happen to the little bugger), the Aussie was met by our regimental sergeant-major, who virtually picked the fellow out of his boots and carried him into the sheds at the back of the dock.

Our colonel was infuriated, and forthwith summoned the adjutant and officer of the day – who was me.

We marched up the gangplank onto the deck of the Australian troop carrier, and searched about for someone to tell us where the Australian regimental officers could be found. We encountered a sailor swabbing a deck on the far side of the superstructure. He told us to "take a butchers behind that door over there …" The colonel was so angry he moved as if to hurl the poor sailor overboard, but we followed his instruction and opened the door. There, in the huge interior of the ship, was the body of the Australian regiment of infantry, some lying asleep in hammocks strung between stanchions, some washing their socks in buckets, others strolling about in underpants and singlets, some bare breasted or in shirt-sleeves pulled up at tables and intent on a card game, laying bets …

No one rose to greet us.

"Where are the regimental officers?" the British colonel demanded. His enraged tone did little to coax the group of soldiers from their lethargy.

"Probably in the ward room," answered one of the soldiers, not looking up as he examined the cards in his hand.

"Stand up when I'm talking to you!" the colonel shouted at the man.

The soldier obviously did not quite understand why he should have to.

He laid his cards carefully face-down on the table and stood slowly, rubbing the back of his head. Like the others with whom he had been playing, this soldier was casually dressed and was unimpressed by anyone pulling rank in such unpleasant fashion. He was wearing a pair of crumpled khaki shorts, a shirt completely undone down the front showing a brawny suntanned chest and abdomen. His feet were bare and he topped the colonel by a good three inches. It was hot even in the shadowy interior of the ship.

"I guess you'll be asking a favour of me, then?" the soldier replied casually. "You'd get it a little faster if you'd trouble yourself to be more agreeable. We're on downtime, here, mate, and you should be able to see that ..."

The adjutant sucked in his breath, the colonel glowered – and the moment passed.

The soldier took advantage of the electric pause.

"The ward room is through that steel door," he said pointing, and pointedly polite. "Follow the passage right to the end, on the left. You'll hear 'em. They were partying until late last night, and I think some of 'em are still at it."

The three of us turned and without a word strode through the companionway. My two senior officers, I noted, had extremely red necks, and I studied the backs of their heads with a certain intensity, looking for small puffs of smoke emanating from their ears ... As the most junior of junior officers I deemed it best to remain neutral, and to utter not the least comment. The soldier's brass had been well shined; I could never have summoned the guts to speak quite so irreverently to a senior officer, but that particular Australian left an impression on me.

The ward room door proved to be a substantial soundproofing. From the corridor we could hear subdued voices when it was closed; when we opened it, the noise was like New Year's in Trafalgar Square. There was a distinct stench of stale beer, and the air itself was dense with a full shift of cigarette smoke. Some twenty men were gathered about in various states of informal undress, and the camaraderie between them all made it difficult to be able to discern any difference in rank, or even between soldier and sailor. It was clear this was something of a farewell party between the ship's complement and the regimental officers, and that it had begun at least the night before.

Our small party, dressed in somewhat more formal attire, was distinctly at odds with the ambient of the room. An Australian lieutenant approached and assisted in singling out the commander of his regiment.

An affable fellow, the Australian commander professed no knowledge at all that he and his men were to be met by a Commonwealth delegation – in the form of an entire British garrison. Beer bottle in hand, he stepped out on deck with the British officers and looked over the rail. Below him, in three ranks stretching two hundred metres up the entire length of the dock, were the exhausted, heat-stricken, demoralized and by now somewhat embittered members of one of Britain's oldest and proudest regiments of foot, the band of which might yet have attempted, if requested, to strike up one more rendering of Waltzing Matilda.

"Kh-ee-rikey!" I heard the Aussie colonel exclaim.

The band did not strike up. Instead, the three British officers marched back down the gangplank and resumed their places within the formation of the battalion.

Without further ado orders were barked out for the entire troupe to move off – to nothing more than the rattle of a single side drum. And so, hang dog and in silence, all the way back to Changi.

☐

26. Mess

Military officers romping with one another during their free time should be filmed, then later (to sober them up) tied to their chairs and compelled to watch the questionable maturity of their antics.

It was one thing to see inside an officers' mess when there were ladies present. The members would be on their best behaviour and for the most part those present would make an effort to act like intelligent – even noble – human beings. But it was when they were on their own that the seemly turned unseemly. Then Bacchus himself might have sallied forth from the hidey-hole of his cave of delights, dancing and frolicking and casting his irresistible spells of temptation, so that it would take only a couple of fingers of what'll-ye-have for an otherwise debonair gentleman of courtly graces to run amok like a satyr at a girls' pajama party. Quite another psyche, one hidden in boyish shames, would take over and dominate all aspects of such an evening. Were small children to behave as these officers and gentlemen were wont to do on such occasions, they would be reprimanded or sent to their rooms without their supper.

The occasion for such behaviour was invariably after "dining-in" nights – the evenings when, after a battalion officers' dinner with no ladies present, and the assembly was well drunken, the lid was removed from a Jack-in-the-Box of sillinesses.

In somber tones the antics performed were passed off as "mess games."

Examples:

Getting around the walls of the dining hall without touching the floor: those participating, usually junior officers egged on by their seniors, would doff their jerkins and shoes, roll up their shirt sleeves, and attempt by any means to do just that. They would walk on the furniture, swing on curtains, curtain rods or pelmets, shunt chairs about by sitting on one and then transferring to another, or by scooting a chair across polished flooring – officer aboard. The efforts were keenly adjudged by the seniors present, the junior completing the task in the shortest time winning the game. But as a result the hall would be turned into a shambles. An evening of these antics, and the expensive furniture of the officers' mess would look about as inebriated as those who had abused it.

Ships and sailors: this game was a big boys' variant of a children's camp game. There would be a caller, usually a senior officer, who would shout out commands the participants would have to obey. The word "ships" meant you had to go down on all fours; "sailors" meant you had to find a partner to ride on your back. "Hit the deck" meant lie down flat on the floor; "man overboard" meant one man on all fours, another man standing on his back in the pose of lookout. "Three men rowing," meant that an instant partnership of three had to be formed to sit on the floor pretending to row; "four men rowing" was the same, but with a partnership of four. There were numerous commands, all of them idiotic, and the point was to catch out people coming in last, or dawdling. It was a much rougher and more brutal version of the popular parlour game "musical chairs," except the music in these games would be the drunken heaving, hefting, pushing, shoving, shouting and swearing of robust grown men letting themselves go. Imagine a group of forty officers playing this childish game with gusto and it is not hard to picture the state of a dining hall (or the officers themselves) at the end of it.

Cabbage football was popular, often played (without rules) with senior officers on one side, juniors on the other. Several cabbages would be required. For aficionados of rugby a similar game of touch-rugby was sometimes substituted, although the similarity of play combined with the confines of the dining hall often made it difficult to tell which game was actually being indulged. Likewise, dining chair polo was a favourite – wooden spoons or canes as polo sticks, an orange, lemon or pomegranate for a ball. Officers would seat themselves backwards astride their chairs and walk – "gallop" – their ponies forward, sideways or to the rear leaning (or swinging) on the back of their seats to take a whack at either ball or competitor. This activity was especially hard on furniture and flooring.

In the 1840's the troopship *Borboleta* was steaming homeward across the Indian Ocean with a full complement of soldiers and their families who had just finished up several years of their service contracts on the Northwest Frontier. A few days out of Bombay there was a fire on board, and the order was given to abandon ship – women and children first. There was insufficient room for everybody in the lifeboats as the ship was going down, so all officers and men of the regiment were called to assemble in formation on the main deck while the regimental band played hymns and stirring marshal music. Later reports of survivors related how the entire regiment had stood to attention, the commanding officer saluting, as the waters closed over the ship and the sharks finished off any who might have bobbed to the surface. Each year after this tragedy the regiment celebrated "Borboleta Day" – and on that anniversary in 1956 I was present when the junior officers of the regiment, following a mess dinner, invented the "Borboleta Game."

This activity was carried out in all solemnity: the six gigantic fans that normally swirled ceaselessly along the entire length of the dining hall, wafting the tropical airs from one end to the other, were shut down. Glasses of beer were then placed along the blades of each of the stationary fans, and all the regimental officers stood unmoving and to attention in small circles under each unit as the ship was toasted.

On command, the fans were switched on.

The destruction was colossal – beer and broken glass flew into all corners of the room. When the fans were eventually shut off again, the adjutant called for three cheers for the regiment.

Mess orderlies, as was usual whenever one of these farragoes got under way, were instructed to have the room shipshape by breakfast the following day.

There were those who adhered to the notion that such high jinx were good for morale, *esprit de corps*, and who is to deny it when everyone from the seniors in command on down condone such behaviour? The sad reflection of a thinking man might be that it was these same buffoons who commanded their juniors so bravely in the field, with the resultant often bullish – *"charge!"* – attitudes that frequently resulted in wanton and unnecessary destruction. For myself (and I was, if I may claim it, by no means a goody-goody) I can now say unequivocally that never, by any remote concept, did I consider such mess downtime substantial or fulfilling, challenging or useful – or even "fun," really.

There were periodic cricket matches, usually between officers of one regiment and another. Seldom would other ranks participate in what was, in effect, an officers' only get-together.

Good cricket can be exciting; bad cricket excruciatingly tedious. Such is particularly the case when some enthusiast out on the edge of the boundary incessantly claps his hands and woofs inebriated encouragement like a hound baying among garbage cans two blocks away. The encouragement does nothing whatsoever to improve the bowler's bowling, the batsman's batting,

Mrs. Queen's Chump

or the level of play generally.

"Good show, old boy – good show!"

The first "good show" would waft hollowly across a stagnant pitch, punctuated now and then by the clack of ball on bat; the second "good show" might be drowned in the suds of the caller's cup-in-hand.

Cricket grounds of sorts had been set up at both Nee Soon and Changi. And in both, as I recall, spreads of open green weed-field were set aside to be used for nothing much except this plaintive effort at British flag-waving during the cricketing season – which was most of the time the sun was out and there wasn't any other work to be done. Then these grounds would be identifiable as playing fields by the array of great white marquees set up along their verges – always at least one tent (sometimes two) harbouring a well-stocked bar, the rest little more than shelters from a sweltering sun where one could nurse one's drink in shade and contemplate the next one.

Imported bottled beer was always available – never draft, much to our dismay – but I always found beer to be a heavy drink to manage in the roaring heat of a Singapore afternoon. Many of us settled for shandy (and lots of 'em) during the hottest portion of a day, a mix of beer and ginger ale, or beer and lemonade. By four o'clock this would be substituted by "gin and it" – a goodly three fingers of gin, with a splash of Italian vermouth or soda. By six o'clock no one, not spectator, not player, would be drawing sober breath.

"Mess" became synonymous with "bar," and I am convinced that had I remained longer in the army than I did I would have become an alcoholic before my twenty-fifth birthday.

Inter-regimental association was not infrequent, and one of the closest to our Singapore garrison was a popular unit of Nepalese Gurkhas. One of our senior officers several times wanted to invite them over to play cricket and was chagrined when told it was "not quite their cup of tea, old boy." The fellow thought they should learn, that it would be to their ultimate benefit, and that if the Gurkhas were such jolly good chaps (which was the word going about) they would be happy to take up the game and show the rest of us they weren't just tribal misfits from the mountains trying to muscle in on an essentially English way of life. They should be obliged, he thought, to make a sincere effort to play "our" game. Cricket, after all, is the very sport that marks one able (or not) to rise above the herd to the level of an English gentleman – even if a bit short in stature and tinted a slightly different shade. Not quite English, old boy, but at least the Indians are prepared to give it a good try, and they've mastered the game alright ... not too bad at it either, actually, which only goes to show ... Anyway "these little beggars" should do the same, wot! Teach a man to play cricket and you teach him how to turn himself into the kind of chap you don't mind taking back to the club ...

But cricket was not the Gurkha way, as many of us and this particular individual were shortly to learn.

Today Gurkha units serve in the armies of several nations. Their overall temperament and military accomplishments are particularly revered in the British Army, with whom they have fought side-by-side since the beginning of the nineteenth century. The best of my own encounters with them was limited to a brief period at the Kota Tinggi Jungle Training School in southeastern Johore where a number of British and Commonwealth troops were amazed by the Gurkhas' demonstrations of bush craft – their ability to move through thick underbrush without making a sound. The skills they displayed with their knives – the *kukri* – were frightening, cutting through a bamboo thicket as if it was soft butter.

Small of stature but powerfully built, the Gurkha soldier is invariably affable and good humoured, smiles easily, takes his orders without question and is unfailingly polite. Each member of a Gurkha unit has been carefully selected. Nepalese tribesmen of a traditionally warrior disposition, they consider it an honour to be chosen to serve; thousands will apply each year to be accepted for the special training that will permit them to seek entry into the British army – fewer than three hundred will be chosen. To make sure an applicant is up to snuff before he so much as dares to apply, senior members of his own warrior caste will test each applicant – an exam that involves the greatest strength and endurance. One aspect of the selection process involves the applicant being timed racing up a steep mountain gradient carrying a load of seventy pounds of rocks in a basket on his back – the only assist being a supporting strap around his forehead.

One afternoon a small group of Gurkhas did take us up on an invitation – not to play cricket but to meet and mix, mostly for them to demonstrate their gymnastic agilities and prowess with the *kukri*. It was a festival day for them, and so many of us were curious. Not knowing quite what to expect, we trundled along to the cricket grounds and took our places on seats that had been arranged as an amphitheatre. At the outset there was the usual

Mrs. Queen's Chump

round of rousing speeches – British officers lauding the accomplishments of the Gurkha units they had known. Many of us quietly took advantage of the moment to make a beeline for the bar tent on the edge of the green, returning to our seats just in time to watch some of the ceremonial dancing.

By the time the afternoon's activities had picked up a bit of steam a group of my friends and I had already made several sorties to the bar. We wobbled back to our seats to see what was going to happen next. Right in front of us a group of Gurkha riflemen was driving four stout wooden pegs deep into the soft earth, corners of a small rectangle. Each shaft showed about two feet above ground.

Mystery – but then we understood what it was for: a buffalo was led onto the field and each of his legs was tethered to one of the posts rendering him absolutely unable to move. For a moment the beast heaved and tugged but then realized there was no point, so stood there slowly turning its head from side-to-side looking at us. We could see it was a young animal, but even so it was well developed – its neck easily the thickness of a stout man's torso.

A Gurkha sergeant stepped forward and saluted our senior officers. He then removed his hat and jerkin and handed them to an orderly standing off to his side. In return he accepted a white smock which he donned, slipping it over his head and tying it neatly around his waist. Reaching behind and under his smock, he drew his *kukri* and stepped forward to the buffalo, presenting its blade to the animal's nose – a movement of honour, a salute. He then stepped back to just under arm's length from the animal, braced his legs and with a piercing yell brought the blade down on the creature's neck.

The buffalo's legs suddenly stiffened as its head rolled forward and broke clean from the body. Blood splashed onto the grass, the gigantic head tumbling into the gore. For a moment the body quivered, still upright, but then sagged to one side, prevented from falling by the way in which its legs had been so tightly tethered to the four posts driven into the ground.

"Oh dear…!" said one of the senior officers, both surprised and aghast at what he had just seen.

Other seniors had known what to expect and applauded politely.

"Bravo!" cried one.

"Jolly good show, wot!" said another as though he had just witnessed a good cricketer at bat.

At that point I gulped downed the last of the shandy in my glass and headed back to the bar.

Later I had the chance to enquire about the details of the ritual I had witnessed, but never received a satisfactory answer. I was told that in the month of October many Gurkhas back in Nepal would celebrate a ritual they called *dasain* in which they would perform a sacrifice much as we had seen – usually with goats. Our event had taken place far too early in the year for this to have been *dasain*, but I was informed that we may have been watching another less important festival – *chaite dasain* – in which buffaloes are indeed the more common sacrificial animal.

In the end, though, I had to be satisfied with incomplete information, and the impression that this particular afternoon's demonstration had been conducted purely as a means of impressing the British officers. Impressing them or scaring them to death, I'm not sure which.

□

27. Train to Kuala Lumpur

The CT's were acknowledged, albeit grudgingly, for their extraordinary audacity. One of their favourite and more regular exploits was to attack the train that chuffed its way between Singapore and Kuala Lumpur. In the early days the usual pattern was to blow the track and, once the train had been brought to a halt or derailed, to rake it with machine gun fire. It was a vital link on the peninsula's south-north axis and as there was no end of opportunity along the track to create havoc through ambush (the line was bordered over much of its route by thick jungle) about the only response the British could come up with was obvious: to defoliate as far back as possible, and arm the train like a belligerent porcupine.

Over the years the communists had been obliged to learn any attack on the train brought about a swift and vigorous backlash; once a train had been forced to halt, any thought of opening up with machine guns had to be tempered by the rapidity of the British retaliation. Cadres of well-equipped soldiers would leap to the ground to give chase, into the jungle and often for days at a time if need be. The soldiers on the CT's heels would be adept at tracking, and there would be lots of them. The speed of such British response operations had some lasting success; they could not altogether stop trains from being derailed, but the machine-gunning was greatly reduced. Dynamiting a train track could be accomplished pretty much at will, but it takes time to set up and dismantle a machine gun post, or even to disburse a team of sub-machine gunners. Such tactics invariably instigated pitched battles, which the CT's soon learned were best avoided. With the trains now defended by well-prepared troops, any group of dynamiters hanging about to deliver a *coup de grâce* by machine gun ran the risk of being caught. They would have to be more than just a little nimble if they hoped to do serious damage to train and track, have their bout of machine gunning and still give themselves sufficient time to escape instant and heavy retribution.

Well-planned derailments did continue, however, despite British efforts to patrol and clear nearby jungle.

If and when needed, relief trains would be sent along the line – from either end. These would be equipped with the necessary gear to clear and mend track, collect stranded passengers and resupply troops. Travel on the

Singapore-to-Kuala Lumpur train was considered hazardous, so Standing Orders decreed all military personnel using the line must be armed and in uniform.

One of my mother's friends lived with her family in Kuala Lumpur and invited me to come north for her daughter's twenty-first birthday party. I accepted, donned my snappiest military uniform, buckled a pistol in its holster to my Sam Browne belt to ensure I complied with Standing Orders, and packed a bow tie and white sharkskin dinner jacket into a duffle bag.

The run north was an overnight journey. All officers were obliged to travel first class – two passengers to a compartment. The railway had a quaint system of welcoming its esteemed guests: the name of each first class passenger was posted on the door of the cubicle in a small and highly polished brass-framed bracket. I humped my bag along the platform trying to find the correct coach; both platform and the corridors of the train were swarming with white-robed Muslim pilgrims heading north and it was only with the greatest difficulty I eventually found my accommodation and saw by the plaque I was to be sharing it with a Mr. Lee.

It was fairly late in the evening so the train staff had already made up the bunks for the night. Seated on the lower bed was the oldest man I'd ever seen, at least up to that point of my life. He was Chinese, dressed entirely in white and with the whitest of thin white hair. His leathery animated face, creased and crumpled like a ball of scrunched-up brown wrapping paper, looked as though it had survived a long lifetime of bad accidents.

Instantly and without the slightest good reason I could think of, I wanted nothing to do with Mr. Lee. It was a visceral thing. In the years between then and now I have attempted to pinpoint why I felt that way, and so suddenly, and I have never been able to come up with a logical explanation for such antipathy. I was narrow, full of the pre-conceived ideas formed during my sheltered schooling – and in situations about which I knew nothing at all I had a brain box filled with a fairly warped and cockeyed confidence. I think of it as something like the little man who becomes aggressive when he knows he can't compete honestly. In addition, I had virtually no experience in mastering the more subtle of social encounters. I had been well trained – "carefully taught," as the song puts it. I had been through an education that championed empire and encouraged elitism. In the end an inculcated sense of superiority is about the only excuse I have for the feelings I now find it so difficult and almost too embarrassing to clarify. Yet only a few short months before I had arrived from Africa where I had had extremely close relationships with the *askaris* serving under me – and a particularly precious friendship with Nyamahanga Boke, the Number Two of my own platoon. In Africa I never felt anything like the antagonism that coursed through me on the instant of walking into that railway cabin and finding Mr. Lee. I had seen and recognized the brutishness of human differences in Africa – raw racism – and had thought myself immune; in no way did I feel in the least threatened. But here in Asia I was encountering something else, or so I thought – and it was. Here I encountered a finer layer of sheer bull – and it was, indeed, extremely threatening. Here the carefully-fostered British mentality of sovereignty was confronted by a people it could easily identify as culturally equal, and possibly even superior. In Africa it was simple, even rational: whites had always considered the Africans inferior. But in Asia anything as challenging or even remotely resembling equality to whites was a most unpopular notion; admitting such a thing could not only mean loss of face, but the loss of any justifiable reason to hold on – and dominate – in this part of the world. Here, far more than in Kenya, the British were confronted by a strong and rational opposition their own intelligence could not deny – no matter what stretch of rationalization was on offer. Racism was the only logical recourse!

I have been in dicey situations at various times in my life but seldom have I been faced by such a deep personal dilemma. It was fear, in fact. There have been a couple of near-drowning experiences that left me quaking in my boots, and that occasion (described earlier) when I had a machine gun firing at me from a few paces to my front. (I have to think the triggerman missed only because he was quite as fearful of me as I was of him.) I experienced fear on those occasions, of course, but it was not the same nauseating fear I felt the moment I saw Mr. Lee. I could well identify the sentiment I knew was in me, but not its reason. Instinctively I saw him as my enemy, a fifth column, and yet here he was sitting in the first class situation I had reserved for myself, presenting himself graciously and openly in all respects. I did not know the word paranoia in those days but here was a man who, with the utterance of barely a word, was managing quite well to define it for me.

"You must be the gentleman whose name is on the door," he said gently. "Mine is there, too – my name is Mr. Lee. I am honoured to meet you."

I spluttered the kind of answer I hoped would not reveal the apprehension I felt in my bowel.

"Ah!" smiled Mr. Lee, his face following me like a sunflower.

In the moment I stepped across the threshold of the small space we shared he looked deep inside me. I could sense it and felt both unnerved and awkward. I could not bring myself to speak. In that instant I knew he understood my confusion, yet he was quite at ease with the mere spark of interaction that had flared between us. It was as if he was sitting on the end of my nose, able to winkle out the thoughts in my mind before I had thoroughly thought them through myself. I am sure we both felt the tension, though I dare say he comprehended it better than I could just then. There was nothing easy about our communication. There were long gaps, spaces when both of us faced one another but neither spoke. He crossed his boney hands in front of his chest, rocked slowly back and forth. Little bows.

"You cannot see my eyes the way I see yours!" he said at last, which was exactly what I had been thinking. I hadn't realized he had been scrutinizing me.

"I see well for my age, but I am an old man, and my eyes are hidden deep inside these Chinky-Chinee slits." He was smiling.

I was flustered, could not see his eyes at all in fact. Didn't want to. Where they should have been were two dark slashes across his ancient craggy face. I needed to be anywhere else, and he knew it.

"I am a most inscrutable Oriental! Ha! Ha! You probably do not know many Chinese, do you Mr. Hespeler-Boultbee ...?"

He said other things to me that were not without humour and kindness, but they did not alleviate my anxiety. Instinctively I recoiled from this man, knowing he possessed a most complete understanding of my discomfort. He gave me no reason to be impolite. I answered his casual questions – questions of the sort any reasonable man might ask of someone to whom he had just been presented; they were in no way invasive and I had no cause to be standoffish, and yet I was. I was sure I was justified in not liking him. It made no sense to me, but the palms of my hands were sweating as I stood before him – and now, looking back, I can easily suppose it was because of fear. He must have understood that right away. He was polite, his attitude humble. But I could not warm to him.

In the years that have passed since these events I have thought many times of the way I behaved with Mr. Lee at that moment of our meeting. I am sure I am not substantially different from other men who recall with embarrassing clarity the stupid things they thought, said or did many years before. My memory of these blunders, once excruciating, has mellowed into something less self-deprecating – inasmuch as I am now able to measure more accurately the man I was, even to find humour there. I had thought myself my cabin mate's superior and had attempted to push this audacity over on him. He smiled and took it, said nothing. He didn't have to. I had the revolver, yet there was never any question that in this situation he was master. My feelings then were undoubtedly the product of the peculiar circumstances that had torn me from my school desk and plonked me, soldier, in Malaya. As an extension to my schooling I had become a specialist in jungle warfare, a hunter of sorts. But interactions, close social encounters – in these I was unschooled and knew it; my lack of grace unnerved me mightily.

I was convinced Mr. Lee was a communist. Communism was a Bad Thing – and I had come to Malaya to combat it. That a communist might also be a human being had not dawned on me yet. We called our opponents in the Malay jungles "CT's" – communist terrorists – and that was about all we were ever required to know about them, except they were bad and the vast majority were Chinese. Mr. Lee was Chinese, and grudgingly I had to admit he was right: I did not know many of his race. In fact he was the first one to whom I had ever addressed more than the directions I might have given a Singapore taxi driver.

I mumbled an incoherent "good night," and climbed into the upper bunk. There I took off my boots and my Sam Browne belt and holster, stretching out fully clothed. Carefully I poked my pistol under my pillow. Mr. Lee had better think twice if he harboured any intent to attack me during this journey.

At some moment in the blackness of the night when the rhythm of my sleep had synchronized itself with the clickety-clack of the wheels passing over the rail joints, the whole train lurched and I heard the terrifying screeching of steel on steel. It was a dream at the point of wakefulness – until I felt my body rolled violently against the portion of cabin wall alongside my bunk, and then continue the roll onto the roof. By that time I was wide awake and conscious the carriage itself was on its side and continuing its forward motion. Instinctively I knew exactly what was happening, and felt a moment of shame for having allowed myself to wallow into a sleep deeper than the dangerous proximity of Mr. Lee should have permitted. Even as we were still in motion I made a grab for my revolver. I was not sure how, but I was certain my cabin mate had something to do with this emergency, that I would be called upon to deal with him.

The exterior noise was deafening. Tearing metal, breaking glass, splintering wood – the little universe that was the compartment had been sent for a spin and lay toppled onto its side. The interior was transformed by the convulsion, a maelstrom of loose objects hurtling like missiles through our total darkness. I could hear the metal of the washstand and the whole apparatus of the toilet installation being torqued asunder by terrific forces, the crashing of luggage and whatever else had been unsecured.

For an eternal moment the impetus of the train's progress through the night had carried us forward – then the whole thing jarred to an abrupt halt, the cabin floor now its wall. There was a silence as the universe settled into a new configuration. I tried to listen for sounds of Mr. Lee's movements or breathing and as I did so began to hear people shouting on the outside of the train. The strap of my Sam Browne had been coiled in my hand as I had slept, and I could feel the revolver still buttoned into its holster. I slipped the strap over my shoulder, buckled the belt as I rummaged through the bedclothes for my boots. I clambered over the edge of my bunk into the bunk area of my companion, half expecting to find myself on top of his body and having to fight him off before I could put a bullet in him. He wasn't there.

Blackness, but there was a movement of night air about my face, and I could gradually make out our door had been wrenched open, the windows in the corridor smashed. I clambered from the compartment into the corridor and out onto the side of the coach. The night sky was not as dark as had been the interior, and standing where I emerged from the wreck I was able to see forward and back the full length of train. The engine and the first three cars had fallen onto their sides, askew and completely lifted off the track bed. Sections of the train, couplings broken and now emitting steam, hissed like a dying snake where it lay in a cutting made through the right of way. The carriages behind my own were askew but still more or less upright and scores of white-dressed pilgrims were emerging to help one another alight and set their feet on solid ground. They called to one another in plaintive muffled voices. Some must have been injured, but I could see none of them. Soldiers who had been riding in the rear coaches were already on the ground and organizing a search for CT's along the upper rims of both banks of the cutting.

Before climbing down to the ground myself, I looked back into what had been our compartment. I could see no movement.

"Mr. Lee …!" I called down. No answer.

Again – "Mr. Lee!"

He was responsible for all this. In some secret way he had notified terrorists on the ground … I'll blow his head off as he climbs out, I thought.

"I'm here, Mr. Hespeler-Boultbee!" I heard a soft voice call from a position on the ground beside the wreck.

I looked down and could see Mr. Lee moving beside the train among a small group of pilgrims, each of whom was helping others to clamber out of windows or to jump down onto the ground.

Fortune had been with us, as it turned out. The track had been blown in front of the engine in the centre of the cutting in such a way that the train simply ran off the track and fell sideways against a high left embankment. The engine had pulled the first few coaches with it, but behind them, though jumping track, most of the train had remained upright. There had been virtually no telescoping, and no car had ridden up on top of another.

The CT's would have known there were soldiers on the train, so had obviously decided against the idea of machine gunning us. They had probably run off and taken cover in the jungle long before the explosion that derailed the train. Even so in the dark and chaos of the wreck, the possibility of machine guns opening up on us did occur to me so rather than seek out Mr. Lee to put a bullet in his head I drew my revolver and huddled the rest of the night, sleepless but quite alert behind a large steel wheel. I did not encounter Mr. Lee again before the relief train came south from Kuala Lumpur at first light.

*

We were a few hours behind schedule getting into Kuala Lumpur. I was disheveled and tired arriving at the home of my mother's friends, but it was nothing a shower, some breakfast and a few hours of sleep couldn't correct. Being a twenty-first birthday celebration, several groups of friends had come to the city from considerable distances. One had even flown in from India; more were to be arriving from elsewhere later in the day, with the party scheduled to begin at supper time. It was an extremely large house and several of the guests, myself included, were staying over. The attack on the morning's train had been widely publicized so my hosts and others wanted to pump me for details. It was difficult to align in my head all the suspicions I had about Mr. Lee, so I chose not to mention him – and was thereafter thankful to have kept my mouth shut. I managed to put him out of my mind while concentrating on the pretty ladies attending the party. By the time festivities got started later that evening I was most handsomely attired and ready to kick up my heels till the wee hours.

The magnificent white sharkskin evening jacket was borrowed – and during the rigours of an energetic Scottish reel, when I was partnered by the enthusiastic fifteen-year-old sister of the birthday celebrant, it succumbed. I was as fit as I have ever been in my life, but that evening I was an unlikely match for the spirited gyrations of this particularly zestful young lady. Swinging around me, she tore the jacket's sleeve where it joined the shoulder and, worse, rent the garment the length of its un-seamed back. I later returned the pieces to its owner, but it was of little more use than to be cut up for a pair of lady's gloves. I was stuck with a considerable replacement bill.

This unfortunate incident was much on my mind as I was leaving Kuala Lumpur and I had put the trauma of the train ride north – and my paranoia concerning Mr. Lee – into the furthest recesses of my mind. Thus boarding the train to return to Singapore it came as a shock to see his name was once more paired with mine in the little brass name plaque on the door to my first class compartment. Surely there must have been some mistake, I thought. This most certainly could not be any mere coincidence. All my forebodings returned with a thump.

"Good evening, Mr. Hespeler-Boultbee …!" his greeting was deliberate, slow, and accompanied by little bows and nods of his wizened old head.

"Mr. Lee …?"

"You are surprised, are you not? May I say, it is a great pleasure for me to see you once again, and as great an honour to be your companion on the journey down the peninsula as it was on the journey up …"

His gentle politeness might have silenced me, but then I said:

"Our last encounter was one I shall not easily forget."

"No, indeed. Our last encounter was unfortunate, and a tragedy for some. Several people lost their lives in the wreck, you know. I hope our return journey will not be so dramatic."

"And so do I," I told him.

Emboldened, I tried opening the conversation a little wider. Perhaps I could find other information of use – though I had no idea what it could be.

"How did you manage to escape the train so quickly?" I asked. "You were already on the ground when I managed to clamber up on top of the wreck."

"The first shock flung our cabin door open. I was thrown from my bunk into the corridor before the carriage fell onto its side. When I looked back you were strapping on your revolver, so I did not think it was very necessary for me to offer you my assistance. I could see you were unhurt. I was unhurt also, and thus could be of use to others."

Indeed, when I had seen him from my position on top of the train, he was busy helping some of the pilgrims climb out of the wreck. His actions at the time were not consistent with those of a political terrorist and now, facing him, I was obliged to review, maybe revise, my notions about him. Vague morsels of churlishness were not making a lot of sense to me. More accurately, I was finding it difficult to discover precisely of what I would accuse him if I could. I knew I did not feel comfortable sharing my accommodation with a Chinese – but would have been hard put to explain why.

Once again, climbing into my upper bunk, I tucked my weapon under my pillow before wishing my companion a good night.

"We will have breakfast together in the morning," he told me.

Trapped.

We were still chugging through northern Johore when the early call came for the dining car. Reluctantly I worked my way along the corridor, Mr. Lee turning over his shoulder now and then to make sure I was following. We settled at a table across from one another – starched white table cloth, solid railway silver, thick porcelain crockery marked with the railway's logo.

"I believe you do not like me very much, Mr. Hespeler-Boultbee, but you have no need to be afraid of me," said Mr. Lee, quietly spreading a napkin across his lap.

Shamed.

"Oh! Mr. Lee! Whatever gives you that idea ...?"

I mostly held my tongue and my breath through the remainder of breakfast as Mr. Lee continued to smile and nod his head and utter little compliments and kindnesses. I winced and tried not to show my unease.

"My car will be waiting for me at the station, so I shall be happy to return you to your barracks," my companion offered.

"It's not necessary ..." I began, futile and probably not even heard over the clickety-clack of the train.

I felt total panic when we finally stepped onto the platform at Singapore and were surrounded by five young men, each in identical loose-fitting black pajamas and black cotton shoes. A word from Mr. Lee, and they picked up all the luggage – mine included – and ran beside us to the entrance of the rail terminal and out into the sunshine. I thought of kidnap ...

Hardly.

Parked across the pavement directly in front of the main entrance was a big limousine – an antique Rolls Royce with a covered cab in the rear and an open cockpit forward for the liveried driver. One of the bodyguards (for that was what the men in black were) opened the door, while another virtually pushed me inside, Mr. Lee following up behind. He whispered a command to the driver through a speaker tube, and the car moved off slowly along the road to the barracks at Changi.

"You will come to dinner with me next week, Mr. Hespeler-Boultbee. I would like to have you meet my family. I shall telephone you."

While we were still seated in the cab Mr. Lee reached out and laid his hand gently on my knee. For the first time I could see into his eyes, and their full expression. They were extremely old, but they danced playfully. He did not step out onto the curb when we pulled up in front of the barrack gate. Instead he leaned forward, gave another of his little bows as he remained seated and nodded his head. The driver had descended, and held the door ushering me onto the pavement in front of the barrack gate.

As he had promised, Mr. Lee telephoned the following week. Once again the Rolls slid silently up to the barracks, this time the chauffeur coming alone. We made our way through the city's complex of streets, then passed

Mrs. Queen's Chump

through a large gateway guarded by sculpted stone dogs. A driveway led across parkland in which there was a mass of oriental artwork, small temples, a type of shrine that housed a lone and silent bell. There was a small pagoda-like building half-hidden behind wisps of light-leafed and open forest. The main house, surrounded by exotic trees and shrubbery, was several hundred metres from where we had turned off the main road between the guard dogs. We swept up to the stairway that descended from the front entrance, and there Mr. Lee was waiting with several members of his family. He came down to meet me and smiled as though greeting a most precious friend.

Taking me by the hand he turned and presented me to his wife:

"This is Mr. Hespeler-Boultbee," he said to her. She stepped forward and bowed low, simultaneously extending to me in her hands a wrapped gift.

"Mr. Hespeler-Boultbee is an officer in the barracks at Changi, and it was he who guarded me so kindly – with his revolver – on my journey last week when the train came under attack by the communists …"

He looked at me from somewhere way behind the slits of his eyes. Now he was not smiling, and I was unable to detect even the faintest humour in his voice. So I smiled at him instead, and thought about forgiveness.

"Thank you!" Mrs. Lee said to me earnestly.

*

The whole family – Mr. and Mrs. Lee, their children and a host of grandchildren – were all present at the dinner to welcome me. Later, taking me into his study, Mr. Lee showed me a number of framed photographs going back to a time long before the Japanese invasion. He had taken his family into exile in Ceylon during those years, he explained, returning at the end of hostilities to resume his import-export trading business. He did not say so but I eventually discovered he was the proprietor of the largest emporium of trade goods in Singapore. Out of curiosity I went there one afternoon – a gigantic store like a market warehouse, its floors extending into rooms and corridors that would take an energetic man several days to explore thoroughly. There was exquisite rosewood and rattan furniture – beds, chests, tables and cabinets. There were lacquered boxes and paintings, carved ivories and statuary executed in all corners of the Far East. Some items were so big it would require a heavy truck to move them; others were small and delicate – beads, stones, tinkling bells, chimes and chains, carved ebony and teak, brass-wear, mirrors, little jewel boxes and paper lanterns.

Mr. Lee was no communist. He was one of the most powerfully established merchants in Singapore, and his wealth and interests extended into every conceivable commercial endeavour throughout the Far East. Without uttering a word of criticism, and with immense kindness, he managed to teach me a most useful lesson concerning bias and ignorance – quite an intense and much needed brush-up, in a way, on a similar lesson Nyamahanga had endeavoured to teach me months earlier in Kenya.

Slow learner, but by now I should finally have got it about right.

☐

28. Alice

We stayed many weeks at Changi, long enough for me to reconnect with the ritual and the excruciating boredom of garrison life. I itched to get back onto operations in the jungle up on the peninsula. Some people were intimidated by the jungle, but I found in it a measure of quiet and peace that was totally absent anywhere in Singapore. The jungle offered a tranquility that could change in an instant, and on a few occasions it did, dramatically. We were fighting a war of sorts; firefights were a constant possibility, and the occasional chase with the Iban trackers was "hardly peace and quiet." It all got the adrenalin pumping, and I think most of us liked a bit of excitement. When the chase had wound down, though, there were the trees and the bush and the rush of hidden streams, and I felt I could look forever into the green canopy. Here at Changi, passing the meantime in a tiresome round of square bashing, mess dinners, mess games, life was tedious. For levity there might be the occasional sortie to the fleshpots and nightclubs of the city, but I was not particularly good at that either.

And yet it was on one of these outings that I met Alice, and suddenly life in the city and within the barracks assumed an entirely different dimension. She was a hostess in one of the city bars we frequented. The first night I saw her I am sure I could neither close my mouth nor take my eyes away from her. She noticed, but instead of making me feel silly she smiled and waved me in. I knew I did not have a whole lot of experience, but if she was going to be the sum total of it that was alright with me. She was Eurasian. I subsequently learned her mother was a Malay, her father a red-headed Scot. As it turned out, by peculiar circumstance, he was the engine driver of the train I had been riding when it had been derailed as I was on my way up to Kuala Lumpur a couple of months before. Alice was eighteen years old. I was sure she was the loveliest girl I had ever seen.

She was working in the bar as an enticement. Her Chinese boss told her it was her job to get the patrons to buy more drinks. She liked neither him nor the work, and told me so the first time she sat down at my table. She said she had decided to leave at the first opportunity; she did not really need the work, but had made a pact with two girlfriends also working in the bar. They had come to the bar together as a team, so she had made up her mind to bide her time and did not want to let them down.

Alice was tall, notably more so than most of the other girls with whom she worked. She walked on long straight legs, and wore a *cheongsam* slit down its left side so that when she walked one could see the best part of that leg all the way up to the top of her thigh. Her right leg was a mystery to be discovered. Her carriage was erect, even stately, so that she appeared to be even taller than she already was. Her face was a perfect oval, a symmetry framed by the sheen of long black hair which, all by itself, even from the back, gave the strongest hint of her Oriental and European racial mix. Her skin was tanned light brown and looked like velvet. There was not a blemish on it.

Most pleasing of all was that she so openly took to me. I was twenty, and up to my age so far I had always been uneasy in new social settings, unsure of myself and far too conscious of the effort I had to make just to get people to warm to me. If and when they did (I thought it happened rarely) it never failed to amaze me. I suffered more than a mere lack of confidence; more like a severe psychosis rendering me totally inarticulate – particularly so with girls. Yet for all my gibbering idiocy, like some kind of mime trying to explain his movements, I was not so stupid that I failed to notice my ineptness.

The realization this beautiful girl was actually turned on to me was not only a surprise, but it gave me such a rush I felt I could easily have danced a jig before my entire regiment. Given the opportunity I could have made a greater idiot of myself than ever before and not given a damn. I felt immensely proud both of her and of myself when I was with her. She had a way of letting me know that I was her man, despite meeting so many other interesting men (or so I imagined) in the bar. I had never had this happen to me before, and I did not suppose it likely to happen again the same way. Not like that. There was something conspiratorial about our contact, a connection both psychic and electric that gave us both a charge. Our thing. Lovers alone in the world.

For several weeks we saw each other most evenings and through many nights. I would always report to the regiment on time in the mornings. I was clever enough never to be missed, but I would not have cared too much if I had been. Several afternoons a week I would skip out of barracks early and take a taxi downtown.

There was an island off Singapore harbour called Blackang Mati and just

Mrs. Queen's Chump

near it, on the seaward side, was another much smaller island where there was a fishing village built of poles and matting and thatch. The houses were raised on stilts above the level of the surrounding lagoon, with ladders up to their open doorways. Alice and I paddled a canoe out to this little Paradise and remained there with nothing to do but to eat sea foods with the locals, swim in the tepid waters, and lounge in the sun. Sea breezes kept bugs away in the evenings, and we would lie on the woven matt flooring and tell one another how happy we were. We had three days and stretched it to an eternity. Then we paddled back to the city so Alice could go back to work and I could report in at the regiment to assure the Empire of my continued loyalty.

Two nights after our island sojourn I walked into the bar and sat at my usual table. Alice's girlfriends sat across the room at another table and watched me as I came in. They did not say anything, but they were all looking at me. And finally one of them came over and asked permission to sit with me. I was puzzled. This had never happened before, but I slid over on my bench and made room for her to sit beside me.

"Alice not come," she said.

"Oh?"

"Not come more."

The girl was Chinese, and her English came in toneless monosyllables.

"She's left? Did she get another job?"

I needed more of an explanation.

"No. She not come. Alice dead."

The girl's face was as expressionless as her words. I felt consternation, helplessness, a frantic anxiety. I wanted to argue but there was nothing to argue about. I was like a fly on the blade of a ceiling fan, powerless to prevent its turning.

"I don't understand!"

"Alice dead," she repeated. "Come work, hit by car."

I studied the girl's implacable face. I simply could not take in the words she was saying.

"Explain to me ..."

The girl looked into my eyes for a moment, and she must have seen my confusion. I looked for some recognition of it in her own eyes, but she was totally without emotion. She turned her head quickly and moved to get up.

"What are you saying?" I demanded.

At the same time I stood up myself and blocked her retreat, for I sensed that she just wanted to get away from me and I needed to know more. She sat there, expressionless, and said nothing. I turned towards her companions across the room who had been watching us in silence. I began to move towards them, intending to question them, but they rose like a flock of startled little birds. They twittered one to the other as I stepped forward, then they bolted *en bloc* behind the stainless steel of the kitchen door and peered back at me through its round window.

These reactions in no way fitted the information and I was quite unable to understand what was going on. Desperately I turned back to the first girl, who was now standing and trying to calculate the best way to get past me.

"Stop!" I said. "Tell me what has happened."

I think by now I was in tears.

"Alice dead," she repeated again coldly. "She dead, Alice, in street ..."

And with that she rushed past me to join her companions behind the kitchen door.

I was stunned by the information, but no less by the manner of its delivery. These girls were Alice's friends and workmates, and all of them knew perfectly well about the two of us, that we were crazy in love and seeing each other every opportunity we had. I had been coming to the bar almost daily for weeks, and on many occasions had stopped and talked to them while waiting for Alice. To tell me this terrible news in such brutal fashion, and then to run away from me, just did not make sense. Surely one of them, at least, would have the sympathy and heart to tell me what had happened.

Apparently not.

Which led me to calculating that nothing had actually happened at all, that they were just giving me – ineptly – an excuse. But Alice did not want to see me again? That I could not comprehend, or didn't want to.

I did not know where she lived. For that matter, I did not even know her family name. There was no way I could go to her home and check out this ghastly story. But I did know her father worked on the trains, and I knew what he looked like. I resolved to find him, and so at the next opportunity made my way to the main train station.

From Alice's description of her father, her knowledge of the derailment through his part in the drama, I knew perfectly well who he was. I thought I had even seen him by the broken cars early on the morning of the wreck. So I hung about at the downtown station for some time, and walked down to the end of the platforms where it was more likely there might be crewmen in the shunting yards.

Sure enough, after a little while, I spotted the man coming from one of the offices. His shock of red hair was not inconspicuous. I was not quite sure what I was going to say or ask but I was determined to accost him anyway, when something in his manner stopped me cold.

He was close, but walking away from me. He carried a jacket and something else that looked like a lunch pail. Beside him were two or three other men, similarly dressed in work overalls and presumably also train personnel. As they walked, a couple of them laughed and spoke good-humouredly. The red-haired man turned to the man at his left and, with a loud guffaw, threw a brawny arm across his companion's shoulders.

I didn't say anything. I stood where I was at the moment I'd first seen them and watched as they walked away together. That, I told myself, was not the act of a man whose daughter had just been killed in a traffic accident.

I was perplexed. I tried to run various scenarios through my mind. His daughter is not dead? He does not know about the death of his daughter? He does not care about the death of his daughter?

I discounted the last two options. I knew from the way Alice spoke of her father, and from what she had told me about him, that he was a good father to his children. Obviously he cared about her. Similarly, sufficient time had passed since the supposed accident that, had anything happened to her he would certainly have been aware of it. He was starting work, I reckoned, not finishing work. Only a half-hour earlier he would have been in his home where there would have been a family's reaction to such a disaster – had it happened.

This left only the first option, the one that was hardest of all for me to accept. If true it would explain the unkind behaviour of Alice's workmates.

And so I convinced myself, right there at the station. For some reason Alice had decided she did not wish to see me again. She, or her girlfriends, had invented this cruel means of getting rid of me. I could think of nothing else, but I resolved to wait a few nights and then return to the bar to see if she showed up at work. I felt that if she would be there I would be quite justified in demanding a more satisfactory explanation.

Three nights later I returned to the bar. I waited in the street at the time Alice normally arrived for work and, when she failed to show, I went inside.

All the girls were there except Alice.

The one who had spoken to me before came up to me and asked if I wanted to drink something.

I could barely contain my tears, and I just looked at her. I did not want to stay for a drink, so I shook my head.

"If not drinking, not sitting at table," the girl said sternly.

Then she added: "Alice not here. Alice dead."

Her face, as before, was totally expressionless. I was convinced she was lying, but there was no point in saying so, nor in pleading with her. Had I made any kind of a scene she would have called for help and I would have been put outside.

I turned and left.

From that day to this there has been no other explanation as to what happened, and long since I've convinced myself I was probably correct: Alice just wanted out.

☐

29. Drill

There's no way to tell what dynamics might come into play when angry mobs swarm city streets.

Who threw the first stone? Who shoved whom? Whose speech actually incited the mêlée? Was it incitement? How does it all get sorted out in the end?

There is a poorly articulated history of events that led up to the Singapore riots during the latter part of 1956, but for those who were first on the ground the immediate trigger was easy enough to pinpoint: some assassins knifed two British soldiers as they explored the backstreets of a military out-of-bounds zone in the city's seamy dockside area. They had been in civilian dress (as if one couldn't tell a British soldier from his haircut!) – and certainly they had disregarded regulations.

But Her Majesty's representatives on the island were not about to allow the culprits to go scot-free if they could help it. After the rumpus had started there was no shortage of infuriated local Chinese citizenry prepared to take on the might of the British Army, and they did so by demonstrating a contemptuous lack of both fear and respect for their colonial masters. The British bided their time.

All soldiers like to go into forbidden areas; it's a combination of curiosity and adventure. They are fit, full of moxie. If the need arises, they can probably outrun any military police who happen along ...

The girls and their brothels, the shadowy nightlife of the backstreets, the glitzy bars, the wheeling-and-dealing – there was no end to enticing and entrapping come-ons, and these were probably not significantly different from the delights that have provoked trouble for soldiers in their off hours ever since war was invented.

Fresh out of the jungles of Jahore after months of operations, starved for action and with an accumulation of pay to spend, it is a wonder half the battalion wasn't sneaking about the city's streets. Garrison life was deadly boring. In the jungle there had been a purpose, a tangible excitement. Now the unit had been pulled out to garrison Changi – an endless round of square bashing – drill, spit-and-polish and rah-rah the flag. The days were long and tedious. The Australians shared the barracks with the Brits, and there were constant fights – not because they particularly disliked one another, but because there was little else to stimulate young men seeking an outlet for their whoopee.

The first person in the officers' mess to hear about the knifings was the regimental chaplain, Rev. Paul Moffat. He left his dinner on the table, scrambled his driver and jeep and headed pell-mell out the barrack gates. (His vehicle was dubbed the Holy Roller – ecclesiastical purple with a great white Christian cross on the hood.) Initial word had not indicated whether or not the men had been killed – only that they had been surrounded on Arab Street and knifed. Whatever had happened, the padre reckoned he could be of service.

No matter what was going on, and there was no way we could know at that stage, the padre was going to need protection, so I also left my dinner and ran across the drill square to the canteen where I knew the members of my own platoon were about to sit down to their evening meal. It was a time of the day when most of the garrison were stood down and relaxed in off-duty kit. About a dozen men was all I could round up in any state of readiness, so I had them grab their rifles and we hopped aboard a truck to take off after the padre. By now he had at least a twenty minute start on us.

We turned a corner onto Arab Street and were met by hundreds of Chinese running towards some scene of action off to our right. From the cab of the truck I could see over the heads of the multitude to a point only about half-a-block distant where the Holy Roller had been brought to a halt by jeering crowds and was being severely rocked from side-to-side. The driver was attempting to hold his place by gripping the steering wheel. Paul was standing on the passenger side of the topless jeep holding onto the upper rim of the windshield and occasionally raising an arm, as if in blessing, trying to calm his tormentors.

The crowd forced our truck to a stop some fifty paces from Paul and his driver, so I ordered the men out. Holding our unloaded weapons across our chests, using them to butt and nudge, we formed a wedge-shaped phalanx and in a matter of a few seconds had carved and beaten our way through to the jeep. The driver had been hauled from behind the steering wheel now, severely knocked about and kicked and was lying semi-conscious in the gutter of the road. Some of the crowd saw us and pulled back, hesitant about taking on what they must have thought were armed troops. Paul, meanwhile, had jumped from the jeep himself. As we approached he was straddling the inert body of his driver using the vehicle's crank handle like a club to keep the attackers at bay.

I looked at Paul's face. His white dog collar and purple shirt were the only indications that he was bent on the Lord's work. His eyes flashed wildly left and right, his jaw set determinedly, and there was a constant scream in his throat.

"Back! Leave him be! Get back!" And the long steel crank handle smashed now into one man's skull, now across another's wrist. The padre's khaki peaked hat had come off and his sweaty hair flew madly.

"Padre!" I shouted, as much to call him back to his senses as to call his attention to us. I managed to get the men with me to surround the jeep, the padre and his driver on the ground.

I could tell there were mixed emotions in the crowd. Some of the Chinese close to us, ringleaders and crowd manipulators, were boiling with rage and certainly of a mind to make an even more violent statement. However, our rifles were much in evidence. There were some children bent on proving their manhood in front of bigger toughs. They were laughing, prancing about provocatively, calling us names and pulling silly faces. But in the main I had the distinct, albeit instinctive, impression that the greater part of the multitude just then was there simply because something was going on and they wanted to know about it – the ghoulish curiosity of a crowd drawn by the smell of blood.

In that instant not everyone in the crowd was hostile towards us. Few were yet confident enough to scream murder. It could turn any which way, of course, boil over in an instant.

I then realized I had a decision to make: how best to get us all the heck out of there.

The men's rifles were good clubs. There was no question of shooting our way out; the last thing we could do was indicate in any way we had no ammunition. There were only a dozen of us, and the crowd by now had swelled to several thousand.

We managed to lump the driver into the jeep's back seat and Paul climbed in with him. One of my men got behind the wheel, started the engine and ground the gears into reverse.

"Slow and steady!" I told him. "Don't stop until you can turn around!"

The rest of us surrounded the jeep and walked with it back to where our truck was stopped. By stationing my men around the two vehicles we managed to get them both facing the way we had come.

"Get out of the way!" I bellowed.

A stern order directed at specific individuals had its effect. It might not have worked at any other time of the action, earlier or later, but the timing was right and the surrounding multitude was not prepared for assault. The curious right then outnumbered the hostile, and for some reason there was a visible thinning in the multitude's ranks in the close vicinity. An old Chinese woman approached me and tugged at my arm.

"Bodies of your soldiers are there," she said, pointing back to a place in the street close to where the jeep had been forced to a halt.

"You better take them with you …"

The hostility had subsided noticeably, at least close to us, and I was able to get both vehicles lined up, their engines running, the soldiers standing guard and ready to board.

Taking four men with me, we walked swiftly back into the thick of the crowd. People now pulled aside to allow us through, and a little in advance of where the jeep had been were the bodies of two white men. Though in civilian dress I could see they were military.

"Put them in the back of the truck," I ordered my men, and at the same time I turned to four Chinese youths standing in the crowd.

"Help the soldiers!" I blazed at them – and they did. In minutes the small convoy was headed back to Changi.

The jeep's driver survived his beating. I saw him several times about the barracks. But Paul I never saw again. We learned later that one of the men he had clubbed with the crank handle had died of his wounds, and I believe our regimental chaplain felt such remorse that he went into seclusion and later asked for transfer home.

The rest of us had no such ticket. Within a day we were ordered onto the parade square to drill for what we were told were our new "internal security" duties.

*

The incident escalated. Every other night or so riots would break out, indiscriminately and in any portion of the city. At first the British garrison held back. Maybe the frequency of the riots would subside. Maybe the citizens of the island city would become disenchanted with the continual agitation and harangues against the British presence. In barracks we heard nothing of an independence movement. This was 1956. Surely the empire was sounder now than it had ever been? Particularly in Singapore. The Raffles Hotel continued to serve afternoon tea; many of us had partaken. Surely the benevolence of Her Majesty's colonial administration was being misconstrued by this minority of backstreet rabble rousers?

But every night?

Although the garrison remained in its quarters so as not to create a provocation, our inaction was itself a goad. The riots continued and the police alone were unable to cope, so now the military ...

"Hold back?"

Not quite. The soldiers remained in barracks, but the senior command had no intention of remaining indefinitely passive. In classes and in drills on the parade square we learned about Lord Wellington's strategy at the Battle of Waterloo. In the sweltering tropical heat we re-enacted variants of his movements, but with certain grisly modern accommodation.

In that famous battle in 1815 the British commander had employed a square formation that faced outwards against the charging enemy. With the command in the centre, each side of this square had three ranks of soldiers virtually shoulder-to-shoulder. The front rank knelt and fired their muskets from the kneeling position, each soldier passing his arm to the man standing behind him – who in turn passed forward a freshly loaded weapon, and himself accepted a loaded musket from inside the square – and fired. The fusillade amounted to a constant volley – precursor, in a manner of speaking, to the machine gun.

Our modern day formation differed in that it was only a one-ranked square, but our firepower vastly exceeded Wellington's. Our formation consisted of nine soldiers across the front, nine across the back, each rank stretched in a straight line extending the width of any given street. More or less the same number of soldiers formed the flanks of the square, depending on how many men constituted the platoon as a whole. As at Waterloo, the command was in the centre – the officer, his sergeant, a justice of the peace with two or three assistants, and four to six "bullyboys" bearing pickaxe handles as clubs. Forty men would have been an adequate number; my own platoon rarely exceeded thirty-four, sometimes thirty-six.

The role of the whole team was to perform a drill. The idea was, at all costs, to present our adversaries with a stoic and immovable force – grim-faced and armed with sufficient firepower to inflict a lot of damage if need be – and looking as though we were prepared to use it.

Spiffed-up and soldierly, the men's boots would be shined, their kit well cleaned and ironed, their cap badges and the brass work on their belts shining like the morning sun. Either marching or standing to attention, those in the front and rear ranks would be side-by-side taking up the full street across. Depending on the width of any given street they might have quite a large gap between them or even touch one another shoulder-to-shoulder. In this impressive formation the whole would march, slowly but with great deliberation, turning the corner into the head of a street and spacing themselves wall-to-wall across it. Their eyes would face unwaveringly to the front, their semi-automatic rifles in the ready position across their chests. Their lines would be dead straight. They marched as a rigid square, but the core in their midst would be fluid, changing position as circumstances dictated.

Invariably, as the team arrived, the crowd – sometimes several thousands – would fall back a little, those directly in front of the troops pressing against the multitude behind them. The soldiers would move resolutely ahead, their front line rigid, unbending, unsmiling. If, as frequently happened, one portion of the line encountered a human obstruction, usually in the form of someone who could not move out of the way quickly enough, the whole platoon would momentarily stop, noisily marking time by stamping their boots on the hard pavement. The front rank might meet virtually nose-to-nose with the people opposed to them at the head of the crowd, but the straight line was not permitted to bend. The command would be given to "mark time" until the crowd fell back, but eventually there came a moment when the force of the troops' progress forward was equalized by the sheer consolidation of the multitude.

At this point the platoon commander would call a halt. In the front rank each man would have already loaded a live round into his rifle chamber; he would immediately fall to one knee and hold his weapon ready at an angle at his side.

The side ranks, each close to a wall, would halt facing inwards – which would permit each man to scan the roofs and windows on his opposite side of the street. Their rifles would be at their shoulders, their heads and weapons turning slowly from side-to-side as they would seek out any movement or threat. Their orders were to shoot to kill anybody throwing missiles (roof tiles, bricks) onto the troops below, or to pick off anyone at all who might look even remotely threatening. Few people chose to show themselves on rooftops or in upper windows – just being there was presenting a target.

The rear rank would halt along with the rest of the platoon, and each alternate man would turn to face the rear. The members of this back rank would be entrusted to cope with any danger approaching the square from behind. This side was usually free of any threat; if the operation was progressing the way it should, the area to the rear of the platoon would be covered by an auxiliary squad of troops.

If at any moment someone from the crowd would be so foolish as to try to enter the square, or even be so unfortunate as to be shoved into it, the troops were instructed not to block their way by moving slightly to one side or another. They were told to hold their positions no matter what, to look straight ahead, eyes front – and permit people through, whether they were coming from the front of the square, its sides or its rear.

Certain death awaited. The bullyboys would spring in swiftly with their pickaxe handles. No questions. They were instructed, without hesitation, to club to death anyone – man, woman or child – who was not one of the squad. Should an infiltrator intend to inflict damage he could best accomplish it from the centre of the square; so the orders were both clear and strict – no tolerance, no exceptions.

Once the troops were brought to a halt, the justice of the peace would be called forward to a position just behind the front rank. His assistants would raise a banner, written in both Chinese and English characters, demanding the crowd disperse – a terse "DISPERSE OR WE OPEN FIRE." This civic official would then read a short form of the Riot Act, which amounted to precisely the same message as on the sign.

All hell would be exploding at the business end of the square. The crowd facing the troops, by now thoroughly alarmed by the businesslike demeanour of the men in uniform, could never disperse as instructed. They would be pushed forward by their fellow demonstrators at the rear who had no reason to fear because they would be unable to see what was happening up at their front. Out of sight at the back of the crowd, they would be unable to take stock of the weaponry arrayed against them and they would not be able to judge the looks on our faces that might indicate our determination and what we were prepared to do with our weapons. In any case, leading like generals who manipulate their cannon fodder from the rear of the action, the instigators of the mob would no doubt reason that a few casualties among their own ranks could only help to enhance and sanction their cause. Militants and fanatics tend to think that way: if there is a point to be made the losses can be justified; damn the consequences.

The tactical philosophy, if that is the correct way to describe the objective of our training, was to present the howling, poorly organized masses in the streets with a determined and immoveable phalanx. To achieve our objective we were required to demonstrate the bullying single mindedness of a unit that, though small in numbers, was nonetheless extremely powerful. Above all we would make it abundantly clear from the moment we marched into the street that we were prepared to dish out maximum force and to die doing so if necessary. Appearances – our turnout, our personal cleanliness and polish, the efficiency of our drill – these had to impress right at the outset, and to be maintained, as a unit, until the crowd was put to flight. There was never any question of using anything like tear gas, for that would likely affect us as well as them and leave our own ranks open to disorder and raggedness – an adverse spectacle to be concealed from our opponents at all costs. The training psychology had a defined "us" and a "them" component to it: and both had to work in our favour. No bluff. No shooting over their heads.

As the people on the ground doing the dirty work we would have to suppose the purpose of our hours on the parade ground was not only to work out the effective method by which a crowd could be scattered, but to prepare ourselves for any eventuality during the process of achieving this goal. In every conceivable way we were being required to act according to a colonial mindset, an attitude I came in later years to think of as the "Amritsar justification."[*] It did not follow that a crowd would scatter either immediately or tidily just because we asked them to.

It is older men who have the time to muse about such things; young

---

[*] On 13 April, 1919, British troops were ordered to open fire on civilians at Amritsar, India. Total massacred: 1,300.

fellows gung-ho to follow orders tend to avoid complex thinking.

*

How could such preparedness avoid calling up the Furies?

It was as if the thoroughness of our "internal security" drills, like some self-fulfilling prophesy, had forced open Pandora's Box.

The multitude rose. We drilled. The people pressed their rising, and we in turn morphed our drill into a grotesque reality.

One evening it is my turn to be called out, and things are suddenly happening exactly according to the precision of our drill.

We wheel into the street. The crowd is alarmed. Terrified. This is not the first time they are confronted by British troops.

My mind is reeling. I, too, am frightened. Supremely alert but terrified. The noise, the shouts of the determined, the wails of those who cannot get out of our way.

The multitude moves back. We come crashing to a halt right in front of them. The width of an office desk does not separate our front ranks.

The portly little magistrate, ashen, shaking, moves around the side of the banner that declares our intent. In words I cannot understand he tries to lift his voice above the clamour. It is brief, and none of his fellow countrymen pay attention to him.

Seconds are like labored minutes.

Over to one side, a wall behind him, a man in a dirty green shirt stands on the hood of a car and shouts his defiance. Yes, it is defiance. It is not encouragement for those about him to move back. He wants them to move forward, to swamp us.

"Number Two Rifleman ...!"

He hears me and I see him tensing.

"... Man in green shirt ... fire when ready ...!"

Number Two waits until he is sure his shot is clean and will not harm anyone other than his target. It only takes a moment.

A loud crack in that street. The man in the green shirt is thrown back. He drops out of sight.

The crowd screams. There is a movement back and away from us. A lurching. Panic.

The surge falters. Those in front are blocked by those behind them.

We move forward – two steps, three … halt.

Just then a woman and her child are pushed between two of the soldiers in the front rank and enter the square. She comes to me and begs to be allowed passage.

Momentarily I turn away from the front rank, take the woman by the shoulder and escort her towards the rear of the square. The woman's child clings to her mother's hand.

Two of the bullyboys step forward to prevent her passing.

"Let her pass!" I tell them.

They stand aside, uncertain, confused.

"See them through!" I tell them again.

My attention is called back to the soldiers in the front rank. Another man in the crowd is shouting above the rest ...

"Number Six Rifleman …! Man in white shirt …"

The target sees the rifleman swing around towards him. His eyes open in fury. He bares his teeth, and pulls the front of his shirt open to reveal his chest, and like this commits himself to those long instants before death.

This time the multitude breaks. They are running to get away from us.

There are stragglers. Some cannot move fast. Some are injured in the press of the stampede.

I wait. I know what I must do.

I call the men into marching formation and we move forward. Now there is no one to confront us. All have run, scattered into side streets. We follow to the first cross street, consolidate our advantage, resume our defensive square.

Within minutes my platoon is relieved by those who have followed behind us. They station themselves at various strategic points in the labyrinth of streets between the buildings.

Mrs. Queen's Chump

We march back along the same street of our action just moments before, toward the trucks that brought us into this zone.

A group of local policemen stand guarding the bodies of the two men who had been shot. Plainclothesmen search for any relevant documentation.

A little further. Bludgeoned and lying in the middle of the street, also guarded now by police, are the bodies of the mother and her child.

"Oh God ...!"

There is a senior officer, a captain, standing with a group of soldiers by the trucks.

"What the hell were you up to?" he demands angrily.

"You know damned well the bullyboys are under strict orders!" he shouts at me accusingly.

"Why the hell were you trying to give this woman a pass out of the square? I saw you! I saw you! She shouldn't have been in there ...! How can you expect this drill to work if you're going to go soft on people who push their way into the square ...?"

Drill. That's what it had been. An "internal security" drill.

*

One of the quirky traditions of the regiment was its boast of accepting more twins into its ranks than any other regiment of the British Army. It was an uncanny feature, amusing at times, but on one occasion during these uncertain days in Singapore it might very nearly have backfired with severe consequences.

Two of the fellows in the regiment had gone to school with me back in Britain – Peter and Michael Flushing. They were identical twins and most people were unable to tell them apart. However, knowing them well I did not have this difficulty.

The peculiar thing in their case was that Michael had risen to the rank of second-lieutenant, commanding his own platoon; Peter, serving in the same battalion but not in Michael's company, had become a lance corporal.

One evening I was surprised at dinner in the officers' mess to see Lance

Corporal Peter Flushing saunter in among the dining tables and take up his place right next to me. He was grinning broadly, and I immediately understood what was happening.

"Sh-h-h! Don't let on ..." he cautioned me, as he sat down. "Michael and I have decided to do this from time-to-time. I get fed up with the miserable fare in our canteen, and tonight I wanted to have a good dinner. Michael's over with the corporals ..."

Bit of a joke. Ha! Ha!

It backfired when Michael's unit was suddenly ordered into the downtown streets to face off against a mob of rioters. There was no time for the two brothers to switch places, so Lance Corporal Peter stood in for 2/Lieut. Michael, and led his brother's men into action in the riot. No one was ever the wiser, and Peter was able to bring his brother's troops back without incident.

"You'd better not try that one again!" I cautioned Michael when I saw him later.

His grin was just like his brother's.

"Yeah! Bit of a tricky one, that ..." he agreed, winking.

*

Within two weeks the madness was over for me. There was a troopship bound for Liverpool and I was on it.

□

30. Out with the Tide

My two-year term of National Service was drawing to a close. I was stationed at Changi barracks for the last weeks of it, continuing to be assigned to "internal security" duties. One morning the battalion commander sent for me. He bade me sit down in his office as if to talk to me more like my old headmaster than the colonel of my regiment.

He noted my service was coming to an end, and he asked me disarmingly if I might consider signing on for another three years. I was surprised but also somewhat flattered when he told me he considered I had worked well during the six months I had been with his battalion. The unit could use young men like me, he said. Signing on would mean an automatic substantiation of my commission and a bump up in rank to full lieutenant.

However, extending my service had not seriously occurred to me. Though my mind was far from made up, I had been entertaining notions of returning to my extended family in Canada. My mother and father had divorced when I was a young child; my mother had assumed custody of my brother and myself, and the three of us had left the country. There were many family members I had yet to meet – my father included. I was pretty sure I wanted nothing further to do with the military, but thought it best not to say all that until I had at least given the colonel's proposal a little more thought. I was totally sincere in telling him I would consider his option, and rose to leave his office in quite high spirits.

He was smiling. Maybe he thought he had secured a recruit.

"By the way," he said, as I reached for the doorknob, "you have a number of soldiers in your platoon who are likewise National Servicemen. See what you can do to persuade some of them to sign on. Good career move for 'em, I'd say …"

"Yessir!" I promised. But my heart sank. I had already spoken to the National Servicemen in my unit, and to a man they wanted out.

However, I had promised to give it a try so in the days that followed I set up a round of meetings with my men to see if I could convince – even just one of them.

I started with Watts, my batman.

"Wot me? Not 'arf!" was his instant reply to my suggestion. "I wants out! Two years in this man's bloomin' army is quite enough, thank you muchly! I wants me old job back."

Watts was an east end Londoner. Not an awful lot taller than his rifle, he was nonetheless one of the toughest and most willing soldiers I had known.

"Go on, Watts! What have you got going for you in London that's better than a life in the British Army?"

Stupid question, and I suppose I wasn't particularly sincere in asking it.

"Me, sir? I was a winder cleaner on Civvy Street. I wants to go back to cleanin' winders when I gets out …" he replied.

"Cleaning windows? You really want to go back to that …?" I was a little too incredulous.

"Yeah – that's for me!" he said. Then he winked and flashed me a naughty smile.

"You'd be surprised to see what I see when I'm cleanin' them winders!"

Needless to say, I gave up – with him and with the others. I was far from convinced that I wanted to remain in the army myself, so I wasn't much of a salesman. In the end I was obliged to report back to my colonel that I had failed to recruit even one of my men.

"And how about you?" he asked as I was explaining these things to him in his office.

"No, sir. I think I need to head back to Canada …"

"Oh, that's a pity," he replied. "I'd have thought you'd want to …"

"Not really, sir. I've given it a lot of thought …"

"Well," he said, "it's been brought to my attention that you have an adverse report to deal with, so what are we going to do about that? You received this adverse report in Kenya, and I am required to submit a second report about you six months after the first …"

I'd not thought overly about it, but that blot on my copybook had shadowed me malignantly since I had left Nairobi. I had hoped by now it would have gone away – but there it was again like, a raven, swooping down

Mrs. Queen's Chump

and cawing at me. My active service in Johore and in the streets of Singapore – had this not been sufficient to erase the black mark ...? The colonel himself had said he was pleased with my service ...

"Not as easy as that, old boy," he said. "Certainly I have no complaints about you, you know that. But I think it's best we have a word with the brigadier, see what he has to say. I'll talk to him myself, see what we can do. Can't have you wandering off with a cloud like that over your head ..."

Again, I left my colonel's office in chipper spirits. I had not anticipated hearing more about events that had happened all those months before on Mount Kenya, but at least my present commander was giving me some benefit over doubt. I felt I had little to fear when, some days later, I was notified the chief of brigade now wanted to talk to me.

"Sit down, Mr. Hespeler-Boultbee – what's this your colonel tells me about an adverse report...?"

The brigadier looked like a reasonable man. He was affable, not in the least aggressive, and he begged me to talk to him "man-to-man" to relate all the events that had gone down in Kenya six months before. He had what I thought was a copy of the report in front of him; there was a dossier on his desk and he glanced down at it occasionally. But I felt no cause for alarm and quite at ease sitting in front of him. I did not know what was in the report; I could only tell him my view of what had happened. I had not done that for anyone before.

He listened carefully, then turned to me and said:

"Your commanding officer tells me he asked you to recruit men from your own platoon to sign on for an extended period, but that you have failed to do it."

"Not for lack of trying. I certainly asked them. I wasn't able to get any of them to sign on, but it was difficult to be convincing when they know perfectly well I shall be leaving the army myself."

"That's my point, Mr. Hespeler-Boultbee," the brigadier continued in reasonable tones. "Why are you not prepared to sign on yourself? Your colonel invited you to ..."

"No, sir, I don't think so. I told the colonel I'd think about it, and that I have. I'm a Canadian, and feel strongly about it. Now I need to go back to Canada. I don't think I should be doing what I'm doing. I have no great knowledge of politics, but I'm of the opinion I'm really in the wrong army. As a Canadian I have no business fighting Britain's colonial wars ..."

The brigadier was not impressed.

"That exhibits a rather poor attitude, I'd say, young man," he said. "I'd have thought you'd be anxious to sign on, to clear your reputation ... Seems to me your first adverse report rather blackened your name. Your commanding officer has to write a follow-up report on you, you know. You are not in a strong position. A man in your shoes should be pleased to have the opportunity to clear his name ..."

"Yes, I'd like to clear my name. But I can only do it by signing on in the British Army for a further three years ...?" I asked.

"It might help straighten out your record."

"But that's hardly fair. The colonel invited me to sign on, sure, but he left the decision to me, and he certainly didn't try to coerce me. He gave me every indication he was pleased with my performance ..."

"Indeed, Mr. Hespeler-Boultbee ... Your commanding officer sent you to me for further evaluation, and for the moment my evaluation is incomplete. That will be all. You may go. You'll be hearing more in due course ..."

And so I was dismissed. I didn't like it, and now had a strong sense of foreboding. The brigadier had lulled me into thinking I was more or less in the clear, but his last comments indicated quite the contrary. The nasty sensation in my bowel, the feelings of depression, of abject failure that had accompanied me as I came down off Mount Kenya came galloping back again – justified or otherwise.

And yet I was excited. I was going home. I would probably hear nothing more on the matter until I arrived back at my regimental depot, and in the meantime there were a number of matters, chiefly a host of farewells to friends and contacts, that turned my last few days in Singapore into a storm of social activity. It all helped to lift my spirits out of the doldrums into which I was sure I was on the brink of plummeting. I caroused with my regimental buddies most evenings and got drunk a lot.

*

Mrs. Queen's Chump

The troop ship on which I embarked, the Empire Warrel, was carrying about two thousand soldiers, the greater number of them National Servicemen headed back to Britain for demobilization at the end of their obligatory two years. There were also many regular soldiers aboard, both officers and other ranks, and in many cases they travelled with families that had accompanied them abroad, perhaps lived in the Far East for several years. Among this latter group was a bevy of lovely girls, many of whom had been attending schools in such places as Japan or at various locations in Malaya and Singapore.

As on the trip out, the ship first headed for Colombo in Sri Lanka, the British Colony then known as Ceylon, where we were scheduled to stop for two days – long enough for a mixed bag of subalterns and some of the regimental daughters to go ashore and seek out whatever fun spots there were.

A group of twelve of us – seven junior officers and five of the ladies – were eager to visit one of the famous beaches that lie along the coast just out of Colombo, and so we hopped into taxis and drove in convoy out to the Galle Face Hotel. There was a heavy surf, but the beach was welcoming and so we changed into our bathing suits in the hotel and picked out a level patch of sand near some rocks, laying out our towels close by the main building.

I was a strong swimmer, so raced ahead of the others into the water and started walking out towards the breaking waves. I had not gone more than a few yards, the water only around my knees, when I realized something was amiss. The sand was being scooped out from below my feet, and the more I tried to retain my balance the more I could feel the pull of the water as though I was wading through the turbulence of a fast river. I tried to walk out of the surf but couldn't. It was as if my legs were being sucked from under me by a strong vacuum cleaner so I started to swim, trying to stay close to the surface. But then a large wave broke over me and I felt myself being pushed down, unable to pull myself to the surface. I had taken a great gulp of air before going under, and all at once realized it was the only air I was going to have until I could fight my way up and out – but try as I might that just wasn't happening. I could feel my body being tumbled across the steep sea bed; one instant my legs would touch down, the next my hips or my head. There was no control and even if there had been I would not have known which way to swim. Totally disoriented, I could no longer tell which way was up.

I was terrified and on the point of gulping my lungs full of seawater. Jagged rocks stabbed at my back. And then a surge of sea spat me to the surface and onto the rocks as if I was no more than a glob of phlegm. My comrades raced over to me with towels and kind words and for some minutes I just lay back gasping for air. One of the functionaries of the hotel came down to join us, and sternly warned all of us not to take the sea for granted. The surf here at Galle was known for its treachery, he said. It had some of the strongest undertows along that portion of the coast. Needless to say we stayed out of the water that afternoon and contented ourselves just lying on the beach and sending up to the hotel bar for liberal quantities of beer. All of us had had a bad fright.

There was another occurrence during the afternoon that further contributed to my sense of mystique concerning the Galle Face beach – something I have thought about many times between then and now.

Walking up and down about fifty yards from us, but studying our group carefully, was a wiry little man dressed in a sarong and with a grubby cloth wrapped turban-like around his head. He walked barefoot, his black skin crisp and shiny like a mummy well-basted in the hot sun. Several of the group had noticed him and commented, for his interest in us was intense and obvious. After hovering at a distance for about twenty minutes, he walked purposefully over to where we lay on the sand and stood directly at my feet. In precise and intelligible English he told me:

"You are not English, and you were born of the third of December, 1935 …"

I was jarred upright instantly. He had my attention in a trice, for the date was correct. At first I was alarmed because it was apparent he had been into the hotel's changing rooms and somehow managed to acquire my identification papers. But then I realized that was impossible. I did not have my papers with me that day. I had left them behind in the cabin of the ship, and my wallet with my money in it was with me on the beach. I had left it in one of my shoes when I went into the surf, but all of our belongings were more or less together and there was constantly someone with them. In any case, my wallet only contained money; there was no identification in it whatsoever. There was nothing about me to indicate my nationality was different than any of the others in the group – my skin is that of a Caucasian, and I was in company with other Caucasians. I studied him hard.

"If you give me ten rupees, we may walk down the beach and I will tell you more," he said – and so I paid him ten rupees and went with him.

Like anyone who has visited fairgrounds and circuses I have always been intrigued by fortune tellers, amused at how they have usually come up with a formulaic babble about long life and riches and beautiful women who'll bare me a flock of children ... But this fellow was different.

"Why have you chosen me?" I asked him.

"Because you are not like the others, and I can see enough about you that makes telling you interesting. Besides," he added with a smile, "if what I tell you is correct you will tell the others, and then they also will pay me ten rupees. In this way I shall earn a good day's wage ..."

He related other things about my past, all precise and accurate; the details are of no consequence to this story, but they surprised me. Though travelling to England now, he told me, I would not remain there. Before Christmas I would be faced with another long journey – and it turned out just as he had said: I spent that Christmas with my father in Canada. I would be married within a year, he said, and I was. I would have children, but would remain less than ten years with my wife; we separated in 1963 – six years on – and were divorced within a decade. There was more, but so much suffices to make my point.

We walked back to the group, and everybody wanted to know what he had told me. One of the girls jumped up flashing her ten rupees, and she walked rather jauntily down the beach with the fortune teller. Sadly, she returned to us in tears and quite unable or unwilling to confide what it was that had passed between the two of them. We tried comforting her but she was so upset we all decided we had had enough of the Galle Face beach jinx, and so returned to the city docks.

There is little more incident from that day that bears relating, but what happened was a "sit-up-and-listen" sort of lesson. It was the first time in my life I had come so breathtakingly close to dying (I discount the earlier machine gun incident because the bullets on that occasion did not actually hit me; in neither that instance nor the train wreck had I been in the least injured); and it was the first time in my life, despite my encounters with Africans' "sixth sense," that I had been forced to take note of what I can only call the supernatural – its insistence and its effect. Both incidents, the undertow and the fortune teller, marked me as if I had been stamped indelibly and rather forcefully. I am not, and never have been, a superstitious person;

but since that day I have found it unconscionable to ridicule the deep superstitions or beliefs of others. Over the years my psyche has been jogged by numerous incidents, but the most important lesson of that long ago afternoon has always been the realization that whatever powers I have, they are minimal and temporal. My story is mine, and I have lived it – I have ridden the train and even made some significant choices. But in the end I have to say the rails upon which my life runs have at no time been laid in place by me.

*

Two days at sea is more than sufficient to allow boredom to seep into the lives of two thousand cooped-up homeward-bound soldiers – and we had already been at sea for considerably more than two days. Quarrels flared. There were complaints about everything from stuffy lower deck quarters to the quality of the food in the mess hall and the fact the soldiers were obliged to rise early every morning for deck PT – and thereafter had little with which to occupy themselves for the remainder of the long days.

We were two days out from Colombo and headed west towards the Red Sea and the Suez Canal. By this time I had made friends with Sparks, the ship's radio operator, and was able to pass an hour or so with him most days as he worked. I was astonished at the number of transmissions that flew back and forth on the radio waves, and it wasn't as though the Empire Warrel was a major fighting ship of the line. Most of us thought of her as little more than a rusted out old tub press-ganged into ignominious service as a troop transporter after her more noble prior years in the luxury cruise line business. At least she had a small swimming pool which provided some measure of entertainment for the troops.

I popped my head around the door of the radio room one morning.

"Any news, Sparks?"

"I'll say there is!" he replied. "A fellow called Nasser has closed the Suez Canal and won't allow any shipping to pass ... We'll get as far as Aden, and then we'll just have to hole up for a while, I guess."

This would mean delays, I thought – just the sort of thing that could trigger an unwelcome increase in tensions among the men on board. They were going home, and most of them were on the point of completing their terms of National Service. They would not take kindly to delays.

As I had surmised, tensions only grew as the ship steamed on for Aden. The long days dragged out in laborious tropical slow motion. It's hard to keep the lid tamped down on men about to be demobilized. They seldom display the usual military formalities, even in a highly disciplined British Army. They can be hard to activate constructively; not so hard destructively. We all recognized that unless kept active they could well become difficult, even unmanageable. A few fights had broken out in the soldiers' salon. Now and then someone's bedroll would be turfed overboard and fed to the fish. The officers were hard pressed to keep their men imaginatively occupied. There were the usual rounds of lifeboat drills and physical training. The evenings spun into a routine of movies, masquerades, bingo – and grog. In the daytime there was the ship's tiny swimming pool, assorted deck games – and grog. One enterprising officer varied the fare a bit by mounting a machine gun on the afterdeck rail. The men would spend hours each day (and quantities of ammunition) taking target practice at coloured balloons loosed off from the ship's stern to bob in the churning wake. When the stock of balloons ran low, seagulls or flying fish proved to be suitable targets.

In Sparks' radio room, messages continued to fly from ship to shore, and back again, but one morning when I dropped in to see him he was particularly glum.

"Bad news," he said. "That Nasser wallah won't allow any ships through the canal, and now comes word that the Brits and French are invading Egypt ... We might have to alter course and go around Africa instead. Round the cape will add six weeks to our overall trip ..."

My first thought was for the state of the troops aboard. They would not take this news kindly. In the officers' salon there was heated debate, but one fellow in particular was cheery enough.

"Damned good show!" exclaimed Gill Budge, and he raised his mug of grog to propose a toast to the health and happy circumstances of the Egyptian president.

Others were outraged.

"I'll not drink to that!" one of the more conservative subalterns blustered. "God, man! Take away Suez and you block Britain's access to the oil fields. England would grind to a halt in a day ..."

"Good!" exclaimed Budge, a worthy Scot. "Who'd notice?"

"We'd go to war for that …" someone else puffed.

"Exactly!" said Budge. "And I think we already have. But the matter's a trivial one, really. If the Gypos won't let us use the canal, we'll just march in and take control of it again ourselves. Simple as that. It's no big deal. We'll have the whole matter sorted out by the time we get to Liverpool. Do you realize the advantages to us? We'd get an extra few weeks of cruising through these delightful tropical waters, weeks more sunshine – and all the cheap booze we can soak up at the bar. Why, lads – we're laughing!"

Indeed, there was a burst of laughter and Budge was suddenly off the hook.

"Ah, Budge! You're off your rocker!"

"And that's not all," persisted the feisty little Scot. "Do you not realize, our two years will be up – we shall all be discharged from service within a day or so of leaving Cape Town. Can you think of anything more ludicrous? A troop ship full of civilians!"

All the subalterns looked at one another. Hm-m-m.

"Hey, he's right y'know …"

"Too bloody right I'm right! And another thing – that wretched colonel in charge of the ship – he won't have the least say over us …! We'll all be private citizens, and the War Office can only bellyache!"

His opinions were amusing because they were so ridiculous, and in the current atmosphere we all appreciated the snippet of surrealism.

The juniors especially enjoyed the reference to the ship's colonel. He was detested by one and all.

A career soldier who had served as commander of an artillery unit during the war, Colonel Wormswold was close to retirement, but looked and acted as though he was already well past it. He was ill-tempered and cranky, constantly pulling rank over even the senior officers aboard the ship, some of whom were his equal in terms of service. He quite openly detested the high spirits of the men going home for discharge, and made no effort whatsoever to hide his feelings. He was one of the unfortunates found in any army whose military abilities and military zeal seem mismatched. In their private discussions the junior officers had come to the conclusion the colonel had probably stayed too long in the army, shunted from one thankless task to another until he had wound up in this miserable administrative post aboard a rusting trooper. He was a defeated and snarling fellow. He had been badly wounded in the Second World War, but not so badly that he had had to be invalided out. Some said he was ideally suited to the command of a trooper – unable to do anything else. His face was horribly scarred; he was minus chunks out of one of his hands, as well as his sense of humour. His disposition was such that smiling was anathema to him, though a few of us had seen something approaching a leer when he had identified one of his own petty personal triumphs. His right leg and right shoulder were twisted out of shape and this threw his bush jacket off centre. It gave a peculiar distortion to what he offered for a salute.

There were strong objections, increasingly voiced openly, to the way in which Col. Wormswold attempted to run the deck like a parade square. Without any particular reason and with no explanation, he had forbidden shore leave passes to half the troops aboard when the ship had docked at Colombo. He took pride, or so most of us thought, in making life aboard the Empire Warrel as unnecessarily vile as he possibly could. The single greatest symbol of his power, the one thing that created the most resentment, was his use of the ship's public address system at any hour of the day or night to voice his petty complaints. The men quickly nicknamed him "Squawker," tore a number of speakers from their fastenings and hurled them overboard in their efforts to silence his voice in at least some quarters of the ship.

At last the Empire Warrel docked in the harbour at Aden. We arrived in port at the south end of the Red Sea just as the Suez War was ratcheting up at the north end. Rumour was rife and there was a growing sense of emergency; then Col. Wormswold summoned all officers aboard to a meeting in the ship's first class lounge.

Here he announced to us that that very morning he had sent a cable to the War Office in London – and volunteered the entire ship's company for active service in the current Suez War.

It was a total surprise to all of us. From the muttered asides of one or two of the senior officers the rest of us understood the colonel's motion had been initiated without the least consultation with any of them. The wretched man had had no meaningful command since the end of the war, and now (God help us!) was his opportunity for a glorious denouement – a heroic hurrah for empire and the colours.

He paid no attention whatsoever to the fact that virtually the entire shipload of us was headed home for demobilization, or that we were also transporting women and children. Most important of all, he had failed entirely to consider we were unarmed.

Having zealously announced his ill-considered intent for us, he banished the junior officers from the salon and ordered the most senior of the seniors to remain behind for what he called a "strategy session."

Those of us so dismissed wandered about the decks and awaited further news, all of us shaking our heads and wondering whether the old coot had gone completely bonkers. Perhaps he would announce his decision over the ship's PA. An hour or so later a group of senior officers re-emerged from the salon talking amongst themselves. Some were shaking their heads as though they had been listening to the carefully-reasoned arguments of an imbecile.

"Barmy!" I heard one of the majors mutter.

We later learned more or less what had gone on at this strategy session. The colonel was enthusiastic, and harangued the senior officers as though he was their battlefield commander about to launch a great surprise movement against the Egyptians. They could not know, he reasoned, that nearly two battalions of British troops were lurking secretly at the bottom end of the Red Sea. We could sneak up this long waterway behind the Egyptians' lines, he told them, and so be in position to surprise the enemy from his rear. He had pulled out maps and charts to augment his plan.

To a man the seniors had confronted him with the several inescapable fallacies of his scheme. In sum these amounted to their demand that he accept we were in no condition to be able to launch an attack on any enemy. But such counsel, the colonel whined, was nothing more nor less than rank insubordination.

Not waiting for him to grant their dismissal, the meeting had broken up with individual officers wandering out of the salon singly and in groups, all of them glowering and casting their eyes to the gods, their heads wagging at the idiocy of the whole concept. Apparently the colonel just continued talking and arguing, persisting with his maps and his diagrams and his convoluted machinations until there was nobody in the room to hear him out.

At one point someone heard the naval captain of the ship comment:

"No way I am going to take my un-armed ship up the Red Sea to deliver this rabble of homeward bound soldiery to the guns of infuriated Egyptians! We'd get halfway there and someone would spot us. We'd be sitting ducks, bombed and then sunk ...!"

The colonel was so sure of the efficacy of his scheme that he demanded the ship's captain maintain the Empire Warrel in port; we would await from London the acknowledgement and sure confirmation of his proposed grand manoeuvre ...

For two days, the two thousand troops aboard were denied shore leave, and were obliged to swelter inside the steel walls of the trooper, broiling under the Aden sun.

London quickly rejected the colonel's idea. Sparks told me. Col. Wormswold fell into an even more morose frame of mind as the ship's captain happily commenced to steer a homeward course around the south of Africa. As we had reckoned, the change of course was to add six weeks to our journey back to England.

By now there was not a man or woman aboard who did not detest our crippled colonel, and who would not happily have pitched him to the sharks.

*

As day followed day the troops became resigned to the delay in reaching home shores. Word soon got out they had been spared the idiocy of the colonel's audacious Egyptian escapade. They began to hoot their derision when his voice came over the PA. Boredom triggered quarrels between men pent-up in the ship's confined space, but by and large the junior officers were able to keep the lid on. Perking.

But then there occurred an incident that unleashed emotions considerably beyond the bounds of the event itself: a service corps sergeant and his wife had become entangled in an acrimonious row over the interest a warrant officer had begun showing the wife. It might have ended quietly had not the wife herself demonstrated she quite enjoyed the warrant officer's attentions. The distraught sergeant sought the assistance of one of the senior officers aboard, and suddenly the whole affair became the ship's *cause célèbre*. It all came to a crescendo one evening when the sergeant went missing. Over a period of days the ship was combed top-to-bottom, blunt-end-to sharp-end;

no sign of him. There was no question of foul play beyond the foulness of the incident itself; it was apparent the poor fellow had jumped. By the time his absence was noted it was far too late to turn the ship around to attempt a search.

We were approaching the equator. The heat was massive; the waters of the Indian Ocean so glassy still they reflected and heightened the temperature. The uncertainty and excitement surrounding the sergeant's apparent death, plus the colonel's incessant announcements, scoldings and punishments had created a disagreeable air and cast the bulk of the men's spirits into the doldrums. Everyone knew he was going home, but the long days passed in a fragile silence. All that could be heard was the constant low rumble of the ship's engines, the intermittent clanging of the dinner gong – and Col. Wormswold's nagging nasally voice coming over the PA speakers. The nights were as hot as the days. Many of the men brought their bedding up onto the decks to avoid the unbearable stuffiness below, but without explanation the colonel put a stop to it. The soldiers grumbled, but did as they were told. In the officers' salon we had begun to think things would remain at a low simmer – probably until we entered the Atlantic and the men could see they were started on the home stretch.

The situation was more or less stable until the day we actually crossed the equator. This was an occasion to party it up – and there was no good reason to deny the men a bit of fun.

The more scholarly British Tommies knew all about the superstitions and traditions involving King Neptune's ancient decree: that those crossing his line – the equator – at sea for the first time must pay homage to him. There was to be a ceremony, so word was passed around and most of the soldiers assembled beside the ship's tiny swimming pool and on the surrounding decks – either to take part, or just watch.

The King Neptune who scrambled over the railing with his queen was a bulbous buck private from the Ordnance Corps by the name of Harry Horner, one of the most prominent barrack room lawyers aboard.

"Oh Lord …!"

Horner and his sidekick, a fellow called Rutter, took their thrones by the pool. The two of them were inseparable and usually troublesome.

In the uniform of the Ordnance Corps Horner was an unconvincing soldier, but his messmates championed him for all that. He was mouthy and forward, and so amused them – though to his seniors he could be a right pain in the butt. As King Neptune he commanded the centre of attention, a position he dearly loved and from which he was seldom absent. Doubtless as a civilian he might have succeeded in life as foreman of a fairground work gang in the Midlands. As a soldier he was altogether too conspicuous, too lazy, too argumentative, too loud – and his formidable bulk tended to exaggerate his perpetually sloppy turnout; Mother Nature had cut him at least one size too large for his tropical denim uniform. But as King Neptune and his queen both Horner and Rutter were in character, clothed only in swimming trunks and girded about with make-believe seaweed and crowns cut from cardboard fruit boxes.

Surrounded by a motley gang of thuggish acolytes, Neptune called for silence. Then he produced a scroll and rolled it out dramatically before him, holding it top and bottom. In as hoity-toity a voice as he knew how to summon, he called out the first of a long list of names – those unfortunates to be sentenced for deigning to cross Neptune's line.

"Thomas Booth, sergeant-major, King's Loyal Regiment, present yer bleedin' arse right 'ere right now before King Neptune!" Horner bellowed as pompously as he could.

And Sergeant-Major Booth, to give him sporting due, complied. He was dressed for it, for he must have had some idea of what was about to happen. He was barefoot and clad only in a pair of khaki shorts. He eyed his subordinate warily.

But for now Horner was king.

"Stand up straight!" he commanded the sergeant-major – who did, but more out of bristle than outright obedience.

Queen Rutter walked behind Booth and tapped him on the shoulder with her wand.

"Make a wish!" she said.

"Drop dead!" growled Booth.

"That's no way to speak to yer queen!" thundered Neptune. "Sergeant-Major Thomas Booth, you stand trial 'ere today on the charge of invading the sovereign territ'ry of Neptune's Deep. Y'not only float yer ruddy carcass across His Majesty's line with all the cheeky brass of a flyin' fish sailin' through an open port'ole, but you 'ave insulted 'is gracious an' loverly queen! Yer fuckin' guilty, mate – have you got anything to say before I pronounce sentence?"

"Bah! Get stuffed!" said Booth.

"Kneel before your king!"

"Like bloody 'ell, I will ...!" Booth began, but Horner was off his throne like a sea lion wobbling down off its rock. Between Booth and the pool Rutter had fallen to his knees in a crouch, presenting his broad back just as Neptune bellied up with deliberate force. Booth toppled backwards over the queen and into the pool. The entire soldierly assembly roared their laughter and approval.

A score of hands were proffered to assist the sergeant-major from the water, only for him to be met by the courtiers' mops and buckets of suds – and to be thrown once more into the pool.

"NEXT!" shouted King Neptune, and Sergeant-Major Booth was left to clamber out onto the deck on his own, encircled now by a group of his friends and supporters laughing and telling him he was a good sport, helping him towel down.

"We'll talk again tomorrow when you've come down off your high throne," Booth told Horner with a menace that was anything but mock.

But Horner and Rutter, centre stage and having fun, weren't hearing it. The courtiers got busy hauling their next victim up for judgement.

Just honest fun, I thought – but with an edge. One by one those who had never crossed the equator before were paraded before the king to stand trial, and all of them were soaped and dunked. The performance went on for over an hour, at the end of which time Neptune and his queen were looking about for more victims. The soldier spectators were getting bored and started to wander away. The lunch gong had just been sounded.

"How about the bleedin' colonel?" someone shouted, and immediately the onlookers became animated again – but now with a deliberation and purposefulness previously absent.

Here we go, I thought.

Suddenly soldiers were streaming back to poolside – scores of them.

"Get the colonel!" they shouted.

"Do 'im!"

Neptune leapt onto his throne.

"Bring 'im to me!" he shouted, flushed by the cheers of his mates and the notion of exercising his dubious authority over (but mostly against) the senior army officer aboard the Empire Warrel.

I was standing with a group of junior officers, but there was little we could do – or, in truth, cared to. A rabble of soldiers eager for the chase and clamouring for a chance to beat up on the hated colonel raced to the companionway that led up to his quarters. Some might have claimed it was all in good sport; but their action tended to stretch the concept of good order and military discipline.

In a moment they all swooped down again, dozens of them shouting and hollering victoriously. Col. Wormswold was fully clothed but for his hat, and though he pulled and tugged to free himself from his captors his frail form was powerless against such a mob. He broke free once, turned to try to say something to the soldiers, but someone grabbed him and heaved him bodily over a broad shoulder, carrying him bottom-first to Neptune's feet and plonking him down on the deck – hard on his butt, the way one might have unloaded a sack of coal.

One of the junior officers, forgetting his dislike of Wormswold, doubtless worried for the safety of an elderly man and probably thinking this a hell of a come-down for someone of the colonel's rank, ran forward to try to persuade the rabble to ease up.

But the mob's blood was a-boil. The subaltern was too late in pushing through to the throne area. Struggling and expostulating, the colonel tried to rise to say something but Neptune's pronouncement was louder. An outsized paint brush loaded with soap suds was sloshed into the colonel's face. Lathered and "shaved" with a theatrical wooden razor, sentence was passed.

"… And I command you be cast into the deep blue sea …"

The queen had moved into position behind the victim. Neptune stepped down from his throne for the unceremonious belly bounce – and Col. Wormswold flew backwards over Rutter's back into the pool.

The ritual was over in seconds, the soldiers cheering and laughing as their bedraggled commander struggled to the surface and clung to the side of the pool. No one stepped forward to offer him a helping hand out of the water, and he had to work his way around to the ladder. When he emerged he looked pitiful in his soaking wet uniform, the more so because he was furious.

"I don't know who you are, soldier. I don't give a damn!" he blazed at the beaming Horner.

Then he turned and caught sight of the subaltern who had tried to come to his assistance.

"Put this man under close arrest!" he ordered. "That's an end to your fun and games. If you had bothered to ask, I would have told you I have crossed the equator more than thirty times."

It was a sad admission, and the troops hooted with laughter. Some cheered, but it was a hollow cheer.

Hard not to suppress a tight smile. Col. Wormswold did not know how to avoid making enemies. He pushed his way through the soldiers milling about the poolside and made his way back up to his quarters.

Horner was led off to the brig complaining bitterly.

"Rotten bastard! No sense of humour in that twisted-up bag o'bones."

Then he turned to those nearest.

"He can slap me in irons today, but officially I'll be on Civvy Street the day after we leave Cape Town, and you know where he can shove his bloody army then! Can't lay a finger on me, he can't – not once I'm on Civvy Street ..."

And so the champion of barrack room lawyers expostulated all the way to his cell. He had a point: by far the greatest portion of the troops aboard the ship were National Servicemen headed home for release from the military; our detour around Africa meant that for pretty well all of us, our two-year contracts would run out long before our newly scheduled arrival date in Liverpool. What would be our status in that event? It was a point worth checking, particularly in view of the volatility of so many of the soldiers and their mutinous attitude towards the authority of the colonel of the ship.

Yet more rumour increased the tensions on board and eventually the matter was taken up by a group of the senior officers acting, the juniors supposed, independently of the colonel. A meeting was called in the officers' salon, and there our status was outlined in no uncertain terms by a small committee of senior officers: army regulations and protocol stipulated that all military personnel would remain in service – even beyond their contract date – until formally dismissed at their home depots. We were asked to pass this information along to all warrant officers and sergeants, with instructions that they in turn were to pass it along to the troops.

With such firm instruction and the especially valued co-operation of the senior non-commissioned officers, morale among the troops was restored overnight. Col. Wormswold was as detested as ever; his voice was heard less often on the PA system (mostly due to the fact that by now most of the speakers had been unscrewed, the units pitched into the sea), but the tense mutinous atmosphere of the lower decks evaporated quite miraculously.

King Neptune remained in the brig all the way to Cape Town. At that juncture he was let out, his status as barrack room lawyer severely tarnished by his abject apology for his effervescence. Col. Wormswold, it seemed, had been softened up somewhat by the insistence of some of the senior officers that it had all been meant in good fun.

Horner's corruptive influence was now as abruptly faded as was the colonel's. Normalcy returned – but many of us feared it might only be temporary. After Cape Town we would have to pass the equator a second time on our way north.

*

There was to be a general shore leave at Cape Town celebrating the first British trooper to dock there since the end of the Second World War. The men needed money to take ashore, so before entering port a pay parade was organized in the lower salon – two thousand men with their personal account books in hand, all to be signed by the day's pay officer – whose post fell to me that day. It meant checking each man's name off against a list, entering the correct sum in the correct space of his pay record, and signing my name into his book. I challenge anyone who has ever had any doubt about his moniker to attempt to sign it two thousand times in a row. At the end, beyond suffering a headache sufficient to ring the church bells, he will almost certainly wish his name to be shorter.

Word had been flashed ashore ahead of our arrival so that by the time we pulled in hundreds of loyalist ex-pat townspeople, many waving Union Jacks, had come down to the quay to greet us. All soldiers were instructed to leave the ship in uniform – and pretty well all of them, as they stepped off the gangplank, were met by welcomers who invited them into the city and to their homes for the day. I think my uniform was indistinguishable enough but Gill Budge, my cabin mate, stepping off the boat with me, wore tartan trews and Tam o'Shanter. No sooner had the two of us set foot ashore we were beset by a nostalgic family who had emigrated from Scotland before the Second World War. They whisked us off on a whirlwind tour of the city, including a ride up Table Mountain, and then drove us to the family home for lunch.

Kind though these people were, we needed to get away to explore corners of Cape Town on our own. We had been told to be back on board ship by six o'clock, and there were many tempting bars between ourselves and the quays. We needed to examine as many of them as we could on our way ...

But the hospitality of the Cape Towners knew few bounds, and before long we found ourselves once again in the back seat of someone's car headed for an obscure and highly recommended quarter of the city. The drinks were liberal and each a goodly four fingers deep. Then the inevitable: at some juncture of the long afternoon Gill got himself tugged one way, I another – and we were separated. Eventually I made it back to the ship, staggering up the gangplank like a dignified camel on a tight rope. I made it to the bunk in my cabin and only regained consciousness when I felt the lilt and gentle movement of the ship as it moved beyond the confines of the harbour and entered the swells of the open waters.

I searched every corner of every deck, but Gill Budge was nowhere to be found.

In the days that followed there were periodic roll calls to which I or one of the other junior officers who were party to his absence responded when Gill's name was called. Certainly none of us was going to report him. It would only cause him no end of trouble. I suppose if we thought he was in harm's way, or dead, we might have said something. But seeing as he was just absent silence was our preferred course of action; if he could manage to wriggle out of his pickle, sort things out for himself, all to the good. He was an enterprising fellow. He'd use his nous and there was always the chance that no one would ever notice. In the meantime none of us need be more involved than covering for him. Bit like the Great Escape; we wondered if he could pull it off.

*

So we steamed out into the South Atlantic leaving southern Africa well out of sight on our starboard side as we passed St. Helena and approached Ascension Island.

One afternoon, as an alternative sport to shooting coloured target balloons from the stern rail, the junior officers decided to challenge their senior colleagues to a tug-o-war. There was much good natured jeering and hooting as space was prepared on one of the upper decks. With eleven men to a side the seniors would outweigh the juniors by several hundred pounds; it would not be much of a contest. But the juniors were confident, adamant – cheeky.

"You guys are out-of-shape!" we jeered. "Lard will never win against sheer youthful brawn and determination of will. You don't have the stamina ..."

The contestants decided between them the winner would be the team that succeeded in hauling their opponents over the centre line three consecutive times. A junior officer and a senior officer would act as umpires.

"You're all so puny ... you don't stand a chance!" the seniors jeered back at us.

So the teams formed up at either end of a long length of heavy rope stretched out on one of the upper decks. It had been salvaged from a locker deep in the innards of the ship.

Both teams went into huddles at their respective ends to formulate strategies.

However what the seniors were unable to see from way down at their end of the deck was how the juniors managed to secure their end of the rope to one of the ship's stanchions and disguise their manoeuvre from view.

Full of confidence, the seniors took up positions at their end of the rope and the contest began. Their anchor, a major of enormous proportions, tied the rope around his great girth and leaned back, his meat-slab bare feet fastened to the deck as if cemented.

At the other end, the juniors fed out the slack until their ruse was taut. The umpires, seeing nothing amiss, knotted the handkerchief in the centre between the two teams, shouted "Pull!" – and the game was on.

Both teams tugged as if their hearts were to break ...

The astonishment on the faces of the seniors was soon apparent. They heaved and they heaved, but no way could they get that team of muscled youth to budge an inch. One by one they scowled and grunted, grew red in the face fit to burst a gasket – and sweated.

To no avail! The subalterns held their deck ...

But then there came the moment when it was time to reveal the hoax. On a single word all members of the junior team stood away and revealed to the seniors how they had been pulling against the steadfast and un-budging stanchion of the ship.

"You cheating bastards!" they shouted, as the juniors doubled over with laughter.

They might have set about boxing our ears except they were so exhausted they didn't have the umph for it. They announced they had no will to embark upon another two rounds of such a futile and unequal contest.

Not all of them had thought the joke so terribly funny.

*

The closer we came to Ascension Island the closer we came once again to the equator, the events of our previous crossing all too paramount in our minds. There had been rumblings that certain intransigents were plotting anew to make our wretched colonel's life even more wretched, and the general consensus among seniors and juniors alike was that it should be discouraged.

Unfortunately Wormswold himself also got wind of the plot. Instead of keeping it to himself and quietly asking his officers to support him, which they would have been prepared to do, the silly bugger resorted once more to his beloved PA system (it still worked all too well in some areas down in the bowels of the ship), and to inflicting an assortment of pre-crime punishments on the lower decks. The pool was emptied of its contents, and during the heat of the days when the troops might otherwise have enjoyed using it they were ordered to muster for hours and hours of lifeboat drill – the sequence of which they had done so many times before they knew it perfectly well.

It was a stupid move, and now not even the senior officers and warrant officers could any longer be certain of controlling the angry and unruly soldiers. Wherever there were groups of men on the decks, insults against the colonel would be shouted out that couldn't help but be heard, even when he was in his quarters. It was always done in such a way that no one person could ever be discovered or accused. On several occasions when the man had stepped away from his cabin, mobs of soldiers would jeer him or even hurl missiles. Not surprisingly he became extremely nervous, would seldom sally out of his quarters. He even ceased having his meals at the head table in the officers' dining lounge – which didn't bother any of us at all. Many of us, in truth, were torn between our concern that he might come to harm and our rather callous wish that someone would toss the son-of-a-bitch overboard – the principal speaker, so to say.

In the end we crossed the line the second time without event, though the mutterings and fierce threats in the corridors of the ship were sometimes quite audible.

*

This last long leg of the journey might have been agonizingly boring for me had I not met on board a delightful girl who was also travelling home, and who (my judgement is hindsight) must have been at least as headstrong and stubborn as I was. We were both young, and shipboard romances have an irresistible urgency about them that is charming. All the way up the Atlantic and into Dakar, we spent our moments together.

Her name was Pauline, but for some reason when we first met I had heard her name as "Bobby," and so that is what I called her for the remainder of our time together. She was returning to northern England with her mother, the wife of a transport sergeant who had remained behind in Korea. Happily for us Bobby's mother had recognized the obvious affection we held for one another, and was quite content to give us her tacit approval. Bobby was a good mixer and so enthusiastically joined in whatever activities were organized each evening in the junior officers' salon. She was extremely self-assured and proved to be popular among the small company of subalterns and the other girls who, as "daughters of the regiment," were travelling with us and had become our companions.

However, one afternoon I was summoned to the cabin of Col. Wormswold. I had no idea what he wanted, so went along curiously cocky.

"You are an officer of a line regiment, sir – a line regiment, and one of the British Army's finest ..." the colonel began sternly. "This girl you are escorting is the daughter of a services sergeant, and thus well beneath your social standing. Bad form, sir, bad form ... Quite unacceptable. You are to cease this relationship forthwith, do you understand ...?"

My jaw dropped, and I wanted to laugh. But I think I did the right thing.

"Yessir!" I barked, without giving him a chance to say another word. Then I threw the stupid bugger a snappy salute, promptly turned on my heels and stepped out of his cabin.

As I left, though, I could see this pallid and sickening little man twist his thin lips into what I supposed he thought passed for a smile, showing me his bad teeth. He was no doubt pleased with himself for succeeding in straightening out the social and moral judgement of a youthful officer hell-bent on going astray.

Without delay I raced up to the lifeboat deck to keep the tryst I had made with Bobby prior to going in to see the colonel. We laughed and snuggled. We had many more delightful things to talk about. The colonel's injunction went overboard with not a moment's consideration, and from that point on neither of us took any heed to hide the fact we were continuing to see one another.

Neither, it seemed, did the colonel have much of an idea what to do about it when he discovered for himself I was disobeying his order. One afternoon he came upon the two of us standing by the rail, dreamily gazing at the horizon, as is the tendency of shipboard lovers. The man was so embarrassed by the encounter he was unable to mutter more than a frail "Good afternoon ...!" as he manoeuvred his hideous disfigurement across the deck.

Mrs. Queen's Chump

We ignored him.

I can't help but think the troop commander must have understood the full complement of the ship was ganged up against him. Indeed, it was. It must have been a fierce feed to his insecurities and paranoia. He issued orders daily which all of us, seniors and juniors alike, treated with contempt.

Nothing was said. The juniors held a good-natured respect for all of the senior officers, and they, to a man, made not the least move to correct us when we paid little or no attention to the ship's commander or anything he said. The order that we rise from our bunks at six o'clock each morning to muster on deck for a half-hour of physical exercise came initially from Wormswold, but was relayed to us by the senior officers – and we complied willingly. No doubt the colonel thought we were obeying him. We did not have that intent; we were obeying the orders of the men we respected, and our senior officers had sufficient wit to not say anything to Wormswold that might have indicated the contrary. The senior officers constituted a group that on more than one occasion had proven the voice of sweet reason. And certainly it was to their account reason had finally penetrated the numb skull of the man who would have had us sail blithely up the Red Sea to Suez.

In due course the Empire Warrel put in at Dakar. Bobby and I went ashore and spent several immensely pleasant hours on the beach there, and later browsing among the city's shops and cafés.

*

In Liverpool, damp and grey, Gill Budge was standing dockside in his tartan trews and Tam o'Shanter. He waved up at us as we pulled alongside and called to him from the deck. He came aboard just as soon as the gangplank was lowered. In the cabin we had shared he gathered his belongings together and told me what had happened to him in Cape Town.

He had had too much to drink, as had I, and had fallen asleep at a moment when our host group had decided to move on to another bar. It was past six o'clock when he awoke and realized he had missed the boat, so virtually penniless he did what he had been trained to do, and was extremely good at: he used his initiative. Friendly Cape Towners had delivered him to one of the bases for the Royal South African Air Force, as it was then known.

The air force took to him warmly, and within a day or so were able to transport him to Nairobi; from there he had had no trouble bumming a ride with the Royal Air Force back to England. He would have arrived unexpectedly and far too early at his regimental depot, and if he had reported in right away he would have revealed his lapse. So he took himself home and enjoyed a quiet and unauthorized leave for a few weeks while waiting for our arrival aboard the Empire Warrel to be announced in the daily shipping news.

No one was the worse for the irregular deviation. The two of us descended the gangplank together and bid one another goodbye there at dockside.

Bobby and I parted then, also. We made each other many and many promises, but our ship had come in and our roads went different ways from that moment. I have often wondered ... but then what's the point? There are times, I am sure, when the sweetest of memories must remain just that, and so serve the lucky anointed a lifetime.

□

31. Home

Two years is a lengthy time to be absent from family, but before going to our homes all of us were required to report in at our regimental depots. My regimental depot was in a small city in one of the Home Counties south of London, so from Liverpool I headed straight there. I travelled down by train, took a taxi from the station to the barracks, and was affably greeted at the officers' mess by a captain. When I told him where I had been and what I had been doing he became quite animated and wanted a firsthand accounting. He insisted the concierge move my kit into one of the bedrooms upstairs, then invited me for a drink in the bar and to join him at lunch. We passed a most pleasant hour together.

That was as far as the affability went. After lunch I was approached by another captain who introduced himself as the depot adjutant. He ushered me to be seated in a quiet corner of the downstairs lounge.

There was a dossier in his hand and he waved it angrily under my nose.

"You received one adverse report in Kenya, and now a second one from Singapore. What kind of a record is that?"

A sudden and intimidating switch in tone, and I was thrown for a loop by the man's aggression. I did not think it would have mattered a great deal what I might have said to him, so refrained from giving him any answer at all; he was steamed up and more intent on delivering his castigation than hearing whatever I might have to say. He paid no attention to the few other members of the mess who were seated in nearby armchairs sipping their after-lunch coffees and gently turning snifters of cognac in their hands. They must have overheard him, and I was desperately embarrassed. The captain could see it, which prompted him to attack with even more venom.

"Do you realize there is now a court martial pending?"

"I had no idea," I told him truthfully. "What does that entail?"

He was working himself into a fury and turning puce. One eyebrow had shot up, his jaw jutting forward as he glowered at me.

"One adverse report is a disgrace; two – my goodness, it's unheard of! This means a court martial is called for – and in the long history of this regiment there has never been a court martial. Never once a court martial in over three hundred years! Can you even assess what you have done, you bloody fool? You have brought this entire regiment into disrepute. You! A mere National Service officer, and a bloody colonial to boot! Ye Gods, man!"

That was a bit over the top, I thought and remember thinking impudently how well he caricatured himself – that he would create an even sterner impression were he to be wearing a monocle.

But by now the man was shouting, and I was alarmed. Court martial? Even the term frightened me. I had no realistic idea of what it was, just the notion in the back of my mind that it was something for which other men were occasionally shot.

The captain stood up, still blazing at me.

"Where are you staying?" he demanded to know.

"In one of the rooms upstairs, I think … I haven't been up there yet."

"Well, go to your room right now and remain there until you are sent for," he barked, and he turned and marched out of the room.

Go to your room, you naughty boy … I wanted to laugh, but actually I was terrified. The other officers in the lounge coughed gently, and turned their backs to me.

Pariah. Bloody colonial.

Very confused and intimidated young man.

Quietly I rose from my chair and sought the concierge in the main hall of the mess.

"Will you show me my room, please," I asked him.

"Of course, sir! I'd be happy to. Come right this way. Will you be staying with us for long?"

He was an elderly man, a well-trained and well-mannered house servant, the sort of fellow who had taken on this job when he himself retired from service in the ranks of the regiment and had become a fixture. I wanted to hug him for being so kindly towards me.

He showed me a small but rather cosily appointed room on the first floor. It had a single bed, scatter rugs on the floor, and a table and chair next to a window that looked out onto a pleasant garden. My kit had been placed on the floor between a chest of drawers and a small cupboard.

"The washroom is just down the hall, sir," he told me. "You may take a shower if you wish, plenty of hot water ..."

Hot water, indeed; I was already in plenty of hot water.

He left the room, all smiles. I guessed he hadn't yet heard I was a regimental disgrace.

It was mid-October and late afternoon shadows were already creeping into the corners of the room. The failing light reflected the emptiness of my mood as I sat alone at the table and looked outside. I couldn't help but turn over and over in my mind all that had passed in the months since I had been last in Britain. Whatever the great adventure, whatever the lessons I might have learned through a host of experiences, the whole now seemed sordid, sullied by the thought of the trouble I was causing. To be perfectly honest with myself, I was unable to put a definitive finger on any of it – not the events on the mountain in Kenya, not the more recent talks with my commander and the brigadier in Singapore. These were the sources of the two reports against me; I could remember and yet could not quite comprehend what it was that I had done, or was supposed to have done – or not done. And the adjutant's anger with me just now – well, he was outside it all. He was infuriated by what others had written about me on those papers he held in his hand. His first thought was for the regiment and his allegiance to it; he could have no real concept, the details, of my predicament – but then maybe they weren't even written on those pieces of paper he carried ...

I sat at the table for a long time and finally, when it was growing dark, I stretched out on the bed. I was awoken shortly when the concierge returned with a tray of food and put it on the table.

"I am told you will be taking your meals in your room, sir," he said. "Is there anything else I can bring you?"

"No, I don't think so. Did anyone say anything else to you?"

I had been in the room the whole afternoon but it was as if he was my gaoler for a much extended period of time, and I needed to know news from outside my pen.

"No, sir. No one's said anything to me, but then why should they? I expect one of the officers will come by at supper time."

He left, and again I was on my own. The plate of sandwiches and the tea were welcome, and I consumed them in silence. Again I stretched out on the bed and fell asleep.

Quite late in the evening I was about to get ready for bed when a lieutenant came to my room. He had a superior air and spoke with an exaggeratedly haughty tone.

"The adjutant has instructed me to inform you that as your conduct is considered disgraceful, so you are to be treated accordingly. You are to be confined to your quarters, which means you are to remain in this room for the duration of your stay here. You are not to venture downstairs to the bar or dining room, nor are you to attempt to socialize with the other officers in the mess. Tomorrow morning the adjutant will come and talk to you again. You are to remain here until he comes. Do you understand?"

"Perfectly," I told him. I was sure I did not wish to speak to this man any more than he wished to speak to me, but then he hesitated at the door.

"You were with the unit in Malaya?"

"I was."

"Did you see any action?"

"Yes."

"Oh!"

For a fleeting moment he looked as though he wanted to open up a pleasantly civilized conversation, but then he apparently thought better of it.

"Well – good night, then!" And he strode out, closing the door behind him.

I slept well enough, and the following morning a substantial breakfast was brought to me on a tray – porridge, kippers, toast and marmalade and a pot of tea. I shaved and dressed – and waited. Pulling a pad of paper and pen out of my kit, I sat at the table and tried to write a letter to Bobby. I couldn't explain what was happening to me right then because I didn't have a firm grasp on it, so I confined myself to words of endearment and said how much I hated to say goodbye to her in Liverpool. I don't know if I ever mailed the letter, but writing it kept me occupied.

Close to noon the adjutant came to my room, opening the door and entering without knocking. His entry was quite theatrical, the deliberate absence of a courtesy rap on the door being a gesture towards civilized behaviour beyond my entitlement.

He carried his dossier of papers, and shuffled some of them out onto the table in front of me. The printed words Court Martial jumped up at me from the top paper, and I wasn't able to pay much attention to whatever else was written.

"You can avoid the disgrace of a court martial, and receive immediate release if you will sign these papers – here – and here – and here …"

He pointed to dotted lines with his finger, and held a pen for me to sign. Without any hesitation, I took it and wrote my name.

"Here is a travel voucher for you to take a train to your home," he said, holding out an envelope.

I took the voucher, saying nothing.

"I speak for all of us here," said the adjutant. "We shall be glad to see the back of you. You are to leave right away. I want this room cleared before noon."

And with that my services to the British Army came to an abrupt end. I took the train to my home station, trying to think all the while that what I actually felt was relief. But it was not quite like that. I felt humiliation in a way I had never felt it before. I was returning home in uniform and had wanted to stand my full height to meet my family. Instead I slunk down the long driveway to our front door, kitbag over my shoulder, feeling like some creature that had just crawled out of the moat.

But Mama came to the door and welcomed me like a returning hero, so I managed to put on a good face. It was weeks before I could summon the courage to tell her what had happened, and even then she shrugged it off.

"They give medals out like candy, darling, but you have to attain the rank of general before anyone will think to show you real gratitude. You did your bit, and I'm sure it was the best you could."

Dear Mama. She had her way of seeing things, took nothing too seriously, and that was that. Yesterday.

☐

32. Aftermath

There was never a court martial.

Months after returning to Canada I received a letter from the War Office in London. It was addressed to me as "Private," and said that because I had voluntarily resigned my commission and been granted a special dispensation to return to Canada, I would be relieved of any obligation to serve a further three years in the British Territorial Army.

It was evident that one of the papers I signed on my last day at the regimental depot was indeed a resignation of my commission, which was doubtless the sole objective of the adjutant's scare tactic. In any case, my considerate action had ensured the three hundred-year-old dignity of the regiment remained as clean and bright as the polished brass shell casings that decorated the entrance to the HQ mess. Bravo!

I had been a very callow man when I joined the British Army in 1954. Embarrassingly, I grew two inches in basic training and had to be issued with a new uniform by the quartermaster. Despite my many adventures I was still extremely unworldly when I was demobbed. Badly shaken (I had not anticipated the second adverse report nor the events that followed at the regimental HQ), I made my way back to my father's house in Kamloops, British Columbia, in time to celebrate my twenty-first birthday.

Signing my commission away was my regimental adjutant's way of getting rid of an embarrassing problem, but it had not been my intent; I would not have done it had I been more alert and less intimidated. When I realized what I had done – and what had been done to me – I promptly signed on with the Rocky Mountain Rangers, set about earning my commission back, and eventually served five years in the Canadian Army Militia. My pride and my confidence had been badly shaken. There was no question of a pension for my active service, either then or later, nor have I sought one – although in my later years I have developed sensibilities concerning the idea of putting one's life and mental stability on the line in exchange for zero compensation and a kick in the butt.

It took some years to come to grips with the train wreck of my personal life. We had an idea about "shell shock" as it was called in those days; but

Mrs. Queen's Chump

"post-traumatic stress disorder" is only a recently recognized phenomena.

While Canada provided me with many, many comforts, and always has, at the time I was released back into civilian life it was not the best place for me to attempt the therapeutic de-briefing – or unwinding – I no doubt needed rather urgently.

Canada in those distant days was something of a social and cultural backwater. I couldn't talk to people about where I'd been and what I'd been doing because no one really understood what the hell I was talking about. Why should they have cared? There was no pressing need to provide for returning soldiers, then; Canada's soldiery hadn't returned from anywhere since the end of the Korean War, and if at that time a soldier wasn't traumatized sufficiently to warrant hospitalization he was always good for beer and a yarn at the bar of his local Legion. A soldier who had served in a "foreign" army was a curiosity long before he was taken as a casualty.

Stories: "You better write 'em down some day, Jer!"

One afternoon I found my father thumbing through the pages of my sister's school atlas to inform himself as to exactly what the divisions of Africa looked like.

"… And the Chinese were trying to colonize Malaya?"

To give relevant answers to questions (on the rare occasion when a question might be asked) proved confusing to the point of risking the wandering eye. His two sons had fought out there somewhere, but beyond that none of it made much sense or had a whole lot to do with him.

It was about that time I read a small filler in a Vancouver newspaper that stated: "There are one hundred and twenty-six bookstores in Canada."

Nowadays there could well be one hundred and twenty-six bookstores in downtown Vancouver, but my point is this: in 1956 when I returned to Canada, Canadians did not read widely, and had not yet become travellers; they knew Lester B. Pearson was Canadian, but of the rest there were no outstanding internationalists most people would have known of. Curiosity was bounded by the size of your paycheque and the type of car you drove. Canada's educational system, circumscribed by a teaching milieu that was a regurgitation of what it had gone through itself in the previous generation (as had the teaching milieu of the generation before that) was the cornerstone of what passed for the country's culture. The populace as a whole tended to the parochial, tightly confined by and within the bounds of the country's extraordinary geography. The outside world through which I had been wandering was a blearingly long way away.

Things were to change drastically in the decade that followed, but that did not do me personally a whole lot of good in the extended instant it was most needed.

The 1960's ushered a radical thinking into Canada, as it did the world at large: the Viet Nam War, long hair, drugs, the victory-V and the raised middle finger – all of these, and more, were indications that the world was turning a social summersault. Restless people started moving out, discovering for themselves what lay beyond the stoop of their own homes in an effort to meet the great wide world; "empire," they were discovering, was a confinement not an edification. They began to doubt, to question the efficacy of the snake oil being peddled (democratically!) by those who had always claimed to be their "elders and betters."

Who am I to complain? Or even to comment?

Well, maybe it is just that question (if it's not the Official Secrets Act!) that causes the Little Man to shut his gob and say nothing. And maybe by telling stories like the ones in these pages, one Little Man is finding a voice he actually had all along.

I have never seen either of the adverse reports that were written about me so many years ago in Kenya and Singapore. They are the smallest chips of that crumbling empire and are of no consequence now, to me or anyone. More important today, though I am in the closing years of my life, is the vindication that comes with the knowledge that at last the world is opening – like a flower – and its people are wising up. It's a slow but unstoppable process. No longer are huge swathes of population dumbed down into silent acquiescence. The correctness of empire no longer suits them. The Little Man no longer accepts being brutalized and bamboozled into "standing up and taking it." He is shoving back.

The real Little Men now (a different littleness) are the politicians, the bankers and corporate leaders – the greedy, arrogant, bullying madmen who recklessly peddle themselves as able, who make desperate efforts to convince the world at large they are the new democrats, they are the new elite and, above all, they know what is best for everyone else. They are the men who have always stood behind Mrs. Queen, and who are responsible for having me sent out to guard their investments in places like Kenya and Malaya. One man gets one vote – first past the post, and the majority wins. Ha! Ha! Till now the real majority has never won, and those who prate about democracy the loudest are the liars of this world – and the most undemocratic. Our institutions are filled with them. Our governments, our churches, the universities, the military – all are choc-a-bloc with "experts" laying down the law and telling anyone who'll listen that they know, they know, they know … They know how to get it all "right" – but then they fail lamentably, and run off with the piggy bank.

And these are the ones, wannabee empire builders, who send the nation's sons and daughters off to war (preferably not their own sons and daughters) …

Grim picture, and yet I take heart. We live in an accelerating world where the blind and oppressed are that segment of the population who really have had to learn to "grin and bear it." They are the democratic majority forever charged with accepting the information they receive as their lot in life. It is they who are now faced with the demands of "manning up." This involves knowledge, education, understanding – and then confrontation in all its manifestations.

With all that, in turn, comes the realization that manning up requires not just the strength to acknowledge errors, but to make corrections.

An optimist is required to deal with all this – someone with the belief that the topsy-turviness of our lives has a tendency to right itself eventually.

I think it was this that always made my dear Mama smile. She was not immune to catastrophe in her own life. In fact she was quite good at creating it. But when her son stumbled home with news of his own bumpy ride, she tended to see the ridiculous before she would bow to the weight of form or stigma. Admitting an element of humour, a familial static slapstick, made my predicament much easier to bear.

Shortly before her death she looked at me over the top of her vodka glass, and winked.

"Bonk!" she said.

She had mothered two soldier sons, and somehow we had all survived it.

Her faculties pickled quite beyond her ability to express herself with complex words, Mama nonetheless felt strongly about all sorts of issues, and over the years had developed a special vocabulary with which to express her exasperation, disgust or contempt. She held a deep dislike for what she saw as bullshit or pomp, so a noise – any expressive noise – uttered with suitable gusto and delivered across her wrinkled nose with unmistakable tones of delight or distaste, conveyed her meaning with utmost clarity. And her deep sense of humour.

Such breadth of expression permitted her to draw on mountains of gravitas, and she had a wide vocabulary of similar words and tones that expressed a full lexicon of sentiments – the content, happiness and warmth of a child at play.

Hers was a remarkable ability, considering she would have to be pie-eyed drunk to enter this mystic realm. But enter it she always did, and it enabled her to revel in the most delightful of optimisms – along with the benefits of a special life-long chautauqua to which, I am happy to say, she invited both of her sons.

☐